D1823422

The Politics of EU Accession

The question of Turkish membership in the European Union (EU) is highly controversial and subject to many misperceptions and misunderstandings on both sides.

This book examines the politics of EU accession which has evolved during the expansion of the EU, from more procedural conditions to provisions of substantive democracy. With a particular focus on the challenges Turkey faces to join the EU, the authors examine the experiences of the newly-democratised and acceded Czech Republic, Hungary, Poland and Slovakia to provide insight and to identify the best possible solutions.

Combining the Turkish and Central European perspectives in one volume, and using a social constructivist approach, the authors address issues including Euroscepticism, EU absorption capacity, women's rights, democratisation, Turkish Kemalism, the desecuritisation of Turkish politics and the problem of Northern Cyprus. This book establishes the challenges the EU, its member states and the candidate countries need to face and successfully address in order to contribute to both their democratisation and the European integration process.

This book will be of interest to students and scholars of European politics, Turkish politics and international politics.

Lucie Tunkrová is an Assistant Professor at Fatih University, Istanbul.

Pavel Šaradín is an Associate Professor at Palacký University, Olomouc.

Routledge Advances in European Politics

The Politics of EU Accession

Turkish challenges and Central
European experiences

**Edited by
Lucie Tunkrová and Pavel Šaradín**

Routledge
Taylor & Francis Group

LONDON AND NEW YORK

First published 2010 by Routledge
2 Park Square, Milton Park, Abingdon, Oxfordshire OX14 4RN

Simultaneously published in the USA and Canada
by Routledge
711 Third Avenue, New York, NY 10017, USA

First issued in paperback 2016

Routledge is an imprint of the Taylor & Francis Group, an informa business.

© 2010 Lucie Tunkrová and Pavel Šaradín, selection and editorial matter;
individual contributors, their contributions

Typeset in Times New Roman by Swales & Willis Ltd, Exeter, Devon

British Library Cataloguing in Publication Data
A catalogue record for this book is available
from the British Library

Library of Congress Cataloging in Publication Data
The politics of EU accession : Turkish challenges and Central European
experiences / edited by Lucie Tunkrová and Pavel aradín.
    p. cm. — (Routledge advances in European politics ; 61)
    Includes bibliographical references and index.
    1. European Union—Turkey. 2. European Union—Membership.
    3. Europe—Economic integration. 4. Turkey—Relations—European Union
    countries. 5. European Union countries—Relations—Turkey. 6. Europe,
    Central—Relations—Turkey. 7. Turkey—Relations—Europe, Central.
    I. Tunkrová, Lucie. II. Šaradín, Pavel.
    HC240.25.T8P65 2010
    341.242'2—dc22
                              2009043137

ISBN 13: 978-1-138-97901-7 (pbk)
ISBN 13: 978-0-415-55549-4 (hbk)

Contents

Notes on contributors

Dr Armağan Emre Çakır is an associate professor at the European Union Institute of Marmara University, Istanbul. He is the chairperson of the Department of Politics and International Relations of the European Union. His research focuses on theories of European integration, and EU-Turkey relations.

Mgr Angelika Gergelová is a PhD student at the Department of Politics and European Studies at Palacký University, Czech Republic, and works as a head of Eurocentrum Zlín. She focuses especially on the *finalité* of the European integration process.

Dr Rabia Karakaya Polat is an assistant professor at the Department of International Relations at Işık University, Istanbul. Her research interests include electronic democracy, local democracy, democratization in Turkey, and securitization theory.

Dr Petr Kučera works as an assistant professor in Near Eastern studies at Charles University, Prague. He held fellowships at the universities in Berlin, Ankara, Istanbul and Princeton. He has published articles on Turkish literature and the modernisation process, and translations from Turkish literature.

Dr Pavel Šaradín is an associate professor at the Department of Politics and European Studies at Palacký University, Czech Republic. His research focuses on Central European political systems and on electoral studies. He is the editor-in-chief of a peer-reviewed journal *Contemporary European Studies*, published by Palacký University.

Dr Ahmet Sözen is an associate professor of International Relations at Eastern Mediterranean University. He is the recipient of the Paul Harris Ambassadorial Scholarship in 1997. He is the founding Director of the Cyprus Policy Center think-tank.

Dr Lucie Tunkrová is an assistant professor at Fatih University, Istanbul, and Palacký University, Olomouc. She focuses on enlargement and theories of the European Union's decision-making processes. She is a member of a research team working on a 5-year grant titled Czech National Interests in the European Union.

Preface

The European Union (EU) is facing many significant challenges today including coping with the failure of the Lisbon Treaty and the impact of the two recent enlargement rounds on the Union's structures. The accession of the Czech Republic, Hungary, Poland and Slovakia in 2004 – together with the other six countries – and the opening of the negotiations with Turkey in 2005 unlocked many new issues and demanded the revision of some existing concepts that need to be readdressed and reassessed. The question of Turkish membership in the EU is highly controversial and subject to many misperceptions and misunderstandings in both the EU and Turkey – the debate has with changing intensity gone through various phases and addressed a number of levels, including political, economic, cultural and security expectations and concerns.

Even though not applied uniformly, East Central European Countries (ECECs)[1] share with Turkey some common problems such as weak societies and volatile electorates, which affect the success of the various instruments of democratic conditionality, their efficiency and attained results. The ECECs are well aware of the fact that they joined a very different EU than the countries before them, largely due to the immense growth in EU legislation and in the areas of EU competence in the past 15 years, of growing political and economic integration. They are also aware of the different impact of EU integration on candidate countries after the introduction of the Copenhagen criteria in 1993. Democratic conditionality has become a key EU accession strategy moving from the originally more procedural conditions to provisions of substantive democracy. The last enlargement rounds tested how they work and when they are effective.

In both the ECECs and Turkey we can observe forces that resist the transnational imposition of norms and values, reflected not only in public opinion but also activities of some political elites and even attempts to mobilize resistance to them. Furthermore, the ECECs and Turkey have experience with non-democratic regimes that had to undergo (substantial) regime change as pre-condition for membership (or promise of future membership) and endorse consolidation of democratic regimes while liberalising their economies. Their experience with Europeanisation is, thus, rather different from most 'older' EU Member States.

We do not deny that there are many differences between the individual Central European and Turkish cases and between their ways of acquiring EU membership but we believe that the vast amount of research conducted on the ECECs accession can be to some extent applied to Turkey. The Turkish accession process is expected to be very long and as such the experience and possible partnership with ECECs is particularly valuable for Turkey while the ECECs can considerably contribute to the future form of European integration with Turkey as a full EU Member State.

The first attempt of the authors to address this topic resulted in a text, which was published by Palacký University Press (Olomouc, Czech Republic, in Czech) in 2008. The interest in the topic expressed by a number of foreign colleagues in Turkey, Central Europe but also in the USA and elsewhere led us to the decision to present its modified and upgraded version. We addressed scholars from Turkey and the Czech Republic with the aim of presenting an overview that would provide the readers with important information surrounding the whole discussion but would also start a more balanced debate on the issue. The text should be seen as a beginning of a broader undertaking in the future – we hope and believe that it will increase the interest in the subject and provide some background for potential venues of research on Central European and Turkish 'Europeanization'.

Lucie Tunkrová, Pavel Šaradín
Istanbul – Olomouc, July 2009

Note

1 The ECECs include the four post-communist countries in Central Europe, the Czech Republic, Hungary, Poland and Slovakia.

Acknowledgements

This text owes much to the dedicated work of all the contributors and we would like to thank them all. We would also like to thank Heidi Bagtazo and Lucy Dunne from Routledge Advances in European Politics series for their patient support and professionalism, and our colleagues for the many invaluable comments and encouragement. We are, however, solely responsible for any mistakes or errors.

The book is a significantly revised and expanded version of a *Turecko a Evropská unie: česká a turecká perspektiva* published by Palacký University Press in 2008.

It was prepared with the support of the Czech Republic's Ministry of Education, Youth and Sports National Research Program II as part of the project 'Czech Republic in the European Union: National Interests and Decision-Making'.

List of abbreviations

ADD	Association for Kemalist Thought
AKEL	Progressive Party of Working People
AKP	Justice and Development Party
CAP	Common Agricultural Policy
CBM	confidence-building measures
CC	candidate country
CDU/CSU	Christian Democratic Union/Christian Social Union
CEECs	Central and Eastern European countries
CEFTA	Central European Free Trade Association
CEI	Central European Initiative
CHP	Republican People's Party
CSDP	Civil Society Development Program
ČSSD	Czech Social Democratic Party
CTP	Republican Turkish Party
CYDD	Support for Modern Life Association
CZ	Czech Republic
DTP	Democratic Society Party
EB	Eurobarometer
EBRD	European Bank for Reconstruction and Development
ECECs	East Central European Countries
ECHR	European Court of Human Rights
ECJ	European Court of Justice
EEC	European Economic Community
EFTA	European Free Trade Association
EOKA	National Organisation of Cypriot Fighters
EP	European Parliament
EPACVAW	The European Policy Action Center on Violence against Women
EU	European Union
EUMAP	EU Monitoring and Advocacy Program
EWL	European Women's League
FKGP	Independent Party of Smallholders, Agrarian Workers and Citizens
FYROM	Former Yugoslav Republic of Macedonia
GDP	Gross Domestic Product

HU	Hungary
ICJ	International Court of Justice
IKV	Economic Development Foundation
ITO	Istanbul Chamber of Commerce
KDH	Christian Democratic Movement
KDNP	Christian-Democratic People's Party
KDU-ČSL	Christian Democratic Union – Czechoslovak People's Party
KIK	Public Procurement Authority
KSČM	Communist Party of Bohemia and Moravia
LPR	League of Polish Families
MDF	Hungarian Democratic Forum
MGK	National Security Council
MHP	Nationalist Movement Party
MIÉP	Party of Hungarian Justice and Life
MS	Member States
MSZP	Hungarian Socialist Party
MZV ČR	Ministry of Foreign Affairs Czech Republic
NATO	North Atlantic Treaty Organization
NGOs	Non-Governmental Organizations
ODA	Civic Democratic Alliance
ODS	Civic Democratic Party
OECD	Organisation for Economic Cooperation and Development
OSCE	Organization for Security and Cooperation in Europe
PiS	Law and Justice
PKK	Kurdistan Workers Party
PL	Poland
PO	Civic Platform
PSL	Polish People's Party
SETA	Foundation for Political, Economic and Social Research
SK	Slovakia
SLD	Democratic Left Alliance
PSL	Polish People's Party
SMK	Hungarian Coalition Party
SNK	Union of Independents
SNS	Slovak National Party
SPD	Social Democratic Party of Germany
SZ	Green Party
SZDSZ	Alliance of Free Democrats
TESEV	Turkish Economic and Social Studies Foundation
TOBB	Union of Chambers and Commodity Exchanges of Turkey
TRNC	Turkish Republic of Northern Cyprus
TRT	Turkish Radio and TV Corporation
TÜSEV	Third Sector Foundation of Turkey
TÜSIAD	Turkish Industrialists' and Businessmen's Association
UBP	National Unity Party

UK	United Kingdom
UN	United Nations
USA	United States of America
UNFICYP	UN Peacekeeping Force in Cyprus
WIDE	Network Women in Development Europe
WWHR	Women for Women's Human Rights – New Ways

1 Introduction

Lucie Tunkrová

In May 2004, ten new Member States (MS) entered the European Union (EU), eight of them former communist countries. Three years later, two more post-communist countries, Bulgaria and Romania, joined the bloc. On 3 October 2005, the EU launched accession negotiations with Turkey, which initiated the final stage of Turkey's journey towards EU membership. This moment in EU-Turkey relations was seen by many as a truly historical event but it also highlighted the many issues that will have to be tackled on the way. The most salient ones directly related to Turkey include political and economic reforms, relations with Turkey's neighbors, and the question of the relationship between Turkish and European identity including the connection between the Christian and Muslim traditions. It will be a difficult and long process, where these and many more pressing problems related to both Turkey and the EU will have to be addressed. Concurrently, the EU is learning to "live" with the 12 new MS, while they are struggling to adapt to the new conditions of membership, facing the problems of persistent division between "old" and "new" Europe, between "us" and "them."

Europeanization can in its widest definition relate to the formation of Europe as a cultural entity, and European integration can be viewed as an alternative way of achieving shared European identity, which in modern vocabulary means "adaptation to (West) European norms and practices," often promoted by "domestic elites with internationally oriented identities and interests" (Featherstone and Kazamias 2001: 4). It simply represents one the many influences the European nation states are exposed to. It also refers to the process of "becoming European," which pertains especially to countries, whose "Europeaness" can be or is on some grounds questioned.[1]

A narrower definition of Europeanization is related only to processes associated with European integration in the framework of the EU. In this respect, we could also distinguish between Europeanization and EU-ization (Wallace, in Haughton 2007).[2] The actors "redefine their interests and behavior to meet the imperatives, norms and logic of EU membership" (Featherstone and Kazamias 2001: 13). Put very bluntly, Europeanization is a process in which countries adopt the broad scope of both formal and informal EU rules (Schimmelfennig and Sedelmeier 2005). It, thus, investigates how the norms are diffused in the domestic environment.

The issue at stake is how we specify norms and values, or more precisely *European* norms and values. We can generally define values as the "conception of the desirable" (Kluckhohn, in Gerhards 2007: 6), as justified preferences, relatively stable over time and abstract (Gerhards 2007), while norms refer to particular standards. There is no explicit definition of European norms, so we define them as the rules, principles, and decisions specified in the *acquis communitaire*, that is, the EU primary and secondary law as stated in the EU treaties, directives, regulations, and case law of the European Court of Justice (ECJ). They also involve certain unwritten and common practices that we find in, for instance, decision-making procedures. Hence, European norms and values refer to a very complex body of formal and informal rules, which play a normative role and serve as a guideline to the MS and the candidate countries (CCs). Through these rules and norms, the EU increasingly limits the abilities of the national governments to act (Ladrech 2002). The pressure for Europeanization tends to be higher in countries, whose norms and values display higher levels of incompatibility with the European norms and values.

The impact of European integration on domestic political systems, known as top-down Europeanization, examines how the EU affects its MS. The EU's impact varies because the countries have their own issues, agendas, and interests and understand or wish to understand the rules and norms differently. How the national level influences the European one is investigated within the bottom-up Europeanization approach, which focuses on the formation of transnational structures and how national processes and structures affect that process providing new opportunities but also posing challenges to various domestic actors. The top-down and bottom-up directions of Europeanization cannot be easily separated for as European integration affects the member state, so does the member state affect the EU.

We can also understand this relationship in a different context where the top-down influence of the EU might empower certain domestic actors, who then attempt at influencing the state's policies from the bottom-up (Schimmelfennig and Sedelmeier 2005). As the representatives of the groups have frequent contacts with the EU, they start to become more Europeanized, developing a stronger European identity. The national and European levels meet and through mutual dialogue transform the identities and perceptions even though this process tends to be more asymmetrical and the national and sub-national level are transformed more than the European one. In the specific cases of democratizing countries, the EU and its conditionality create an opportunity structure that the domestic actors can use to pressure the political actors towards reforms. Still, Green Cowles and Risse (2001) show that change is likely to occur if the pressures from the EU coincide with the interests of particular domestic groups. Otherwise, change is dubious.

CCs engage in the accession process, which involves the adoption of a "set of rules, norms, institutional structure, ideas and meanings, interests and identities" (Lendvai 2004: 320). Once it starts, domestic and European issues become more intertwined due to the continuing impact of Europeanization. The steps towards Europeanization can be initiated either at the domestic or at the European level. Action can also be taken at both levels simultaneously that reinforces the whole process of rule adoption (Schimmelfennig and Sedelmeier 2005). On the domestic level then, "Europeanization is both a cause and an effect of action . . . The mode of reaction of the different states highlight not only the importance they attach to Europe, but also their understanding of what 'Europe' is" (Featherstone and Kazamias 2001: 2). European questions slowly become domestic political issues. The discussion becomes more salient as the negotiations touch on the more sensitive issues of integration and it culminates in the ratification process.

With the deepening of European integration, the CCs are exposed to much higher pressure of Europeanization than in earlier times. Simultaneously, the CCs are exposed to many external and internal forces – globalization, international orga- nizations, change in public perceptions and expectations, in social norms, values, beliefs. The perceptions on how to define citizenship, how to conduct foreign policy and neighborhood policy, how to define rights of minorities, how to understand gender equality, develop and change. It is hard to define what role the EU played in this process as we cannot isolate its influence from that of the other actors. Societies develop and change over time, it is a constant process affected by both internal and external factors.

The effect of Europeanization on the CCs is always asymmetrical (Pridham 2006; 2007; Featherstone and Kazamias 2001, Hughes, Sasse and Gordon 2004) – the CCs need to adopt EU rules and regulations to satisfy the requirements for candidacy, for opening negotiations, and, finally, for membership, while they have virtually no power over the content of these rules and regulations, that is, the top- down force is much stronger than bottom-up, mainly because the CCs do not have any say in the EU decision-making process and are only beginning to participate in the various EU structures. The EU's power over the CCs is higher than over its MS because the former face the threat of being denied membership whereas the possible sanctions for the latter are relatively mild. The European Commission's regular reports on the CC's progress evaluate their advancement towards member- ship in purely EU terms. In the case of Eastern enlargement, their specific situation of extensive reform project gave the EU "a unique position to impose [on the CCs] its system of governance" (Diez 2000: 6) both formally and informally. Lane (2007) argues that the EU had a lot of influence on the political and economic development of the East Central European Countries (ECECs), partially as a result of condition- ality and the connection of the membership prospects with domestic politics.

In addition, the negotiations are intergovernmental in nature and as such conve- nience the national governments and bureaucracies over the parliaments, interest groups, and other political actors. They also lead to the fragmentation of domestic society (Featherstone and Kazamias 2001) since accession negotiations' outcomes create both "winners" and "losers." This does not need to be translated into eco- nomic terms only but should be understood as (dis)empowerment of particular sec- tions of the society, which can be "felt in social, cultural, economic and political terms as change and continuity are juxtaposed as domestic fault lines across the domestic system" (Featherstone and Kazamias 2001: 13). The empowered groups will use the EU requirements to reinforce their position in the domestic system and will try to use them to limit the power of the veto players defined as those who oppose or try to block change in the *status quo* and have the institutional power and will to do so. The more the pro-reform actors and the more vocal they become, the higher the chance of the requirement not only being met but also implemented for it has been internalized by at least some of the social actors. The EU does not "create" these domestic actors but can help empower them.

The various theoretical approaches to Europeanization include rational choice institutionalism and sociological institutionalism (social constructivism). Rational choice institutionalism applies a minimalist view of the role of institutions with states acting as rational actors with fixed sets of preferences, who try to maximize their self-interest, while the institutions lay down the rules of the relations (rules of the game). As regards Europeanization, it maintains that state compliance is achieved by providing positive and negative incentives, the so-called "logic of consequences." In the accession process, rational choice institutionalism highlights the importance of the stick and carrot approach, where the EU membership is the carrot and the denial thereof, the ultimate stick. It also works with the notion of external incentives, where the outcome of the negotiations depends on the relative power of the actors defined in terms of information available to them and the ratio between the benefit coming from the agreement and the possible alternatives. It also works with the concept of adoption cost, that is, the country will have a better compliance record if the adoption costs are low and vice versa. If the government faces zero adoption costs, it is assumed that conditionality is not necessary. However, the costs are not stable and might change with, for example, a change in government.

While respecting the strengths of rationalism, that is, the ability to conduct detailed research on the individual phenomena of European integration, we believe that it basically excludes important aspects closely related to the issue of enlargement, notably the questions of "identity, community and collective identity" (Christiansen et al. 1999: 533). While rationalism works with the idea that the actors can evaluate the real costs and benefits, that is, they follow the "logic of consequences," social constructivism states that actors behave in a certain way because that is how things are done in their view, that is, follow the "logic of appropriateness," choosing from the range of available choices the most legitimate or "appropriate" one.

Thus, while accession is governed by rational actors, the outcome is also influenced by other factors such as socialization and adoption of certain norms and rules. The EU will not be able to impose its regimes on the CCs despite its power and the asymmetry in their relations (Diez 2000) if the CCs are not willing to accept it. Therefore, the CCs will follow the stick and carrot approach of the EU but only under certain conditions and only up till a certain point. It also leads to the idea that if EU enlargement is to be successful, more attention needs to be paid to the norm adoption so that we avoid the so-called Potemkin harmonization. The extent to which the CC listens to the EU depends not only the former's material interests but also on the extent to which it identifies with the latter (Diez 2000).

Social constructivism assumes that values, norms, and rules provide an important part of explaining political processes and events because they affect identities, behavior, and interests. Constructivists define norms as "shared, collective understandings that make behavioural claims on actors" (Checkel 1999: 551). Actors try to discover the existing rules and follow them, through the "logic of appropriateness" and "rule-governed action." Sjursen (2006: 9) argues that the "logic of appropriateness" results either from habit or particular identity or from "rational assessment of morally valid arguments." For the purposes of our work, we are not as much concerned with how European norms are created as how they interact within the accession process, how they affect the CCs, and how they become internalized and diffused.

CCs adopt EU norms because they believe in their legitimacy and because they identify with the EU. Unlike rational institutionalism, which argues that norms will be adopted as a result of offered incentives (or fear of punishment), social constructivism holds that they will be adopted because domestic actors see the EU norms as legitimate and suitable solutions for existing domestic issues (Schimmelfennig and Sedelmeier 2005). Social constructivists argue that the willingness to accept external norms increases if it concerns an area where such rules were absent or delegitimized, that is, there will be minimum opposition, or where the CC believes that the EU rules match with its image of "good policy" (Schimmelfennig and Sedelmeier 2005).[3]

They are also interested in discourse analysis. Diez (1999: 602, 610) argues that "speech acts have important social and political consequences" and notes that the future of European integration does not depend only on the national interests of the MS but also on the "translatability of the discourses on European governance that the relevant political actors are embedded in." Thus, language represents an essential device for social constructivists because it "shapes our social and political realities" (Tunkrová 2008). How we name things becomes important for our understanding and communication. Social constructivists accentuate the power of negotiation, persuasion, and contestation in the EU negotiations. The regular reports on the progress of the CCs prepared by the Commission use language not only to evaluate the country in question but also to inspire further changes and reforms using "constructive criticism" to pressure the governments for more reforms but not to demotivate them. Just like in the actual negotiations, not only "what" is said but also "how" it is said is crucial. However, this is often measured not in absolute but relative terms, compared either to the previous year or over a longer period of time and it also differs from country to country (Hughes, Sasse and Gordon 2004).

What needs to be highlighted here, though, is that constructivists do not argue that discourses "cause" but that they "enable" and that they are not rigid (Diez 1999: 611). Applied to EU practice, "directives and communications from and to the European institutions speak a specific and unique language which is normally only understood by a limited circle of insiders" (Christiansen et.al. 1999: 541). Hughes et al. (2004: 141) argue that the CCs' elites need to learn to "'speak European' but also become acculturated and assimilated into European norms and 'ways of doing things.'" Verney (2006: 40) utilizes the example of Greece in demonstrating the importance of talking about enlargement for influencing its outcome, when the original rather strong opposition to Greece belonging to Europe[4] changed into a "moral mission" to democratize the country through EC membership. She further believes that at this point promotion of democracy became "a major new legitimating strategy for the European Community" (Verney 2006: 40) and that already the second enlargement – what she calls the "Greek precedent" (Verney 2006: 41) – showed that the European Economic Community (EEC) did not perceive itself as a problem-solving entity but rather a "value-based community founded on a conception of a common European identity and the rights-based post-national union" (Verney 2006: 39). Ever since 1981, democracy promotion became an important argument in all subsequent enlargements, with the exception of the 1995 European Free Trade Association (EFTA) enlargement.

What language the EU and the MS choose and how the CCs understand the message involves the process of social learning. The language of individuals and the various groups together with the different approaches to constructing the environment result in different set of languages being used, a "discursive web surrounding each articulation" (Diez 1999: 603). Our understanding of the meaning is subjective and exposed to the understandings of the other actors in the process defined by our and their contexts. The attitudes about cause and effect may alter without open coercion resulting in the redefinition of interests and/or identity (Checkel 1999). A reason for such change can be, for example, recognition of a policy failure, which needs rectification, a choice of different approach. This can extend from minor policy issues to large shifts in, for instance, foreign policy orientation or choice of a predominant economic model. For social constructivism, social realities are "fragile, changeable, and contestable," are more "local than global" and "are confined to a limited time-frame" (Christiansen et. al. 1999: 530). Similarly, identities change and develop, or as Sjursen (2006: 14) puts it, "identities are malleable entities and they are shaped and reshaped through communicative processes." Delanty and Rumford (2005: 16) describe them as not "forever fixed or immutable" but rather as "social realities . . . shaped in conditions of contestation and negotiation."

For social constructivists, people understand the world through "world views," which "give meaning to social situations" and are "real myths produced by institutions and used by actors" (Jachtenfuchs 1995: 119). Thus, the Copenhagen political criteria are not uniformly applied and are ideologically biased but they are defined as a basis of European political identity; therefore, the CCs are required to fulfill them. These norms become embedded in the community as universal values and they refer to the EU in the framework of a rights-based conception. The Eurobarometer (EB) surveys have, for example, repeatedly shown that EU citizens want the CCs to meet the Copenhagen criteria in order to be admitted and we can also often find such statements in the speeches of the EU and MS representatives. In addition, people "'imagine' their social surroundings" (Delanty and Rumford 2005: 16) within certain socio-cultural frameworks – for instance the Czech population sees itself as belonging to the Western Christian tradition despite the very high levels of atheism in the country. Defined politically in terms of democracy, human rights and rule of law, or culturally, the CC needs to understand the EU and itself within these terms. Hence, the EU's attachment must be coherent and credible and the CC must place itself within these terms and consider them the source of a shared identity.

The EU embraces several competing world views, where the three dominant ones are intergovernmentalist-federalist debate; secular-Christian; and liberal-social market. For some it is primarily a process of creating a supranational, democratic polity based on a set of democratic principles and respect for human rights, for others a cultural entity, and yet for others a market. These various conceptions of what the EU is/should be confront each other in the public sphere through discourses, yet the actors involved cannot control them, "they are generative of the very terms of the debate . . . There are no authoritative definitions of what constitutes the 'we,' the 'other,' 'inside' or 'outside'" (Delanty and Rumford 2005: 19). The CCs also become – even though still marginally – more and more involved in these debates as the point of accession draws near. All three conceptions affect them not only indirectly through EU policies but also directly as the CCs' compatibility with these "camps" will affect the MS' approach and support for or resistance to their membership.

For example in Germany, the Christian Democrats (CDU/CSU) support the cultural and normative world view and the Social Democrats (SPD) the rights-based political union. Chancellor Kohl, who once called the EU a "civilizational project," often mentioned with respect to the ECECs the shared values of Western Christianity, Renaissance and Enlightenment, cultural kinship, and reconciliation. With the SPD coming to power in 1998, the rhetoric changed to an emphasis on universal rights rather than cultural association and the government shifted its attention from Germany's immediate neighbors to a more general support for enlargement, including Turkey (Zaborowski 2006). In this regard, Kohl once said that a Muslim country like Turkey does not belong to Europe (Lundgren 2006: 121) and it is rather obvious that Turkey would not have been granted candidate status or start the negotiations had a CDU/CSU government been in power in Germany in 1999 and in 2004.

Every enlargement, but more so the last two rounds and the ones to come, lead to questions about the nature of European values and to some extent also what defines Europe, and where the term "Europe" is equated with the EU. So, does the accession to the EU mean that the country reached a sufficient level of "Europeaness" or is "Europeaness" a basic pre-requisite for starting the negotiations in the first place? And, finally, does "Europeaness" matter at all? The proponents of these three approaches, political, cultural and economic, would provide quite conflicting answers to the questions. We can, though, claim that the last two enlargement rounds have changed the EU, which is no longer "exclusively based on a narrow western conception of modernity" (Delanty and Rumford 2005: 20).

Delanty (2003) argues that Europe does not have political or cultural identity and the national identities are being transformed by Europeanization and globalization. Europe is not a homogenous continent, neither are its regions, and, in many cases, nor are its countries. Despite some commonalities such as a predominantly Christian heritage, Europe's nations differ economically, politically, and culturally. Referring today to some shared values and norms defined by the Copenhagen criteria is problematic as regards their unquestionable application in all EU MS.

Europeanization is believed to have the potential of promoting policy convergence (Featherstone and Kazamias 2001). Taking into consideration that the adaptation to European values, norms, and rules depends on their domestic context, a certain level of convergence with "European" values could be expected (Wiener

2006) but the data indicate otherwise. Arts and Halman (2004: 47) note there are many "varieties in cultural heritages, languages, religious and ideological traditions, and differences in political and education systems" across Europe. Their research on the European Value Surveys also indicates that we cannot observe a "unique trajectory of values change"; therefore, even though they find some pattern of conversion to post-materialist values, it is not a general one. As the heterogeneity of the EU increases with each subsequent enlargement, convergence becomes a moving target. Other surveys, however, are more optimistic.[5] If the EU values and norms were stable and shared by MS, the EU should have been providing clear signals to the CC, however, the MS do not share a clear set of values and norms, which results in often ambiguous enlargement preferences. The EU institutions and MS have at times divergent inclinations and as such, the CCs are facing an uncertain environment.

Focus of our research

We want to concentrate in this volume of the effects of Europeanization prior to accession, that is. during (and even prior to the initiation of) the accession process, on the CCs. Countries aspiring for membership have to meet the terms of the EU as part of the conditionality demand for receiving the status of a CC and later for full membership. Schimmelfennig and Sedelmeier (2002) identify four areas of enlargement research: applicants' enlargement politics; member state enlargement politics; EU enlargement politics; and the impact of enlargement. We are concerned with the last one, impact of enlargement. The key issue is "how does enlargement change the identity, the interests, and the behavior of governmental and societal actors? Under what conditions do they conform to the norms of the organization?" (Schimmelfennig and Sedelmeier 2002: 507); and how do the embedded structures of the country affect the process of Europeanization? Apart from individual case studies on selected countries and/or single issues comparing the Central and Eastern European countries (CEECs), the possibility of comparing the experience of the ECECs[6] and Turkey has been to a great extent neglected. The conclusions of the existing research on Europeanization are in this respect still inconclusive and exhibit relatively elevated levels of fragmentation. This volume focuses on the perspective of the CCs and Europeanization in these countries and as such belongs to "accession literature." We try to identify how Europeanization understood in the more narrow definition of the term affected the ECECs and Turkey and what lessons we can draw from their experiences.

The EU actively promotes certain rules, values, and norms perceived as essentially European, generally believed to be derived from the West European heritage of humanism, rationalism, and secularism, which the CCs have to comply with and the EU regularly assesses their observance in the Commission's reports on their progress. It becomes a basis for receiving the status of a CC and for opening and closing the accession negotiations. In its enlargement policy, the EU has used political norms and values as defined mainly by the Copenhagen criteria for assessing the CCs' congruity with EU norms and values. The Copenhagen political criteria are currently the dominant factor in EU enlargement policies with respect to determining the CC's belonging to "Europe."

The effect and implementation of EU norms varies across CCs and among their various social groups. While some internalize the norms, others adopt a rhetoric supporting the values and norms because they expect some benefit often without a true conviction in their validity. Moreover, domestic politics, the distribution and relative power of veto actors in the society, and the actors' expectations play a vital role. During the accession process, the debate takes on various forms and is shaped by the realities of the negotiations and the domestic and international environment.

While we believe that rational institutionalist approach to the ECECs' and Turkey's accession provides much important insight into accession literature, we predominantly adopt a social constructivist approach to understand the role of assessing their democratic and economic capacity in their accession negotiations. The ECECs were new democracies, emerging market economies, and carriers of many negative legacies of their communist regimes. They belong to the Eastern periphery while Turkey belongs to Europe's South-Eastern periphery. Distant from the economic centers, these democratic "newcomers" are economically relatively weak and burdened by the negative heritage of autocratic or authoritarian regimes.

The ECECs seem to have little in common with Turkey[7] but at closer look we will see that there are many things these countries share. Both come from a political culture where the state was superior to the society and as Sadurski (2004) shows, they have suffered from weak public administration, widespread corruption, civil servants' arrogance towards the public, government party control over the public media and business manipulation of the private media, slow and corrupt judiciary, internal security service interfering with politics, and members of parliament hiding behind parliamentary immunity. Lundgren (2006) argues that the main difference between the Central and Eastern European candidates and Turkey is the human rights and democracy record rather than the often mentioned problem of "cultural closeness."

We deliberately limit our selection of the former communist countries to the so-called Visegrad group only. It makes our work manageable and more focused. They were seen as the accession "winners" and as such provide better contrast to Turkey than latecomers such as Bulgaria and Romania. They are also similar enough to provide a rather consistent group – reason for excluding the Baltics. Slovenia will not be considered as it is a rather odd case for many reasons – it is a former Yugoslav republic, economically strong, small, and a relatively homogenous society. The four countries we investigate – Czech Republic, Hungary, Poland, and Slovakia – provide a number of fields where comparison with Turkey is possible. In all five cases, we can argue that Europeanization was seen as means of completing modernization and democratization, where various actors in the domestic arena actively referred to the EU as a source of inspiration, justification, and point of reference when internalizing the norms and beliefs related to European integration.

A CC's path to accession can be divided into several phases starting with focusing their policies to Brussels, a process which culminates in the formalization of this relationship in association agreements. For ECECs, this stage was completed with the signature of the association agreements in the first half of the 1990s. The second phase was marked by the pre-accession negotiations (1994 to 1997). The third phase commenced with the signature of the accession partnerships, the first evaluation reports prepared by the European Commission in 1997, and the opening of the negotiations in 1998 (2000 for Slovakia). The fourth phase started upon their accession to the EU in May 2004.

Turkey signed the association agreement, the Ankara agreement, in 1963. In 1973, a detailed customs union plan was signed but the 1974 Turkish occupation of Northern Cyprus and the 1980 military coup froze the relations between the Turkey and the Community. The association process was revived in 1986 and Turkey applied for membership in 1987. The Commission endorsed Turkish eligibility in 1989, customs union was established in 1996, and it was granted CC status in 1999. Accession partnership was signed in 2001 and the negotiations officially commenced in October 2005, while the actual negotiations started in June 2006. The Commission, however, included a safeguard clause, which stipulated that the negotiations could be suspended if the reform process in Turkey came to a halt.

In the ECECs, the desire to "return to Europe" dominated their foreign policies since the fall of communism and constituted a reconstruction of their identity from a socialist to a democratic state and as European citizens. In Turkey, the motivation to enter the EU falls within the long process of Turkish modernization as defined by the Republic's first leader and its architect, Mustafa Kemal, who saw westernization (and the related Europeanization) as the future of the new Republic and a source of a new, modern Turkish identity. For Turkish elites, membership in western organizations, including the EU, has always been considered a natural continuation of the modernization plan. The broader understanding of Europeanization developed over time into the more specific one, explicitly related to the goal of EU membership. Even though political and economic problems at times strained the EC-Turkish relations, since the establishment of the European Economic Community (EEC) it has been one of the chief aims of the Turkish Republic to be fully recognized as a European state via joining the EU.

While economic reasons played an important role for both the ECECs and Turkey – at the point when the negotiations started, Turkey was more economically integrated within the EU structures than any of the ECECs, mainly due to the establishment of the customs union in 1996 – political motivations seem to be the dominant determinant in their effort to join the EU. The ECECs wanted to decouple from their communist (Eastern European) past, Turkey wanted to decouple from its Ottoman past, the Middle Eastern connection and the fear of being "left behind" after the end of the Cold War. EU membership was to serve both as a final confirmation of their belonging to the (West) European tradition and civilization. While they shared the desire to join the EU, the ECECs and Turkey also shared a certain level of distrust towards the West – the Turks talk about the "Sèvres syndrome/complex," Hungarians about the "Trianon trauma," the Czechs have their "Munich trauma," and Poles feel a prevalent distrust towards the Germans as a legacy of World War

II; all ECECs blame the West for not supporting them during their anti-Soviet uprisings; and Turkey for "deserting" it after the end of the Cold War.

In the EU's approach to the CCs, in the case of the ECECs, there was the feeling of responsibility to integrate countries that were involuntarily excluded from the European project. In addition, the EU was hoping that their membership would ensure that the political and economic reforms were irreversible. In the Turkish debate, there are voices claiming that the EU should award Turkey with membership for serving as a buffer against the potential Soviet attack in Europe during the Cold War, as a reliable North Atlantic Treaty Organization (NATO) partner and an island of relatively high stability in the neighborhood of wobbly Near and Middle East. In both cases, the EU also followed economic reasons – creating a larger market and investment opportunities. Still, some negative images were hard to overcome. The ECECs as members of the former Eastern bloc represented recent enemies. In the second half of the twentieth century, Europe's main spook was communism and 20 years ago, the ECECs were, as a part of the Soviet bloc, the main dangerous "other." In the case of Turkey, history books make it into a major enemy of Europe's in the past and, more recently, Islamophobia has turned the country's Muslim faith into a scary ghost of today. Actually, as the communist threat vanished, Turkey rematerialized as the major "other."

The impact of Europeanization on the post-communist countries was far greater than in the previous rounds of enlargement not only because of the deepening in the second half of the 1980s and in the 1990s but also due to the process of transition from communist to liberal societies as the EU had a unique opportunity to help form the new structures, policies, and institutions of their societies involving both democratization and liberalization of the economies. Some authors, therefore, distinguish between "Europeanization West" and "Europeanization East" highlighting that even though the two have certain common features, the latter had many specifics because it involved CCs and not MS and a transition to liberal market economies with the need for substantial institutional reforms. Furthermore, the monitoring of compliance was much more rigid in the case of CCs because the Commission started to publish detailed annual reports on the CCs' progress.[8] Turkey is not undergoing such dramatic development but the EU is trying to apply many of the instruments developed for the CEECs in order to help Turkey complete the long-awaited process of full democratization and economic liberalization. Still, for some the required reforms in Turkey do represent "radical progressive democratization" (Avbar et al. 2007: 336) and some even call the political and economic reform process and change between 2000 and 2004 a "refolution" (Benhabib and Isiksel 2006).

Yet, we do not try to argue that these cases are identical. The authors are aware that there are many differences within the group of the four ECECs and between them and Turkey. We realize that cross-country comparison of such multilevel variables as Europeanization leads to a high level of simplification and generalization. The countries do not have the same institutional structures, they react differently to the adaptation pressures, they have diverse political cultures, there are different veto players in their societies, and the accession process has empowered different sectors of their societies. Their ability to utilize the accession process has also varied. These problems raise the question of method. We combined data published by the EU, the MS, CCs, and both national and international NGOs. We also used results of previous research on either individual case studies of particular countries and/or policies or more extensive attempts at understanding these forces. We are aware that the data are not always fully comparable but believe that they provide a framework solid enough to present substantial conclusions.

Literature review

The EU accession process brought about broad political, economic, and social changes in the CCs' societies. A good number of publications have been dedicated to the accession process in Eastern and Central Europe and Turkey. Most of the literature available on Europeanization of CCs focuses on the experience of the CEECs prior, and now also after, their accession to the EU. Examples of more systematic analyses are Green Cowles, Caporaso, and Risse's (2001) *Transforming Europe. Europeanization and Domestic Change*, which focuses on the impact of Europeanization on the domestic systems; Featherstone and Radaelli's (2003) *The Politics of Europeanization*, which contributed a good deal to the clarification of the concept of Europeanization; and then Schimmelfennig and Sedelmeier's (2005) *The Europeanization of Central and Eastern Europe*, which applied the concept of Europeanization to the then CCs both theoretically and empirically. Hughes, Sasse, and Gordon's (2004) *Europeanization and Regionalization in the EU's Enlargement to Central and Eastern Europe* presented a strong empirical comparative work in the CEECs uncovering some of the over-exaggerated claims regarding EU conditionality, which allowed many of the previous unclear assumptions to be corrected and/or modified.

Comparative approach to the ECECs can be found in a great deal of works too – apart from the several works of Grabbe (2001; 2002; 2004) and Pridham (2006; 2007; 2008) that focused mainly on the implications of conditionality for EU enlargement policies and democratization, Sadurski (2004) examined whether Europeanization provided a "democracy dividend," de Ridder (2008) analyzed the power of national governments in the Czech Republic and Slovakia within the EU's democracy promotion efforts. Riishøj (2004) compared the impact of Europeanization on Euroscepticism in Poland and the Czech Republic, while Elgün and Tillman (2007) analyzed the relationship between Europeanization and public support for EU membership. Neumayer (2008) looked at how the EU was used in domestic political competition in the new MS; Goetz (2001; 2005) looked at its effect on central administration and also more generally at the level of Europeanization in the CCs, which he identified as present but much weaker than in the MS. Strazay (2003) investigated the relationship between nationalist-populism and democratization, Epstein (2007) the democratization of civil-military relations, and Piana (2009) the judicial reforms in CCs. Johns (2003), Rechel (2008), and Schwellnus (2006; 2009) examined the issue of minority rights. Manning (2004) compared the social policies in the ECECs in light of their transition and Europeanization and

Borragán (2002; 2003; 2004; 2006) has done extensive work on Europeanization of interest groups and civil society in the ECECs. Also gender policies have attracted quite a lot of attention.

The numerous works on the ECECs have been more recently accompanied by growing literature on Europeanization and the case of Turkey. Authors both from within and outside of Turkey have paid special attention to issues such as minority rights, civil-military relations, gender equality, social policy, civil society development, and Turkish foreign policy. The impact of Europeanization on democratization in Turkey was for the first time introduced in a more detailed manner and taking into consideration the previous conclusions of the research in the 2005 special issue of the *South European Society and Politics* journal titled "Turkey, Europeanisation and Civil Society" edited by Thomas Diez. Schimmelfenig, Engert, and Knobel (2003) compared democratic conditionality in Latvia, Slovakia, and Turkey showing that in all three cases, but mainly in the latter two, conditionality critically contributed to their democratization and Kubicek (2005) looked at the relationship between democratization in Turkey and the EU process. Still, most of the works on Turkey and the EU focus either on the impact of the accession process on Turkish politics – less so economy – or the relationship between the EU and Turkey and how the EU will be affected by Turkish accession institutionally, politically, economically, and culturally. The research areas mostly address selected topics, such as the possible implications of Turkish membership for the EU or its impact on Turkey, they analyze the relationship between democratization and liberalization in Turkey (without closer relation to the experience of the post-communist countries); Turkish foreign policy and the EU; of specific issues such as terrorism, identity, or citizenship.

For example, out of the many publications available, Joseph's *Turkey and the European Union: Internal Dynamics and External Challenges* (2006) provides a good overview of the key problems on the Turkish road to membership but just like Arikan's *Turkey and the EU: An Awkward Candidate for EU Membership?* (2006) it concentrates mostly on the possible accommodation of the European and Turkish structures. Similarly, Lake's *The EU and Turkey: A Glittering Prize or a Millstone?* (2005) examines the macro level of the Turkish-EU relations, once more discussing the key challenges (economic, social, cultural) from the more general point. Keyman and Icduygu's *Citizenship in a Global World: European Questions and Turkish Experiences* (2005) is a great resource for grasping the Turkish understanding of state, modernity, and democracy, vital for appreciating the Turkish context.

The attempts to compare the experience of the Central European countries and Turkey have been very sporadic. Most of the comparative efforts – out of the very few – focus on comparisons with the Balkans or the Mediterranean periphery countries (for instance Featherstone and Kazamias 2000; Warning 2006; LaGro 2007; Grigoriadis 2008; Öniş and Grigoriadis 2009). The publication by LaGro and Jørgensen *Turkey and the European Union: Prospects for a Difficult Encounter* (2007) includes a chapter on the experience taken from previous enlargements but it presents a rather general approach. Very few authors connect the ECECs and Turkey on other than random basis. Even then, the approach is either case- or country-specific – comparing mainly Poland and Turkey – for example in the works of Adam Szymanski, Chris Rumford, Åsa Lungren or Ziya Öniş.

One of the first more general attempts was Hughes' (2004) paper "Turkey and the European Union: Just Another Enlargement? Exploring the Implications of Turkish Accession" claiming that the Turkish accession will have some similarities with the CEECs. Tocci (2007) recently edited an interesting report on the conditionality and prejudice in Turkey-EU relations from the perspective of several MS, including Poland, Slovenia, and Turkey. Haughton (2007) looked into how conditionality would affect the EU's ability to bring about change in Croatia and Turkey and LaGro (2007) made links between Europeanization and the enlargement process in the CEECs and Turkey. There is also the recent book by Verez *D'un Élargissement à l'Autre: la Turquie et les Autres Candidats* (2005) but here the CEECs are used mostly as a point of reference, which seems to be the prevailing approach. A more consistent analysis of the Eastern and Turkish enlargement rounds is a volume edited by Helene Sjursen (2006) *Questioning EU Enlargement*, which explores the connections and similarities between the ECECs' and the Turkish accession experiences. Jürgen Gerhads (2007) in his book *Differences between Old and New Member States of the EU and Turkey* looks at the cultural similarities and differences between the countries. The work is interesting working with three groups of variables – modernity, culture/religion, and political and institutional system – but the data he works with are rather outdated and the book relies too heavily on generalizations.

Structure of the volume

As a background to all the chapters, the volume opens with a chapter "Becoming European: Kemalism as an Ideology of Westernism" by Petr Kučera, who shows how the Kemalist modernization project created specific images, which have been embedded in the historical development of the Turkish Republic and became the collective memory of the nation. The chapter discusses how the constructed images of East and West were formed and provides a historical introduction to Kemalism as a westernization ideology, elaborating on its connection with the late Ottoman westernization movement and Kemalist social engineering attempts when constructing Turkish "Europeaness." Instead of focusing on the well-covered impact of Kemalist ideology on the modern Turkish Republic and contemporary Turkish politics, the chapter highlights one specific dimension of Kemalism, that is its westernist element, which wanted to turn Turks into "Europeans." Kučera introduces the concepts discussed in the following chapters, providing the necessary background of issues that continue to resonate in the Turkish society. He argues that despite the various evaluations today, it should be seen as more than simply a modernization ideology but an indispensable part of Turkish identity.

The following chapter "Democratization and EU Conditionality – A Barking Dog that Does (Not) Bite?" looks at the link between Europeanization and democratization showing that the direct effect of conditionality needs to be accompanied by the indirect forces of elite socialization. First on the example of gender equality, it demonstrates how in both the ECECs and Turkey the accession process introduced positive legal instruments of gender equality. However, in the ECECs the non-governmental actors remained relatively weak while in Turkey they have been much more active – as a result of the so-called cognitive Europeanization, attitudes towards gender equality in Turkey started to change and some new topics entered the agenda. If such players are absent or weak and powerful veto actors exist, the importance of the problem will remain low and implementation poor, as the other case study on corruption shows. The failure to give the fight against corruption high political salience resulted, in both cases, in the enduring high occurrence of corrupt practices despite the public's disapproval and the legal measures introduced after the pressure from the EU and other international bodies. The chapter concludes that Europeanization significantly encouraged important legal changes within political conditionality, provided pro-reform forces with strong additional instruments to help define and highlight the agenda but without sufficient political will in the CC, its effectiveness can be overestimated.

The following chapter on desecuritization by Rabia Karakaya Polat "How far away from Politics of Fear? Turkey in the EU Accession Process" analyzes the developments in the challenge of securitization, which is for many observers one of the main obstacles for Turkey in developing a European identity and joining the EU. While the reform process opened a number of issues that were previously considered taboo in any political discussion and as Polat says were "dramaticized," this process of desecuritization still leaves behind many problems such as freedom of speech and the widespread hostility towards granting right to the various minority groups in Turkey. The reforms caused some of the previous restrictions to be restated and that slowed down the process such as the "reform" of the infamous Article 301 of the Constitution.[9] Also, certain problems are used by the securitizers to reverse the process and they use speech acts to fuel long-planted fears in the population. She claims that "although the EU has been successful in inducing formal change, i.e. legislation, its influence on political culture through changing values and norms has been so far limited."

Ahmet Sözen focuses in the chapter "The Cyprus Question in Turkey-EU Relations" on the Cyprus issue, which has been occupying a very important part of the Turkish foreign policy for the past 50 years and is closely linked to the Turkish EU accession process. The official Turkish foreign policy towards Cyprus has changed several times in parallel to the changing international conjecture. In order to understand where the two conflicting sides in Cyprus are today, Sözen provides an overview of the evolution of the Cyprus negotiations in the past four decades with a more detailed analysis of the more recent events. The chapter presents a summary of the conflict paying special attention to the role the EU has played in the conflict and how it has affected EU-Cyprus-Turkey relations. The author shows how the two sides have at times used speech acts to achieve their goals and how the Greek Cypriots (ab)used the talking about European values to postpone the solution of the problem and to pressure the involved sides while Turkish Cypriots have partially lost their faith in the EU. He concludes with outlining what this represents for the future of the settlement.

The dynamics in the CC-relations are reflected in the public opinion. The chapter "The Challenge of Euroscepticism in the Accession Countries: The Good, the

Bad and the Shaky EU" compares the trends in public and political party attitudes towards EU membership in the ECECs and Turkey. Despite some differences, many similar developments could be found. The chapter shows that it is not as important what the EU is but what the CCs think it is, how they perceive it, and what they anticipate. Much depends on the different expectations and variations in the interpretation of meaning, including the meaning of norms, and the effect of cultural differences. The reactions and development of the communication process changes with experience – not only the norms develop but also their relative meaning.

The last two chapters of the volume investigate the issue of Turkish accession process from the perspective of the ECECs. Armağan Emre Çakır and Angelika Gergelová focus on the discussions of absorption capacity and Turkey in the official positions of the ECECs while reconsidering these discussions in the more general context of the EU-wide debate. Their chapter examines the official documents of the four countries in three main areas – institutional, economic, and cultural. They conclude that the ECECs are generally supportive of Turkish membership even though their past positions and some observed concerns would indicate otherwise. The authors explain this support by the ECECs' recent memories of candidate countries and by the relative remoteness of Turkish accession when many issues are still left unresolved, thus, the institutional and economic statements are rather broad and open for possible future changes. As a result, the cultural arguments seem to dominate the debate infected by the ECECs' own ambivalence about the nature of their "European identity." The authors believe that the generally positive approach to Turkish accession will persist in the short and medium term and that it might be only later revaluated as the "conditions of Turkish membership become more specific," which could possibly lead to a situation when "the enlargement agenda collides with other policies and interests."

Finally Pavel Šaradín investigates the support for Turkish EU membership within a broader debate in the ECECs, including non-governmental parties and representatives of the civil society. He then puts the findings in the framework of the Eurooptimist-Eurosceptic debate. Even though the discourse on Turkish accession is in these circles more vivid and controversial than is the case of the official country positions, he comes to a very similar conclusion as Çakır and Gergelová, that is, the debate is for the time being rather vague and will intensify in the future. He also claims that it will be especially the opponents of Turkish EU accession whose voices we will heard most often and most loudly. In the conclusion called "The New European Union," Pavel Šaradín reflects on the past 20 years of the ECECs "experience with Europe," while putting into the perspective of their Europeanization and democratization. He highlights the current debates and how the Turkish accession process falls within these discourses.

This volume attempts to establish that there are a number of potential future venues for research into EU enlargement, in particular the possibility of using the accumulated and growing knowledge and research about Eastern enlargement(s) for assessing future rounds, the benefits but mainly the challenges the EU, its MS and the CCs need to face and successfully address in order to contribute to both their democratization and the European integration process.

Notes

1 In the late 1930s, Hans Kohn (1937: 259) actually used the term together with "westernization" and defined it as "the political, social, economic and intellectual transformation . . . in process in all countries of Asia and northern Africa," thus, applying it to non-European states.

2 The second term failed to be used more widely in academia.

3 Examples of policy failure is in the case of the ECECs the legacy of the communist regimes, in the case of Turkey the disillusionment with traditional nationalist Kemalism as it failed to deliver full democracy and stable and strong economy. EU's effect is stronger if political values change or the environment/idea that underlines the policies is discredited. The negative perception of the regime's legacy was much stronger in the ECECs than in Turkey, which made it easier for their governments to change old and apply new rules. In Turkey there was general support for democratization but once the process touched upon some sensitive issues the support became less upfront.

4 There were many voices in Europe that did not consider Greece "European enough." Opposing those, who stressed the legacy of Ancient Greece, they pointed to the Greek incorporation in two Eastern empires, first Byzantine and then Ottoman, to Greek Orthodox religion, its geographical belonging to the troubled Balkans, unstable democracy, that is, Greece was seen by many as one of Europe's "other." The country was also suffering from many problems such as patronage, clientelism, and corruption. Also in the case of Spain and Portugal, their transition to democracy was accompanied in the EC by "fears of possible revolution, civil war, a right-wing coup, a communist takeover, national disintegration, a reversion to fascism" (Howard 2002).

5 A 2008 survey on the values of the Europeans showed that the three most important values shared by Europeans in the EU-27 were peace, human rights, and respect for human life, which coincided with the values of the ECECs and Turkey in a 2003 EB survey. Peace was also on the top in EU-15. For EU-27, the values representing the EU were human rights, followed by peace and democracy, again similar to the results of the ECECs and Turkey in 2003 (European Commission 2004b; 2008a; 2008b)

6 ECECs refer to the four former communist countries in Central Europe while CEECs, include all post-communist countries in Eastern Europe.

7 Despite a number of similarities, we choose not to compare and apply the accession experiences of South Eastern Europe to the case of Turkey. Greece, Spain and Portugal entered the EU before the expansion of the single market. They have been MS for about 25 years and during this period the nature of the EU and Europeanization has shifted significantly.

8 For a more detailed discussion of Europeanization West and Europeanization East, see Heritier 2005.

9 The Article 301 prohibited insulting Turkishness, Turkish ethnicity, and Turkish government and state institutions. It stated that "a person who publicly denigrates Turkishness, the Republic or the Grand National Assembly of Turkey shall be punishable by imprisonment of between six months and three years" and "a person who publicly denigrates the Government of the Republic of Turkey, the judicial institutions of the State, the military or security organizations shall be punishable by imprisonment of between six months and two years." If a Turkish citizen committed the crime, the punishment was to increase by one third. However, is also said that expressing your thought to criticize was not a crime. The amendment from April 2008 stated that to open a case under Article 301, the permission of the justice minister was required, it changed the maximum sentence to two years and the word "Turkishness" was replaced with "Turkish nation." The amendment was criticized both at home and abroad. The inadequacy of the amendment was revealed in the number of new cases opened – between January and April 2009, 719 cases were sent to the Minister for Justice (then Mehmet Ali Şahin) and he gave permission in 76 cases concerning 96 people. One of the cases concerned ten people, who called Turkey a "murderous state" when criticizing prison operations nine years ago (Bianet 2009).

2 Becoming European

Kemalism as an ideology of Westernism

Petr Kučera

The term Kemalism refers to a set of principles and reforms which were formulated by Mustafa Kemal (Atatürk, 1881–1938) and his comrades-in-arms during the Turkish War of Independence (1919–22) and in the first decades of the republic. They constituted then, as they continue to do now, the foundations of the state ideology of Turkey. The very first sentence of the preamble of the Turkish constitution refers to "reforms and principles . . . introduced by the founder of the Turkish Republic, the immortal and incomparable hero Atatürk," and Article 2, where the form of the republic is characterized, further mentions the "loyalty to Atatürk's patriotism." References to Kemalism as a normative ideology can be found another seven times in the text of the constitution.[1] Although several of the tenets of Kemalism began to be gradually challenged in the 1950s after the electoral victory of the Democratic Party, they are in its main outlines still valid today and are espoused by both the governing Islamic democrats (AKP),[2] as well as the opposition.

An important role in the Kemalist modernization project was played by the construction of specific conceptions of "Western civilization" into which Turkish society was to be incorporated by the reforms. These notions were later projected into the emergence of an imagined East as an undesirable form of Turkish society. Over the course of the historical development of the republic these images were inscribed deeply into the collective memory of the nation and in many ways still shape Turkish identity.

This chapter should serve as an introduction to the analysis of the relationship between Kemalism and Westernism (i.e. a modernization ideology which takes the West as its model) in the early Turkish republic. In the first part, we will outline some aspects of the Westernization and nationalist movements at the end of the Ottoman Empire, which Kemalism to a certain degree drew on. Consecutively, a brief discussion of Atatürk's reforms and their impact on the society is presented. Finally, using the examples of theoretical reflections on Kemalism by two prominent conservatively inclined republican intellectuals, Peyami Safa and Halide Edib Adıvar, and some general observations on the "Kemalist prose" we will attempt to show what kind of images of the "West" and "East" emerged in the Kemalist period and how they fit into the Kemalist discourse of alterization.

This account does not claim to provide an exhaustive analysis of Kemalism, nor does it offer a completely new reevaluation of this ideology. Its aim is, first, to draw attention to those features of Kemalism that show it as an ideology of Westernism and second, to serve as a historical framework which will help the readers of this volume to better understand the roots of contemporary Turkey's unflinching struggle to find a firm place in the European political and cultural structures.

Ottoman-Turkish Westernism after the Young Turk revolution

Kemalism was undoubtedly a fundamental break in the course of development of the Turkish society; however, it would be incorrect to view it without connecting it to the Westernization movement which emerged as one of the three dominant ideological currents – next to Turkism and Islamism – after the Young Turk revolution of 1908. And as we will see also the boundaries between the westernists and Turkish nationalists in terms of their perception of the West were at least permeable, if not wide open.

Westernists (*Garpçılar*) had in this period a close relationship with the preceding philosophical-literary group, The Riches of Sciences (*Servet-i Fünun*), which at the turn of the century tried to strongly anchor in Ottoman society the Western literary tradition and its aesthetic sensitivity, and displayed affinities with Turkish positivists, whose first exponent was Beşir Fuad (1852/3?–1887), the *enfant terrible* among the Ottoman man of letters.

The relationship between the West and the Ottoman Empire was described by the westernists as that between a strong and a weak, or a rich and a poor, where the latter was trying to achieve the same status as its more successful counterpart. Their goal was to westernize the "Asian minds" (*Asyaî kafalar*), as they believed that without this transformation no progress could ever be achieved. In accordance with the aesthetics of the "New Literature" (as the members of *Servet-i Fünun* called their literary movement), they wanted to transform the society by focusing on behavioral changes and on altering the individuals' way of thinking, and therefore tried to spread the knowledge of European customs and habits, promoting them even with the help of pictures in magazines such as *Free Interpretation* (*İçtihad*) or *Intelligence in the Twentieth Century* (*Yirminci Asırda Zekâ*). Some among the more radical westernists even voiced the opinion that one of the biggest obstacles on the path to modernity was not only the old Ottoman-Islamic traditions and institutions, but also religion as such, and in their articles they openly championed Darwinism and materialism (Hanioğlu 1992).

As soon as 1908, Abdullah Cevdet, one of the leading personalities of radical westernists, published a translation of a book by the Dutch orientalist Reinhardt Dozy, *Essaî sur l'histoire de l'Islamisme* (under the title *Tarih-i İslamiyet* [*A History of Islam*]), which explains Muhammad's prophetic mission through psychopathology. Strongly influenced by the psychological-anthropological theory of Gustav Le Bon on races and their mixing, he came at one point even to the conclusion that crossbreeding of races leads to the creation of stronger and more viable races, and therefore Turks should mix with "advanced races" (i.e. Europeans) (Ülken 2001: 256).[3] Another resolute westernist, Baha Tevfik, formulated around 1909 under the inspiration of Nietzsche and Büchner, whose works he had been translating into Turkish, his theory of "immoralism" (see especially his *Yeni Ahlâk* [*New Ethics*]), which called into question Aristotle's rational ethics alongside the mystical ethics of al-Ghazzali and stated that morality in the idealistic sense did not exist – it was solely a mechanism of man's control over his instincts. Baha Tevfik "distinguished" himself among his contemporaries also by his absolute lack of interest in the Ottoman-Islamic culture and his exaltation of everything coming from the West. In the first issue of the magazine *Philosophy* (*Felsefe*), which he had founded in 1912, he described his mission in the following manner:

> In our country there does not exist a philosophical language, and I am trying to create it. I want to break down the zigzags between the East and the West, I want to announce that Eastern sources can no longer bear any new fruit. The superiority of life in the West has its parallel in the superiority of its philosophy.
>
> (Ülken 2001: 234)[4]

In the same year, the westernists published an article in *İçtihad* called "A Very Awake Sleep" (*Pek Uyanık Bir Uyku*), which contained a detailed program of modernization anticipating in many ways Atatürk's subsequent reforms. It suggested changes in dress (a ban on wearing the fez and turbans with the exception of religious dignitaries; women would be free to choose what to wear), in religion (the end of segregation between the sexes, shutting down dervish convents, closing the madrasas and replacing them with modern educational institutions, persecuting charmers and sellers of talismans), in law (granting women more rights; directly adopting a European-style civil code), in the army, in language (simplification of the grammatical rules of Turkish and a consolidation of the lexicon). Moreover, it also called for bringing up Ottoman princes in the manner young European monarchs were being brought up and prohibiting them from having concubines. Other reformers further proposed in a number of periodicals that the Arabic script should be significantly modified in order to better fit the phonetics of Turkish or that it should be replaced by the Latin script.[5]

Probably the most elaborate and comprehensive theoretical text of the late Ottoman westernists is the today less known work of Tüccarzâde İbrahim Hilmi *Europeanize. The Causes of Our Catastrophes* (*Avrupalılaşmak. Felâketlerimizin Esbâbı*, 1916), showing why and in what way the Ottoman-Turkish society must "Europeanize" in its social and family life, in culture, economics, and politics. The Ottoman society is in a deep crisis, says İbrahim Hilmi, as the "oriental way of life" and the "oriental administration of the state" has long since become bankrupt and its remains are being destroyed by the "dreadful waves of civilization" sweeping from the dynamic West. For İbrahim Hilmi the dreary state of society, the territorial disintegration of the Ottoman Empire and the expansionism of the Western powers was only another evidence of the strength of the West – a power he believed the Ottoman Empire lacked due to its adherence to the "Eastern" way of life (Tüccarzâde 1997).

İbrahim Hilmi saw the causes of "our catastrophes" in the fact that while the West had gone through Renaissance and Enlightenment, in the East, the "gates of *içtihad*" (free interpretation of texts) had been closed and the East fell into lethargy and stagnation. The original energy of the Ottoman Empire burned out at the moment when its "Asian" features, stemming from its intercourse with the Persian, Arab and Byzantine cultures, prevailed and the "Asian spirit" expanded to all levels of society bringing along fatalism and excessive adherence to the past (Tüccarzâde 1997: 40). Turks made a mistake in that they succumbed to this "Asian spirit" and did not devote themselves to "science and technology." If the Turks

> had, as the Hungarians and the Bulgarians did, entered Europe from the north and never mixed with Asians and did not live with them and accepted Europe as their homeland, they would have become without a doubt the most important and strongest nation and state in the Balkans.
>
> (Tüccarzâde 1997: 47)

However, when the Turks finally got into Europe, they were already too infected by the "Asian spirit" and were not able to Europeanize (Tüccarzâde 1997: 47).

The westernists (and moderate Islamists) shared many similarities with the Turkists (*Türkçüler*), who also spoke about the necessity for a radical transformation of the society, about rejecting the old way of life and accepting a new life which would be based, on one hand, on "authentic" Turkish values, and, on the other, on the values of Western civilization. The sociologist Ziya Gökalp, a leading theoretician of Turkish nationalism and a prominent figure of the Turkists, summarized this into the famous motto: "I belong to the Turkish nation, to the Islamic community (*umma*) and to the Western civilization." In his perception, the "social revolution"[6] the Turks should go through meant primarily the development of a national consciousness which would draw on the ancient Turkish history and culture, reputedly still surviving in folk culture, and include the adoption of the universal Western civilization.

By turning their attention to the local, largely forgotten "authentic" Turkish culture, suppressed for centuries by a foreign (Eastern, Persian-Arab) culture, Turks would paradoxically strive towards Westernization – Ottoman-Turkish society would become Western even by joining (albeit belatedly) the process of national awakening of European peoples. Gökalp was convinced that the adoption of Western civilization would not in any way threaten Turkish culture, but rather strengthen it, because it better relates to its spirit. He claimed that the Turks had in the past gone through two civilizations: in antiquity they belonged to the "Far-Eastern civilization" and during the Ottoman Empire to the "Eastern civilization." Through their entry into the Age of Nations, they would naturally enter Western civilization as well (Gökalp 1970).

Another key text of the Turkish national movement, was Halide Edib (Adıvar)'s novel *Yeni Turan* (*The New Turan*, 1912), a nationalist-romantic utopia about a renascent Turkish community called Turan living in harmony with ancient national traditions. It reveals, notwithstanding its nationalist agenda, the author's deep admiration for the Anglo-Saxon puritan model of education and behavior. She sees even the patriotic sentiment as most strongly developed among the "northern nations and especially among the Anglo-Saxons," whom she also believes to possess the "most sympathetic, most humane form of civilization" (Adıvar 1924: 68).[7] The Turanic community in Halide Edib's novel is, in theory, based on the revival of "the spirit of Turkishness," while in practice modeled on the pattern of advanced Western societies. Thus, the "national education" all Turanians receive is in fact a combination of a thorough knowledge of ancient Turkish culture, history, and customs, with an upbringing of the Anglo-Saxon Puritan type, which is presented here as a mixture of piety and temperance in dressing, eating, and behavior, on the one hand, and activity, hard work, and tenacity on the other.

Moreover, every part of Turan, has its "Friday schools," based on English and American Sunday schools, wherein children gain "religious, moral and useful knowledge" and master the teachings of Islam which "in no way contradict European civilization" (Adıvar 1924: 15).[8] In wearing "national dresses" which their forefathers allegedly used to wear two thousand years ago, Turanians are said to express their adherence to the "original" community of ancient Turan, yet Halide Edib later admitted that she used the simple clothes of the Quakers as a model (Enginün 1995: 165–66). By the same token, the villages in Turan with their tree-lined avenues, Alpine-like wooden chalets decorated with flowers, garden patches, vineyards, comfortable hotels, or a funicular to the top of a nearby mountain look like – as the narrator says – "Swiss villages" (Adıvar 1924: 151, 154). Despite that, the author steadily assures the reader that these villages have been built in the spirit of authentic national architecture and their doors are covered with Serjuk-Turkish designs.

Halide Edib's novel surely does not break away from the rather schematic pattern of nationalistic narrations of this period. Furthermore, one could easily find in it structural similarities to the nineteenth or twentieth century founding myths of other nations whose goal was to highlight the "authentic," "unspoiled," and "progressive" traits of a nation. Yet what is interesting about this novel (and about many other texts of Turkish nationalists) is the aforementioned duality: it is the way they stress national purity, search for "original" Turkish practices and reject "foreign" influences while presenting a positive image of the West as a role-model, which the vision of the future form of the nation is closely affiliated with.

The national ideal was from its very beginning founded on the awareness of belatedness vis-à-vis the civilizational progress of the West and has always been strongly tied to the conception of the West as a measure of progress. The utopia of the Turanic community was in the end designed to show that Turks are capable of integrating with advanced European nations, or even more: that they indeed *resemble* Westerners. Even for the late Ottoman Turkish nationalists, therefore, the national identity was uniquely connected with the West – which Ziya Gökalp later confirmed with his theory of the universality of Western civilization and the locality of national cultures.

Kemalism: the secular religion of the Turkish Republic

The new Turkish Republic, declared on 29 October 1923, adopted in many ways the existing late Ottoman institutions and reforms and leant for support on military and civil elites, bearers of the modernization project, who had been educated in the new schools established in the Tanzimat and early post-Tanzimat period. As we have tried to demonstrate, many of the basic principles of the new republic were in rough outline formulated already by the westernists after the Young Turk revolution and some elements of the later Kemalist imagination present in the writings of the Turkists. Despite this continuity, the changes the Turkish society underwent under the leadership of its first president Mustafa Kemal (Atatürk) cannot be labeled other than "cultural revolution."

The Kemalist reformers radically ended the hesitancy of the nineteenth-century reforms that were carried out by the Ottoman government and that were expected to lead to modernization without significantly affecting the domain of culture. After the collapse of the Ottoman Empire, secular nationalists "who no longer had a divided mind" came to power and took upon themselves the task to transform the dissolved multi-national Islamic empire into a modern, secularized, Western-oriented republic (Findley 2005: 205). These reformers indeed used nationalistic concepts created during the Young Turk period, but in principle surpassed Gökalp's thesis about the difference between the technological – and therefore universal – civilization, which must be embraced on the macro level, and the local culture, which every nation treasures unchanged for centuries on the micro level. This idea might still have been presented as valid on the official level, but Atatürk himself soon realized its insufficiency: to separate Western culture from Western civilization was a mistake which "we would never repeat again" (quoted in Kahraman 2002: 168).

Immediately after the proclamation of the Republic in 1923, the modernization reforms focused on several areas. Their first goal was to undermine the influence of religion on society on the institutional, legislative, and symbolic level. This was achieved by establishing state's firm control over religious foundations and Islamic clerics, closing religious schools and dervish convents, dissolving Sharia courts, adopting the civil, criminal, and commercial codes from the Swiss, Italian, and German models respectively (1926), revoking Islam's position as the religion of the state (through a constitutional amendment in 1928), or by canceling religious titles, banning the wearing of turbans, and "nationalizing" Islam by having the Koran translated into Turkish and ordering the recitation of the call to prayer in Turkish.

A number of other "revolutions" (*inkılap*, or later *devrim*), as each reform was called, were to support the spirit of modernity and affect every sphere of society and the life of individuals from the time measurement to city planning, from dressing to language and script, and from relationships between men and women to one's relationship to his or her body: we would find among the many manifestations of this "re-coding" of inherited societal norms in the 1920s and 1930s beauty contests, sport events, promotion of a healthy life in the circle of a nuclear, secular family (polygamy was banned and civil marriage made obligatory in 1926) with Western dressing, eating and behavioral codes serving as the ideal to be embraced and supported by the famous "Hat Law" (*Şapka Kanunu*) in 1925 and a number of other regulations. These included legalizing the production and consumption of alcohol for Muslims, declaring Sunday the day of rest instead of the Muslim Friday, replacing the Ottoman-Islamic calendar and system of measurements and weights by "international" ones or placing women under the Kemalist male "state feminism," which granted them basic political rights, sent them to co-educated schools, and highlighted women-pioneers, as, for example, the first Turkish female pilot.[9]

An enthusiastic supporter of Kemalism, Munis Tekin Alp, commented on the law on surnames (1934) that required all citizens to choose a family name and prohibited the use of Ottoman titles such as bey, pasha, or efendi as follows:

> Le noveau Turc portait toujours le même nom, comme au temps ou il était théocrate, oriental et rétrograde. Il portait le même nom que les Arabes et les Persans et tous ses frères de religion. Sa nouvelle tête, sa nouvelle culture et sa nouvelle âme se rattachent à travers plusiers millénaires d'histoire nationale, aux frères de race et de sang, tandis que son nom le confond toujours avec la famille des peuples musulmans, dont il vient de se séparer au point de vue culturel, pour rejoindre son histoire millénaire et la civilisation occidentale. C'est évidemment une ombre du passé dont l'effet psychologique est certain.
>
> (Tekin Alp 1937: 145)

External changes were, on one hand, to cause internal changes, i.e. changes in the mind of each citizen who carried the symbols of "modernity" directly on his or her body, and, on the other, it was also a gesture towards Europe showing that the Turks belong to it and proudly profess their belonging.[10] Yakup Kadri (Karaosmanoğlu), a writer and politician with close relations to Atatürk, described in his biography of Atatürk (1946) an incident that supposedly led the later president to enforce the reforms in dress. According to his account, the young Mustafa Kemal was overwhelmed by shame during his first trip to Europe (Paris) in 1908, when his friend and fellow-traveller became a target of ridicule and contempt for wearing the oriental fez. The conclusion Mustafa Kemal drew from this bitter experience was that Turkey must cease being that oriental country which is captured in European travel guides and ethnographic treatises with a mixture of fear, admiration, and mockery, that it must cease being that world which the French novelist Pierre Loti spoke about with the same affection he was showing for "the blacks of Madagascar, monkeys from Ceylon and butterflies on the Hawaiian islands" (Karaosmanoğlu 2005: 93–95). Or, to put it in the words of the novelist Ahmet Haşim that he wrote down in his diary on a journey to Frankfurt in 1933: "[I]n order for a person to receive the right to be considered a European, he must wear the 'uniform of civilization' – a jacket, trousers and a hat."[11]

The transition from the Arabic script to Latin (1928) also had both a "practical" and a "semiotic" side. Its aim was to increase literacy, but maybe even more importantly to break Turkey's ties with the Islamic East and facilitate communication with the Western world. This was soon followed by the "language revolution" (*dil devrimi*) under the direction of the newly established Institute for Turkish language, which with a surprising success "purified" Turkish from most of its Perso-Arabic lexicon. The language reform and the change of script definitively cut Turkish society off from access to its Ottoman past and culture, recorded in hundreds of literary and historical works, archival documents, or inscriptions on buildings. The Ottoman history and culture became that of the exotic "others," lost its connection with the reality of the modern Turkish citizen and was to be reserved for the academic investigation of Turkish orientalists.[12]

Later on, several Kemalists (especially the group of the so-called "Turkish humanists," supported in the late 1930s by the then Minister of Culture Hasan-Âli Yücel) even suggested on – with some success – the need to introduce obligatory Latin and Greek classes in high schools and to cancel Ottoman literature classes so that young Turks would be from early childhood brought up in the ideals of European humanism and lose all ties with "oriental" literature and culture.[13]

Even the apparently formal changes, such as the Turkification of the *ezan* (call for prayer) had a deep psychological impact. They cut off the bonds that had tied together the international Muslim community (*umma*) and invaded its forms of solidarity and communication, replacing them with "national" ones, whose symbolic and ritual manifestations were, however, derived from the West.[14] One conservative critic of the Turkish Westernization project aptly noted that for the "Europeanized" elite, dance replaced the ritual prayer, balls replaced mystical ceremonies, national holidays replaced Islamic holidays, conferences replaced sermons, universities replaced the madrasas, the hat replaced the turban, and the European hairstyles replaced the headscarf (Doğan 2001: 66).

Parallel to the language reform, the so-called "Turkish historical thesis" was developed, which stressed the pre-Islamic roots of the Turks in Central Asia and "rediscovered" their ties to ancient civilizations (the Sumerians, Hittites, and Etruscans). The state-run Institute for Turkish history, founded in 1925, arranged in Ankara in 1932 under Atatürk's patronage the First History Congress. The participants of the congress more or less agreed that in the pre-historical period Turks created a rich civilization in Central Asia, which became the basis for all following civilizations of humanity. They also concluded that Turks significantly contributed to the development and expansion of Islamic civilization, but a wrong interpretation of Islam in its result prevented the emergence of a "Turkish renaissance."

Following up to the Historical Congress there emerged dozens of historical works and novels which were to support this thesis and revealed the Turkish origin of the advanced civilizations of antiquity.[15] Studies influenced by European race theories (especially by the work of the Swiss anthropologist Eugéne Pittard) and showing that Turks had a brachycephalic skull and therefore belonged to the European race gained in popularity in this period. The most prominent of the advocates of this theory was the spiritual daughter of Mustafa Kemal and one of the leading historiographers of the republic, Ayşe Afet İnan, who, in 1939, finished under Pittard's guidance in Geneva her doctoral thesis on anthropological traits of the "Turkish race."[16]

All these pseudo-scientific historiographic, linguistic, and anthropological theories must be seen in close connection with the whole complex of the modernization reforms, whose single objective was to create a modern Turkish society, which was to become a Western society. The Kemalists were convinced that the coveted modernity could be gradually installed from the top down and from the outside into the inside: if conditions similar to those in Europe are created, if Turks look, behave, dress, and eat *like* Europeans, they will sooner or later *become* Europeans. This is why the reformers devoted a significant part of their efforts to transforming Ottoman cultural institutions and codes and re-creating the physical space in which people lived in order to make it closer to the European environment, for they believed that this would make it easier to form the behavior of individuals (Kasaba 1997: 24). In this sense, Kahraman and Keyman (1998: 67) correctly describe Kemalism as a "nationalistic discourse derived from the global hegemony of modernity," which shall in its result re-create this modernity.

Though it exceeds the scope of this chapter, let us briefly note that it would be nevertheless a mistake to see Kemalism solely as a radical rejection of the Ottoman past and culture and of Islam. It is more accurate to say that many Ottoman-Islamic elements were reformulated, placed in a new context and given a new symbolic value rather than being completely negated. This conception was vigorously promoted, for example, by the quite influential intellectual group of "conservative modernists," which crystallized in the 1930s inside the Kemalist elite. In contrast to the dominant positivist-enlightenment concept of modernity promoted especially by the socialist inclined group *Kadro*, they derived their political philosophy from "other" European traditions, particularly from Bergsonism, and pushed forward the romantic idea of the eternal "national creative spirituality" and "vital energy," gushing forth to the surface in the Kemalist revolution.[17] In opposition to the mainstream of Kemalist intellectuals, the "conservative modernists" sharply rejected atheism and the materialistic tendencies of republican positivists. Stressing a philosophical reevaluation of Islamic theology in the light of Kemalism "[t]hey anticipated a new, modern Turkish citizen who was perfectly capable of absorbing a degree of religious activity without abandoning the secular spirit of the Republic" (Irem 2002: 100).

West and East in the Kemalist modernization project

A close look at early republican reforms and ideas, no matter how they were interpreted by any of the ideological factions of Kemalists, reveals a ubiquitous structure of attitudes and references to the "West" and the "East" as two almost mythical constructs that were endowed with a series of constant, unchangeable characteristics derived from Western perceptions of the Orient as a place ontologically different from Europe. In this economy of derived stereotypes the "Eastern" nation itself, not some far-away territories and foreign peoples, becomes the "Other" of the nationalistic struggle and is designated for subjugation and transformation. The writings of two outstanding personalities of the Kemalist "conservative modernists" and distinguished novelists and essayists, Peyami Safa (1899–1961) and Halide Edib (Adıvar 1882–1964), are among the most intriguing examples attesting to the presumption that this conception was shared both by "radical" as well as "conservative" Kemalists. Both Safa and Halide Edib left behind detailed accounts of their understanding of the Kemalist revolution, and a brief discussion of these texts may help us to better grasp the fabric of Kemalist Westernization thought.

Halide Edib significantly contributed to the Turkish national awakening in the late Ottoman period and was a leading figure of the Turkists, as we have mentioned in connection with her novel *The New Turan*. After the Greek occupation of Izmir (1919) she joined the national forces (*Kuvva-yi Milliye*) and as a corporal actively participated in the War of Independence, which elevated her to a symbol of the emancipated, patriotic, "new" Turkish woman. Her novels, some of which still enjoy wide popularity, have long since become a part of the national literary canon.[18] Despite the fact that she later came into conflict with Mustafa Kemal and "voluntarily" went into a long exile in France, the UK, and the US, she did not question Kemalism as such, just placed greater emphasis on the role of Islam in Turkish society. Her theoretical texts, published primarily for Western Anglophone readers, such as *Turkey Faces West* (1930) or *Conflict of East and West in Turkey* (1935),[19] are interesting not only for their noteworthy interpretations of the historical developments in Turkey, but also for the highly Orientalistic tone that permeates their lines.

Not very differently from other Kemalists, Halide Edib understood Turkish history as a constant conflict between the East and the West, as a clash of Eastern and Western elements, which climaxed in the Kemalist revolution with the triumph of the West. Obviously borrowing from the vocabulary of European ethnographers, she defined two kinds of human beings, both representing a certain interpretation of the Eastern and the Western civilization: the "Eastern man" and the "Western man."

In her view, the mind of the "Eastern man" is turned inwardly, seeks inner peace, spiritual balance, and avoids changes at all costs. He is therefore overly tied to traditions and rejects everything that is not in agreement with them. The "Eastern man" is concerned only with the "true essence of life," but at the same time underrates life's material aspects and has therefore become dependent on the West. The essence of the Eastern mind was to be found in ancient India, which Halide Edib (in contrast to Safa) admired and praised. The Hindu mind was, according to her, the one most connected to the invisible and the spiritual – here the "East" could be found in its purest form (Adıvar 1935, 4–5 and passim).

The "Western man" is, by contrast, completely devoted to this world and prioritizes material values. Christianity was supposed to spiritualize this Roman-Pagan approach, but Western Christianity, in Halide Edib's view, departed from Christ's teachings – originating in the East – and was ultimately altered in the West. The foundational principles of Western civilization are "struggle" and "movement." The essence of the Western mind was to be found in ancient Greece, with the human body as its symbol. The amazing material progress of the West and the exorbitant emphasis on the spirit at the expense of the body in the East led to the fact that the West gradually dominated over the East – and thanks to its ability to constantly change, the West can seize this opportunity to enrich itself by Eastern spirituality (Adıvar 1935, 6–9 and passim).

Similar to Safa, Halide Edib assigned Turkey a privileged position in this diagram: Turkey is a link between both worlds, though in her view Turks had always been much closer to the West that any other "Eastern" nation. In a surprising agreement with the later "Turkish humanists" Halide Edib saw significant parallels between the Greco-Roman administration of the state and the early Ottoman statehood and emphasized the continuity between the Roman and the Ottoman Empire. She underlined the fact that Sultan Mehmet II (1451–81), the conqueror of Constantinople, spoke Greek and Latin, compared the training of the janissaries to the Greco-Spartan method of raising warriors and emphasized that the early Ottoman statesmen must have studied Plato's *Republic* and derived from it their ideas on political leadership (Adıvar 1935: 21–22).

She, thus, contended that it was a mistake to call the Ottoman civilization an Islamic civilization, for it was more a civilization of the Eastern Roman Empire (Adıvar 1930: 31). However, Turks made in her view a fatal historical mistake when they assumed Greco-Roman civilization through the Arab interpretation: "If the Ottomans had gone directly to the Byzantine Greek scholars for learning, probably the Renaissance would have started in the Near East" (Adıvar 1930: 31). Despite that, the face of the Turks was always turned towards the West and thanks to this the Turks were very close to being European. Their true nature was only hidden for a time "behind the colourful and forceful Ottoman façade" and fully emerged thanks to the Europeanizing reforms after the founding of the Republic (Adıvar 1930: 49–8).[20]

In 1938, the year Atatürk died, Peyami Safa published a treatise on the different ideological movements preceding the Kemalist revolution and the emergence of the Turkish Republic and on the position of the Turks between the "East" and the "West." *Reflections on the Turkish Revolution* (*Türk İnkılâbına Bakışlar*), still one of the most significant sources of Turkish conservative thought, provides us again, as Halide Edib's writings, with fascinating insights into Kemalist Westernism.

Peyami Safa identified two determining principles in the Kemalist revolution: nationalism (vertically binding Turks with their – especially pre-Islamic – past and the present) and modernism (horizontally connecting Turks with the Western civilization, its way of life and thought). Safa first and foremost criticized the pre-Kemalist Ottoman reform attempts as heedless imitations of the West lacking any coherent program and leaving the outmoded "Eastern" institutions intact. The late Ottoman reforms created, in his view, a chaos in the name of preserving tradition by introducing dual institutions (two judiciaries, two systems of education, two ways of dressing, and two ways of life) and therefore directly contradicted the conservative faith in the urgency of maintaining order against anarchy (Öğün 1997: 120).

Whereas Safa, in contrast to many other Kemalist intellectuals, placed great emphasis on the historical continuity between the republic and the Ottoman

Empire, he believed that the traditions and historical experiences of the Turks must be incorporated into the *Western* concept of progress, modernity and civilization. Without this framework, they would be bereft of meaning and would condemn Turkish society to stagnation:

> The mystery of the East and its thought is void. If there was no Europe Asia would never know what rights it had. The being known an Asian is not even capable of putting together a map of the country he would like to take possession of.
>
> (Safa 1988: 78)

Culture and civilization are, according to Safa, inventions of the "European mind," and this mind was formed by three basic factors: Roman social discipline, Christian moral discipline, and the discipline of Greek intelligence. Europe is therefore

> every place where the names of Aristotle, Plato and Euclid have a meaning, where the names Jesus and St. Paul are mentioned in prayer, where Caesar, Trajan and Virgil had left traces. Each place which has been gradually Hellenized, Romanized and Christianized is Europe.
>
> (Safa 1988: 78)

Europe defined in this way is the sole bearer of civilization and progress and other cultures gain meaning only in comparison to it.

The "East" could be, according to Safa, defined analogously to Europe with the reservation that it lacks its unity, and consists of many religions and cultures. The East is everything that is not Europe, it is "non-Europe" and is defined *exclusively* by its relationship to the West. Despite defining the "East" mostly in negative terms Safa ascribes to the "Orient" a number of positive attributes, which are hidden under its surface. Viewed from the outside, the East could appear to be passive, rigid, sleepy, but in its essence is thoughtful, has the gift of metaphysical insight and an ability to see things as a whole. "The Orient dreamed of what the West made reality" – it is the "unconscious sphere of the West," wrote Safa in one of his later essays from the 1950s (Safa 2000: 197).

However, to be able to include Turkey into the realm of the West – and Safa firmly believed that Turkey had its place in the West – he further divided the concept of the East into two completely opposite worlds: the Far East with a backward "Asian" (Brahman-Buddhist) mentality, and the Islamic East, which was at its core European. In *The Great European Survey* (*Büyük Avrupa Anketi*, 1938) Safa spoke with contempt about the "primitive" Japanese thought and script and explained the rapid development of Japan by the fact that it accepted European technology as a readymade product, which can hardly hide its backward Far Eastern way of life (Safa 1938: 66–69). In contrast, the Islamic East is a Mediterranean civilization, which has always possessed a rational and scientific approach to the world, and it was precisely this civilization that is the birth of modern Europe by mediating Greek philosophy for the West. Moreover, Islam was not an antithesis of Christianity, but rather its completion, and Turks are not "Asians" in their origin but Indo-Europeans, who founded the oldest civilizations of humanity, such as those of the Sumerians and the Hittites concludes Safa. It was only for a series of unfortunate historical developments, such as the *Reconquista* forcing Muslims to retreat from the Mediterranean center of civilization further towards the East and the victory of al-Ghazzali's and Ibn 'Arabi's mysticism over rationalistic philosophy, that Islamdom abandoned its tradition of rationality, that Muslims came into close contact with the "backward" Far East and that the Islamic East consequently underwent its "Orientalization." Had all this not occurred, Safa claimed, the Islamic world would have been a strong part of the West today (Safa 1988: 94). Through westernizing, he believed, Turkey was doing nothing else than returning to its true roots.

The theoretical works and essays of authors such as Peyami Safa and Halide Edib, in spite of the different ideological points of departure, resonated with the official rhetoric and its strategic use of images of West and East in the construction of Turkish identity. The Kemalist discourse of alterization is even more strongly present in the novels of this period, manifesting itself in the unforgiving conflict between religious obscurantism and revolutionary progress. It included an almost militant approach to all those "reactionary"' layers of the society, that the reformists considered to be closely connected with the "Oriental" past and which it was consequently necessary to remove (religious leaders, dervish sheiks, traditionalists), or radically change (Anatolian villagers).

Novels such as the highly popular *Strike the Whore* (*Vurun Kahpeye*, 1923) by Halide Edib, *Green Night* (*Yeşil Gece*, 1928), written by Reşat Nuri (Güntekin) reputedly on Atatürk's initiative, or Yakup Kadri's *Stranger* (*Yaban*, 1932), to name but the most exemplary texts, reiterate basically the same plot: a young, modernly educated teacher (Aliye in *Strike the Whore*, Ali Şahin in *Green Night*) or a freedom fighter (Ahmet Celal in *Stranger*) comes to a conservative, backward, fanatic Anatolian village/town, bringing alone the "light of civilization" and Kemalist ideals, but meets with stiff resistance by the local "natives," who accuse him/her of being an infidel, invader, or a total stranger. Our hero, however, is unwavering in his/her civilizing mission. Coming to the village of Sarıova, "a den of religious scholars," where "one mosque, one prayer hall, or one madrasa falls on every twelve households" (Güntekin 1928: 10, 12), Ali Şahin discards his turban (he is a madrasa student turned zealous revolutionary), unfurls the "flag" of modern civilization (instead of the green flag of Islam) and is resolute to turn the terrible "green night" of religious backwardness into the bright night of modernity. "I will put out the candles on the graves of the saints. And the town hall will be forced to light lanterns in its place," he calls out and promises that he will teach the children only "positive sciences" (Güntekin 1928: 11).

This "textual conquest" of course coincided with a real subjugation: the people were re-educated and transformed to the Kemalist ideal in the people's houses (*halkevleri*), the village institutes (*köy enstitüleri*), the new schools, cultural centers, official buildings, linguistic and historiographic institutes, universities or modern apartments of the new settlers in Ankara's *Yenişehir*, the New City, physically and mentally separated from the old Ankara (*Engürü*) of the "natives": all these institutions took on the role of centers of "cultural colonization" and by using a series of coercive methods and legal measures were spreading a new language, a new *etiquette*, a new dressing style, a new architecture and a new physiognomy of *the* citizen.[21]

All of the aforementioned texts together with political and social measures supported a certain conception of citizenship, whose every sphere (the style of dress, interpersonal relations, hygienic habits, physical appearance) came under the close control of the Kemalist elite, who consequently judged it according to an idealized image of a European city dweller, determined the normative pattern of behavior of the new citizens according to this the model, and criticized or tried to resolutely remove those elements which don't match this pattern (Şenol-Cantek 2003: 230–31).

Conclusion

In this chapter attention was paid primarily to one dimension of Kemalism in the period from the 1920s to the 1940s: its radical Westernism, which alterized all "Eastern" elements of Turkish society. Hasan Bülent Kahraman (2002: 177) concluded from this "epistemic violence" of the Kemalist reading of society that a whole number of texts, historiographical studies, political speeches, or novels of this period were structured by latent as well as manifest Orientalism as a logical consequence of the Kemalist discourse of alterization of its own society. In this Orientalism, at first the West, not the East, was identified and formulated, and subsequently the attributes of the Turkish society that contradicted this representational West were ascribed to the East. Although it is certainly justified and productive to subject Kemalist texts to a reading that lays bare their "orientalist" structures of enunciation, it leaves out the interconnections between Western dominance over the modes of production of knowledge and power and the dependence and resistance of non-Western societies to it. The words of the Turkish historian Tarık Zafer Tunaya (2002: 799) might be instructive here in terms of illuminating the inherent antagonism within Kemalist Westernism: "Turks fought the West to become Westerners."

Therefore I would rather argue that Kemalism produced a certain version of "Occidentalism," as a *reaction* to Western dominance and Western Orientalism, defined by Xiaomei Chen (2002: 2) as "a discursive practice that, by constructing its Western Other, has allowed the Orient to participate actively and with indigenous creativity in the process of self-appropriation, even after being appropriated and constructed by Western Others." The Turkish Occidentalism combines, to paraphrase Chen, Western construction of Turkey with the Turkish construction of the West, with both of these components interacting and interpenetrating each other. As with the Chinese Occidentalism, this particular Kemalist Occidentalism served different purposes: it was, outwardly, aimed at legitimizing and defending Turkish nationhood and aspirations against Western prejudices and imperialistic ambitions by stressing the historical connections and affinities between the Turks and the West, or even by showing that most of Western achievements had their roots in ancient "Turkish civilizations," as we have seen in the second part of this chapter; and, inwardly, it strove to awaken the "national consciousness" and to mobilize it against Western imperialism (as it happened in the War of Independence), only to later subjugate and re-create the domestic Self using the very same notions of the West. In other words, it is necessary to read Kemalist Occidentalism in the specific context of its utterance, since it served different – and often contradictory – purposes at different times and places.

The ability of the Kemalist ideology to adapt to different patterns and to strategically use the different "Occidentalisms" probably enabled it to become, as Süleyman Öğün put it, a "cultural formation that enjoys a surprising social support" that made it almost the "only element of legitimity of sociopolitical culture." Thus, Kemalism, "virtually as a *secular religion,* took over the role that Islam had played for the Ottomans (containing Islam itself)" (Öğün 1997: 103) and turned into a "common imaginary horizon" (Çelik 1999: 34). That is why despite the justified critique in the ever growing body of theoretical literature on Kemalism challenging it on the grounds that is undemocratic, patriarchal, orientalist, forced upon the society from above, and ignoring the historical and cultural experiences of minorities inside Turkey (Bozdoğan and Kasaba 1997: 3–4), Reşat Kasaba is right to state that thanks to the "civilisational shift" of Turkey towards the West, the institutional, ritual, symbolic, and esthetic manifestation of modernity have become since the late 1920s constituent elements of the Turkish collective consciousness. These manifestations "have also come to set the official standards of exterior form and behavior against which people, ideas, and events have been measured and judged" (Kasaba 1997: 5).

Even if there has been a talk about the corrosion of Kemalism since the 1950s, and the recent electoral victory of "Islamic Democrats" is often interpreted as a "revenge" of all those strata of the society that Kemalism and its Westernization project degraded to an inferior rank, it is important to keep in mind that Kemalism has long since become an integral part of modern Turkish identity and all discussions around it concern more its reformulation in a new context than its rejection.

Notes

1 In Articles 2, 42, 58, 81, 103, 134 and in the Provisional article 2. The entire text of the constitution can be found at the web pages of the Turkish Parliament, http://www.tbmm.gov.tr/anayasa.htm.

2 I intentionally use the term 'Islamic democrats' (after the term "Christian Democrats"), so as not to confuse them with Islamists in the sense of 'fundamentalists'.

3 For Abdullah Cevdet's biography and works see Süssheim 1938.

4 For more details on Baha Tevfik see Ülken: 233–46.

5 For a list of reforms see Safa 1988: 33–35; and partially Lewis 1968: 236–37.

6 Gökalp speaks about the social revolution (under the pseudonym "Demirtaş") in his article "Yeni Hayat ve Yeni Kıymetler," *Genç Kalemler,* II(8). Reprinted in Parlatır 1999: 236–239.

7 The novel was first serialized in *Tanin* (1912), and shortly after that it came out as a book. Following the success of the novel, a short-lived magazine with the same name was published (1914). As early as 1916 the novel was translated into German by

Friedrich Schrader (*Das neue Turan, ein türkisches Frauenschicksal von Halide Edib Hanım*).

8 Halide Edib suggested the establishment of Friday schools in the Ottoman Empire as early as 1909 in one of her articles in *Mehasin* (no. 6, February 1909) (Enginün 1995: 168).

9 For a list of the reforms see, for example, Shaw and Shaw 1985: 384–88.

10 For an excellent analysis of this topic see Göle 1997: 57–82.

11 *Frankfurt Seyahatnamesi*, 1933; newly republished with other texts by Ahmet Haşim as *Bize Göre*. Istanbul, İnkılâp 1992, p. 144.

12 For the language reforms see Lewis 1999.

13 For the relation between Turkish humanists and Kemalists see Akyıldız and Karacasu 1999.

14 Some professors from the Theological faculty of Istanbul University were so swept up by their revolutionary passion that they proposed making Muslim Friday prayers and Islamic religious services similar to Christian Sunday services: Koranic recitation would be replaced by organ music, the requirement to take off shoes before entering the mosque was to be revoked and benches placed in mosques so that the believers could pray while seated – the complicated movements of the Muslim *namaz* would have to be simplified accordingly. See Adıvar 1930: 231.

15 Kemalist construction of Turkish history in the 1920s and 1930s was not an easy endeavor and led to intractable conflicts: there were efforts to create a new Turkish identity freed from its Islamic-Ottoman dimension by refocusing on Asian, pre-Islamic roots of the Turks, while at the same time the Kemalists, in order to dispel the nationalist demands of the Greeks and Armenians, had to emphasize that the forefathers of the Turks came from Anatolia (which would assume that the Hittites – "the forefathers of the Turks" – first lived in Central Asia). See Copeaux 1998: 15–54.

16 See Copeaux 1998: 32–35, and also Aydın 2002. For a revival of the theory of the Anatolian origin of the Turks and their contribution to the formation of the ancient Middle Eastern civilizations in the 1980s see Aydın 2003. For a critical evaluation of the role of craniometry in the search for the European origin of the Turks see Maksudyan 2005.

17 See İrem 2002.

18 For Halide Edib, see the excellent study by Durakbaşa 2002.

19 A modified version of *Conflict of East and West in Turkey. Extension Lectures delivered at the Jamia Millia Islamia in 1935* was published in Turkish as *Türkiye'de Şark, Garp ve Amerikan Tesisleri*. Doğan Kardeş, Istanbul 1955.

20 Halide Edib (1930: 82–83) further explicitly states: "[The Ottoman] thought *foreign* thoughts, spoke and wrote a language, which had *changed* not only in its structure, but also in its spirit. *The estrangement* was complete" (emphasis added).

21 See Şenol-Cantek's (2003) excellent analysis of the transformation of *Engürü* to Ankara.

3 Democratization and EU conditionality

A barking dog that does (not) bite?

Lucie Tunkrová

Introduction

The EU as a normative actor creates a link between Europeanization and democratization of its candidate countries (CCs). The CCs' political elites believe that EU membership will contribute to their democratic consolidation whereas the EU expects the CCs to internalize democratic principles and to become liberal and not solely electoral democracies. This is done directly through the so-called conditionality but also indirectly through elite socialization followed by norm diffusion in the domestic environment given that these elites are open to such influence and that it coincides with their interests (Grabbe 2001). By applying for EU membership, the CCs willingly put themselves under the pressure and scrutiny of the EU, recognizing the obligation to commit to democratization and the protection of human rights.

The EU does not set up the democratic structures in its CCs but contributes to "ensuring that democratic institutions [are] really accountable and stable, that the rule of law [becomes] entrenched and that political pluralism and minority positions [are] fully tolerated" so the rules would become institutionalized, internalized, and finally disseminated in the reformed political culture (Pridham 2006: 394) acknowledging that norm internalization requires a longer period of time. In both the ECECs and Turkey, "Europeanization is treated as synonymous to 'democratization' or pressure to enhance and deepen liberal democracy and to activate appropriate citizenship rights" (Sofos 2001: 248, Müftüler-Bac 2005).

The EU enlargement policy has repeatedly aimed at supporting the democratic regimes of the CCs. The EU defines its core values as democracy, human rights, the rule of law, and social market capitalism – the Preamble of the Lisbon Treaty states:

> The Union is founded on the values of respect for human dignity, freedom, democracy, equality, the rule of law and respect for human rights, including the rights of persons belonging to minorities. These values are common to the Member States in a society in which pluralism, non-discrimination, tolerance, justice, solidarity and equality between women and men prevail.

These core values are exported beyond the EU borders and the process of enlargement is its most successful tool. The CCs that have a recent legacy of undemocratic regimes expect the EU to both anchor the democratization process and trigger the process of democratic consolidation. The major reasons why ECECs and Turkey applied for EU membership were both political and economic in nature. The ECECs' dominant foreign policy goal from 1989 to 2004 was to enter the EU, the so-called "return to normal order" or as it is better known, to "return to Europe." It was coupled with the decades' long perception that everything coming from the West, as opposed to the East (Soviet Union), was good and involved the idealization of the West, not seeing it for what it really was but mostly normatively (Okey 1992). The EU was haunted by what many saw as a moral obligation to accept the CCs from Central (and Eastern) Europe.

Sadurski (2002) shows that this moral obligation, the perception of ECECs as "legitimate Europeans" of the "immediate neighborhood" returning to the European family was, however, accompanied by the fear that their undemocratic past contaminated their belonging to the common European heritage and many doubted whether they could be trusted. For some it was as if they left the continent and their return without losing their way was not certain. Sadurski (2002: 345) states that the new conditionality was affected by the fear of "contamination" and the "tightening of the club membership rules [were to] ensure that no barbarians get inside." Thus, suspicion in the EU-15 about the genuineness of ECECs' democratization surfaced in the arguments, which claimed that the countries were forced to adopt the EU norms and values without internalizing them and that the actual implementation varied (Pridham 2007). Accordingly, for some circles in the EU MS they were not "European proper" but European "rookies" about to *return* to Europe, whereas Turkey was later to become for them a European "wannabe," that wants to *join* Europe.

To address the problem of democracy and EU membership, which reflected the increasingly political nature of economic integration and the political realities of the post-Cold War environment, where democracy and human rights had become "an international concern" (Pridham 2006), the Accession criteria (better known as the Copenhagen criteria) introduced in 1993 demanded that the CCs meet political and economic conditions, together with the acceptance of all obligations of membership. The political criteria (stability of institutions guaranteeing democracy, the rule of law, human rights, and respect for and protection of minorities) are crucial elements of the membership conditions because on their basis the European Council decides whether to open the accession negotiations with the CC or not.

Both ECECs and Turkey had to go through a transition to democracy and then its consolidation accompanied by key economic reforms. While the ECECs had to build up new democratic institutional structures, Turkey had to democratize the present institutions so that they could meet the requirements of modern liberal democracies. The countries had to prove that they "are moving in the right direction" (Pridham 1999) and that they will become consolidated democracies in the future.[1] The major difference between the two is that in the case of Turkey, the enlargement approach shifted from enlargement pragmatism to enlargement ideologization, when the past and present positions and world views become often more important than current actions. With the ECECs, the MS and the EU realized that a "fresh start" was hardly possible and that the legacies of the past regimes would continue to taint the reform activities including the attitudes, norms, and beliefs of the elites and the general public. This has become directly reflected in their approach to the Turkish accession process.

Europeanization and democracy

Democratization, understood as a process of consolidating democracy, has been defined as "stabilization, routinization, institutionalization and legitimization of patterns of democratic behaviour" (Gunther et al., in Pridham 2006: 378).[2] Thus, it includes not only democratic institutions and processes but also development of a democratic political culture and the adherence to democratic values and norms. It is tempting to draw a direct line between EU conditionality and democratization of the CCs but evidence suggests otherwise. While EU conditionality, both formal and informal, can be seen as a strong incentive, its ability to work based on the "carrot and stick" principle is limited by certain conditions. Domestic forces represent one important factor. The sole support for accession among political elites is not sufficient to provide for successful Europeanization of a CC for the various social groups in the country need to believe in the validity of European norms and values in order to implement and internalize them. This is the point where policy dialogue and consensus building are vital in creating support for reforms so that they are not perceived as an EU dictate (Checkel 2000). Hence, the reforms must be adopted by the government and passed in the parliament but their implementation requires cooperation of a much wider range of actors and institutions. Political will must be coupled with determination, i.e. belief in the validity of the norm, and domestic pressure.[3]

Europeanization of the elites is a closely monitored process, when attention is paid to how they socialize, internalize the EU values, and take on some form of European identity. During the accession process, national and sub-national elites, including political parties and the representatives of civil society start to have much more frequent contacts with their European counterparts. As a result, they not only learn the "language" of the EU but also become more socialized in the EU environment. The extent to which the national political but also economic and social elites and the media become "Europeanized" plays a crucial role in determining the outcome of accession. Guillen et al. (in Lendvai 2004) call it "cognitive Europeanization." Lendvai (2004: 321) referred to this as a "meaning-making process" where "changes happen in the way policymakers construct, speak, discuss and act on social issues. New vocabulary, new discourses, new meanings and new agendas are constituted during the accession process." The result is a change in how things are "handled, discussed, thought of and made." For the success of this process, the elites also need to feel that they are being treated as equal partners. If the elites gain the "we" feeling, they can then help diffuse the European norms to the people (Hughes et al. 2004).

The level of socialization should be seen as beneficial mainly because the accession process tends to favor the executive and the administration over national parliaments and civil society. During the pre-accession period, national political parties and NGOs become members of transnational networks. The transnational contacts of political parties and NGOs increase as these actors identify with Europe – become a "part of Europe" (Schimmelfennig, Engert and Knobel 2003), and/or believe that their interests can be better served by extending their activities to the European level and by their country's membership in the EU. They start to internalize the norms and to demand reforms from their governments, i.e. partially counterweighing the EU bureaucratization effects and compensating for the asymmetry in the in the EU-CC relationship.

Benhabib and Isiksel (2006: 222) argue that the combined effects of the EU reforms and the "tremendous development of an independent and vibrant civil society" led to a drastic change in the public debate in Turkey, where issues previously banned from any political discussion would be addressed and ever more openly discussed. The existence of a vibrant civil society as a precondition for successful democratization[4] was recently highlighted by the Turkish chief negotiator, Egemen Bağış (TRT-World 2009) and praised by the EU Commissioner for Enlargement, Olli Rehn (2006), who said that they "have spread the European spirit by promoting democracy, human rights, good governance and the rule of law. Together with independent media, they have resisted nationalism and fundamentalisms, and helped building bridges of inter-ethnic confidence."

The EU and the accession process help and support the pro-reform groups to achieve their goals. At the same time, some actors, including members of the civil society, also represent the anti-EU and/or anti-reform forces. Examples of such NGOs are the Association for Kemalist Thought (ADD) – closely linked to the Turkish military – which requested the ban of YouTube, later tried to ban Google and claims that to "oppose Kemalism is to oppose science"; and the controversial Support for Modern Life Association (CYDD), whose leader Türkan Saylan was well-known for her extreme anti-religious views. In addition, the numbers and strength of the NGOs should not be overestimated. According to 2008 data, while there were around 80,000 NGOs[5] in Turkey and membership levels reached 12 percent of the population, most of them worked in social welfare (42 percent), religion (18 percent) and sports (17 percent). Human rights, women, children, the elderly, and environment represented only marginal areas of their activities; and many were subject to existential problems due to difficulties with financing (*Hürriyet Daily News* 2009a).

The EU also had a negative impact on the development of the civil society. While its aims have been rather ambitious, the nature of the accession process that favors the executive and is highly technocratic often undermined the civil society capacities. Thus, Grote (2009: 14) argues that in the ECECs, the pre-accession and early accession periods were a disaster for the NGOs and that the benefits of Europeanization of civil society might actually be a by-product of membership rather than result of "explicit politics of empowerment and support." Still, the accession process might have cut off some domestic sources for them, but it opened to them the European arena. The NGOs frequently address international (European) institutions and associations such as the EU, the European Court of Human Rights (ECHR), the Organization for Security and Cooperation in Europe (OSCE), and the transnational interest groups for support, know-how, and extra leverage.[6]

The CCs' governments and social groups frequently use the EU card against certain veto actors or opposition, which applies particularly to politically highly sensitive issues. They often refer to "European values" and "European standards" when criticizing their governments (Grabbe 2004) but also emphasize the wide-ranging benefits for the entire society. Avci (2006: 211) shows on the example of the reform process in Turkey that whereas the EU process changed the political bargaining positions, redefined interests and led to difficult political decisions, this became possible because the reforms were claimed to be based on universality, for they were not explained as (only) a result of the wish to join the EU but because they were good for the country. The political elites have on several occasions stated that these reforms needed to be implemented not (only) because of the EU but because Turkey needed them, for the sake of the country.[7] On the other hand, the elites often use similar statements to show that they are not being pushed around by the EU.

To use "Europe" to implement difficult reforms requires a "strong support for and identification with Europe and the European order" (Green Cowles and Risse 2001: 235) but when such strong attachment is missing, the reforms need to be shown as primarily good for the country. This will be stronger in the CCs who perceive the EU as "less granted" and more visible in policy areas where the CC sees the policy (change) as legitimate but dislikes outside interference. Many of the reforms implemented in Slovakia by the Dzurinda government after the 1998 election were not motivated solely by getting back on track with the accession process. Conditionality was successful here because it coincided with the interests of the new government and was strengthened by the work of other international institutions such as the Organisation for Economic Cooperation and Development (OECD), OSCE and Council of Europe (Sadurski 2004).

Schimmelfennig and Sedelmeier (2005) distinguish between democratic conditionality referring to the EU's democratic rules and values, and *acquis communautaire* conditionality, i.e. compliance with EU legislation. The latter becomes predominant with the approximation of the accession talks, while the former is a precondition for the talks to start. They, however, note that in many cases, the latter begins to apply before the former is fully satisfied. This could be said about virtually all the CCs in the Eastern enlargement round including the forerunners. They come to the conclusion that the EU contributes to democratization but that the "EU democratic conditionality was not sufficient to bring about democratization and democratic consolidation" (214), not even when we include the empowerment of the pro-reform political actors. Other positive factors must be in place such as sufficient interest in EU membership and a relatively close and credible prospect of accession. We, thus, argue that the EU works both as an anchor and a driver of reform.

In both the ECECs and Turkey, the EU stimulated the reform process but it also depended on the societal actors. The specific goals and specific targets leading to the ultimate "reward" of membership provided the EU with the power to induce reforms – as was the case with Turkey between 2000 and 2004, but not all countries react to the incentive to socialize and to adopt "European values" positively or at least not at all times. They become (temporary) "reluctant democratizers," such as Slovakia under Mečiar (Kubicek 2005: 363) or Turkey between 2005 and 2009, when the government tried to please the EU with reforms, which were for the most part merely repackaged authoritarian rules (Benhabib and Isiksel 2006). Thus, the carrot works but the "the EU's democratization agenda [is] filtered through [the] state's domestic politics" (Kubicek 2005: 363). We can as a result identify in individual policies and in particular periods early reformers, partial reformers, and rhetorical reformers. It is usually the public that turns its back to the "false" or sluggish changeovers.

With conditionality, language and the transferability of the message become crucial. The lack of a clear definition of what is expected or mixed signals coming from the EU as to what is expected can lead to ambiguous results. The discrepancies in understanding the various concepts such as minority rights can cause problems in meeting the conditions. Pridham (1999: 1235) shows in the case of Slovakia, how understanding the EU language is vital to the progress of mutual relationships, when taking diplomatic language for praising led to a "dialogue between the deaf." Language also becomes the instrument of increased pressure when resolutions and declarations seem to fail. Governments promising reforms do not like to be criticized in the media for failing in the attempt. Dislike of criticism can lead to avoiding situations for which it can be criticized and the EU is aware of it and uses it as leverage. This leads to the observation that even simply talking can contribute to compliance with democratic norms. Concomitantly, using the leverage of criticism should not be overstepped as it could also be abused by people opposing membership in both the EU and the CC in order to prevent enlargement or to hinder the reform efforts.

While the CCs adopt EU rules and norms, they must see them as politically acceptable and they need to adopt them without triggering off harmful effects at the domestic level, i.e. damaging their own position or empowering anti-systemic forces. Language should then be used not only to criticize but also to provide moral support for the reforms (Lundgren 2006: 125) as the EU can use it "to express solidarity, to show commitment, to encourage, to cooperate and be involved, to give advice in a constructive manner, and to send positive signals," etc. Therefore, as Checkel argues (2000: 18), this will work if the one who is trying to effect change does not try to lecture the state or demand change but "acts out principles of serious deliberative demand," or to be precise, leads to a constructive debate which allows the actors to change their attitudes while keeping "their face."

A major problem of EU conditionality as regards democratization and the Commission's reports today is that while progress is being praised in the reports, it is often followed by bold statements on part of the Commission, the European Parliament (EP) but also individual MS that none of that really matters unless other conditions are met. It was this "lack of clarity" together with the feeling of unwelcomeness that the president of European Bank for Reconstruction and Development (EBRD) identified in 2005 as the reason for increased difficulties with promoting reforms in both Turkey and the Balkan states (in Pridham 2007). Öniş (in Lundgren 2006) shows using the examples of Poland and Turkey that while the positive language used with the former made the reformers' job much easier, the much more critical language used when evaluating Turkey led to the very opposite result and undermined the reform effort.[8]

The EU can help the process of democratization but cannot reverse an unfavorable trend. When the reform forces are absent, weakened, or under threat, as was the case of Slovakia under Mečiar and more recently the Turkish AKP government, the elites express their support for EU membership and dedication to the reform process but without sufficient activities – when criticized, they blame the EU for not understanding their "special situation" and arguing that the EU was only saying so to deny them the prospect of membership. In order to keep their political power, they postpone or even stop the reforms.

Case studies – gender equality and corruption

The problems of the ECECs were often identified as very similar to the ones in Turkey, even though at times on a different scale. Sadurski (2004) lists them as weak public administration, widespread corruption, arrogance towards the public, government party control over the public media and business manipulation of the private media, slow and corrupt judiciary, internal security service interfering with politics, and members of parliament hiding behind parliamentary immunity. We choose two sensitive policies, closely monitored by the EU – gender equality and corruption. They represent examples of a positive relationship between the absence of a developed norm and the failure to implement the rules in the domestic environment. They also involve deeply embedded habits and attitudes that require relatively long periods of socialization. They negate the argument that reward or punishment provides the EU with a sufficient EU leverage because they fail to get translated into action unless the norms become internalized, or turned into actual practices.

Gender equality

Gender (in)equality refers to a wide range of issues from gender barriers, male domination, labor force inequalities, low pay, prejudice, and domestic violence. Equal representation of men and women in social, economic, and political life is an inherent principle of any democratic society. In the context of the EU, it was first reflected in legislation on equal pay and later included into directives regulating equal access to employment, training, and promotion, to equal working and living conditions, to non-discrimination in sex and sexual orientation, balance between family and career, etc. Gender equality belongs to human rights issues, which have often been used as the key argument against accession of poorly performing democracies. Especially in the Turkish case, the position of women has raised many criticisms and attracts a lot of attention not only of the EU institutions and MS but also the public.

In the ECECs and Turkey, emancipation of women was part of a socialist and Kemalist, respectively, revolutionary project and the ideologies for several decades submerged gender equality issues to the dominant goals of the state. They included their understanding of feminism within their ideologies while actual individual women's concerns were unimportant given that the states had "higher goals" to achieve. Women's struggle had to be understood within the state's struggle. Women were at times used and "chosen" to represent the new "ideal" woman of the new regime and to add to its legitimacy while actual women questions were marginalized. Women who did not fall within the category of an "ideal woman" were excluded from the public sphere.

Traditional Kemalism and socialism treated the women's question as resolved within their own mindset and had their own version of "correct" masculinity and femininity, which contributed to the construction of the "new" state or nation. In both cases, women had to first understand that the societies were oppressing them. The demise or weakening of the authoritarian/autocratic regimes led to an increase in feminist activism, which together with the process of democratization – and as a part of it – and desire to join the EU led to significant improvements in gender equality. This has to some extent paradoxically been more successful in Turkey than in the ECECs, which can be partially explained by the worse conditions of women in many spheres of life and the earlier mobilization of the women's organizations in Turkey. For the ECECs, in many cases even today the societies believe that feminism is a western "import" unnecessary in their societies.

Protection of women's rights has been a relatively contentious issue in the Turkish accession process because the public and some MS consider the women's issue one of the main obstacles on its way to the EU. We often witness the argument that violations of gender equality in Turkey provide the evidence that Turkey does not belong to "western civilization." The widespread belief is that the West must liberate the "other woman" (Berktay 2004).[9] At the same time, Turkish women have been much more active in participating in the EU accession process and have their voices heard and interests addressed than women in the ECECs. Unlike in the ECECs, where few women NGOs were formed during the socialist era and women's rights were interlaced with human rights in general, Turkey had a long tradition of women's movements and in the 1990s also had a female Prime Minister, Tansu Ciller,[10] something the ECECs are still waiting for.

In the ECECs, Marxism equated women's active participation in the labor market (emancipation through paid employment) with liberation and recognized the second wave of feminism in Western societies and its drive for female emancipation as hostile to Marxism. It defined equality ideologically. Many women had full-time jobs as the socialist-planned economy required a large workforce. They experienced the so-called triple burden – work, household, and compulsory political participation. As Vaknin notes, communism had use only for a "superwoman," or as Ruml, said, "socialism gave woman actually only one right, the right to work a lot" (in Kotlandova Koenig 1997). Women were still perceived as the primary caretakers even though in the sense of "working mothers," as producers and reproducers (Rangelova 2003). The concept of patriarchal family survived in most places until the end of communism. Gender discrimination and stereotypes persisted in educational and vocational choices, horizontal and vertical segregation was highly visible and the pay gap was relatively high (20 to 30 percent) (Rangelova 2003).

The regime included many women in the labor force, ensured relatively high levels of education among women and a generous system of child care services with maternal leave of 18 to 36 months but "there were no laws against domestic or spousal violence, trafficking in women, organized crime prostitution rings, discrimination, inequality, marital rape, date rape and a host of other issues" (Vaknin 2002: n.p.). They also lacked the opportunity to develop a women's movement and to actively contribute to the debate on women's issues. Few women's organizations existed and the scarce state-established organizations were closely linked to the state ideology and the communist party (or their equivalents). In the 1980s, new organizations emerged but the women's question was mostly included under the umbrella of human rights' demands and the dissident movement.

In the aftermath of the revolution, many women turned to the private sphere where they hoped to find more equal status. However, the emerging market economy environment deprived women of social benefits guaranteed by the communist regime. In addition, the Marxist approach to feminism was superseded by neo-liberal thinking, which Hašková (2003: 2) labels with respect to feminism as "genderless (gender blind) individual rights." The societies exhibited high levels of distrust towards Western feminism, which was for many "too ideological, often Marxist, too extreme, family-disparaging and man-hating" (Vaknin 2002). For many women, the term feminism was closely related to revolutionary Marxism – for instance, the Hungarian Women's Association discussed intensely in 1990 whether it wanted to identify itself as feminist (Huland 2001).

The EU accession process in the ECECs brought some positive changes in terms of gender equality. It facilitated the adoption of laws on equal treatment of men and women at work and provisions on parental – rather than maternal – leave. At the same time the ECECs failed to implement the most generous scope of the laws and the EU's influence could, thus, be labeled as fragmented and inconsistent. For instance, in the Czech Republic the government established a Department for Gender Equality, which brings together representatives of the public and private sphere aiming at finding solutions to current problems and disseminate information to women allowing them to take full opportunity of equal treatment. However, even the amended Labor Code still listed professions where women could not work, which did not apply to men in any sector. Hašková (2003), therefore, argued that the special bodies and units established by the various ministries served only the purpose of meeting international standards and not of implementing equal opportunities for men and women.

Gender equality represents an example where civil society has a lot of potential. Europeanization of gender issues in the ECECs started in the mid-1990s, when many NGOs started to expand their activities to the international level and a number of them engaged in gender mainstreaming. Forest (2006) explains it by their limited access to national governments. Other factors include high fragmentation of these organizations and the need to redefine feminism in terms of advanced societies.

They were also framed by a large number of discourses related to gender issues such as economic rights, homosexuality, abortion (particularly in Poland where the debate was affected by religious organizations), political engagement, employment policies, sexual harassment, etc.

They first became acquainted with the policies and instruments available at the European level and then started to create national and regional coalitions. They exchanged information and experience and pooled resources. In the Czech Republic, for instance, 20 NGOs united in the Association for Equal Opportunities and they regularly commented on the documents of the government related to pro-motion of equal opportunities of women (Hašková 2003). Regional organizations such as Karat[11] registered in Poland, aimed at lobbying for the interests and needs of women in the region at all levels of decision-making. The main focus of orga-nizations such as the Polish Women's Lobby, Women's Rights Center, Democratic Union of Women, La Strada Foundation in Poland, Women's League, Network of East-West, and the many more local NGOs was to influence government policy. However, these organizations still kept a rather low profile facing much skepticism, lack of general awareness, and continuing relatively limited access to the domestic centers of power in their countries.

Just as in the ECECs, the women's emancipation in Turkey was imposed from above as part of the revolution/modernization project. The official line of the repub-lic that labeled itself a "feminist state" was that women's position improved with the new policies introduced after 1923 even though the women's movement appeared already during the late Ottoman era.[12] The "Kemalist" woman was to be a mother and a worker, a "new" Turkish woman, an idealized stereotype (Eylem 2007). The republic introduced the concept of state or republican feminism, which suppressed any other form of feminism. Women were encouraged to unveil and the heads-carf was banned from all public institutions. The "ideal" woman was educated and active in the public sphere (professionally and politically) as defeminized subject dedicated to the cause of the Republic but passive in the private sphere where she would succumb to the dominance of the male (Gökarıksel and Mitchell 2005). The active women's participation "represented the values and interests of a small group of urban, middle-class citizens" (White, in Eylem 2007) and most of the advan-tages were until relatively recently available only to a small minority of women (Pope 2004). She was to represent the new secular republic and bring up the "ideal Turk." Women were also used to increase the appeal of Turkish nationalism – first the mothers of soldiers who fought for the republic, later during the Kurdish con-flict as mothers of Turkish soldiers killed by the Kurdistan Workers Party (PKK) insurgents.

The society remained "socially conformist" (Eylem 2007) where women were subject to the cultural norms of patriarchy and the society had to wait till the 1980s to see a rise in the feminist movement that would replace the early republic's "state feminism," which they criticized for giving rights to women not for their own sake but for the sake of the state, turning women into "breeders and educators of the new generations" (Eylem 2007). The 1980s saw the rise of feminism, focusing on both the individual and collective rights of women. In the next decade the movement became more heterogeneous representing the various interests of women in Turkey but also more institutionalized. In other words, women began to establish organizations to encourage the feminist struggle for independence. Especially this "third wave" was to some extent influenced by Europeanization and the growing interest of the EU and its institutions in the gender situation in Turkey. The fragmentation to some extent weakened the movement(s) but the women civil society organizations were still able to utilize this increased pressure to demand further reforms from the government. In the early years after 1999, women were especially positive about the EU's ability to promote democratization in Turkey, which could be attributed to the belief that the accession process will help the women's emancipation process (Aybar et al. 2007).

In Turkey, the reform process after 1999 brought many positive legislative changes. In 2001, gender equality in marriage was introduced,[13] followed by a revision of laws on violence against women in 2004. In the same year, a Constitutional amendment was passed providing for equality between men and women. While Turkey passed a law to protect women victims of domestic violence in 1998, a Penal Code amendment from 2004 abolished reduced sentences for honor killings (even though not in all instances), rape was changed into a crime against a person rather than crime against society, it widened the definition of sexual assault, and criminalized sexual harassment. Despite these positive changes, many issues went unaddressed and even more importantly, the legislative changes were only the first step towards a social change and a widespread acceptance of equality between men and women.

When examining the Commission's reports, we would see that they first took a rather reserved position on gender equality but the issue grew in importance over time. The 1997 report on the Czech Republic, Hungary, Poland, and Slovakia did not mention gender equality at all. The same was the case with the 1998 report except for Poland, where one vague sentence expressed the "need to make progress on national policies improving the treatment of women." The subsequent reports adopted more or less critical positions on unequal pay and labor discrimination, political underrepresentation, and domestic violence. They also addressed the problem of slow implementation. The reports were often inconsistent in evaluating the situations and seemed to be downplaying the problem. By the year 2000, only the Czech Republic and Hungary (plus Lithuania) made significant progress in transposing the nine Directives on gender equality into their national law. Huland (2001) explained this slow development by their short experience with democratic and liberal regimes and by the lack of tradition to fight for women's rights. She argued that in order to internalize these norms, they needed NGOs to raise awareness and to intensify public debate so that a shift in attitudes would occur with the assistance of the EU and transnational networks that would provide them with assistance and expertise.

The Commission's reports on Turkey have also dedicated relatively limited space to the issue (less than a page). The 1998 report actually says that "the status of women . . . is increasingly in line with that prevailing in most EU countries. Remaining legal discrimination is being done away with." The only specific problem mentioned was domestic violence. In 2000, only one paragraph was dedicated to the issue focusing on high gender disparity, high illiteracy rate among women (but also men), persisting discrimination concerning family, and problems with domestic violence. The 2001 report only very briefly addressed the positive legislative changes and labeled the problem of violence against women as a remaining "issue of concern."

The 2002 report is almost as brief and after listing the amendments to improve gender equality, mentions specifically the problems of labor market inequality, political underrepresentation of women and honor killings. The 2004 report was more extensive. While again listing the positive developments, it noted that "discrimination and domestic violence . . . remains [*sic.*] a major problem." The other problems listed were discrimination based on lack of education and high illiteracy rate, mainly in the Southeast, and political underrepresentation. The 2005 report for the first time explicitly mentioned the issue of women participation in the labor market,[14] while highlighting that women's participation in some professions such as academicians, lawyers, or doctors is relatively high.[15] The 2006 report noted that while the "legal framework was overall satisfactory," the implementation continued to be a problem. It for the first time mentioned the socioeconomic situation of women highlighting problems such as poverty and displacement. There have been no major changes in these highlighted issues since.

The reports have repeatedly praised the activities of the civil society in Turkey. Organizations such as Women for Women's Human Rights – New Ways (WWHR) and KAMER were established in reaction to the UN conferences on human rights in Vienna in 1993 and the UN Beijing conference in 1995, which also fueled the gender discourse in the ECECs. In 2000 and 2001 WWHR acted as the secretariat for the campaign on full equality between men and women in the amended Turkish Civil Code and later in the amendment of the Penal Code.[16] Their activities led to the ban on virginity testing and over 30 amendments in the Turkish Penal Code and full equality between sexes in the Civil Code. KAMER is, together with three other organizations, a member of the Committee for Monitoring Violence against Women. It centers its attention on the east and southeast of the country and pressures mainly the local government there. While gender equality policies are able to provide opportunity structures, organizations such as WWHR and KAMER use the resulting window of opportunity, which makes the government more responsive to their demands and starts to implement some very important reforms.

While some argue that EU accession process fueled the gender equality reforms, many are convinced that it was the results of decades' long work of women's organizations (Eylem 2007). A member of the WWHR, Pinar Ilkkaracan, said that the situation of women has improved over the last decade mainly because of the "determined and successful advocacy efforts and campaigns organized by the women's movement". She also explicitly denied the role of the EU in their activities when saying that "we have never used potential EU membership as a strategy to push for full recognition of women's rights in our campaigns" to make the people understand that these reforms are not for the EU but the women of Turkey and to avoid any potential voices who would then label the activities as "the agenda of the West."

She, however, stated that the EU membership would be a good guarantee that these reforms would not be rejected in the future (quoted in Jones 2008). Pope (2004) claims that thanks to the NGOs, the issue of gender equality now has a firm place in Turkey-EU relations. We can assume that the membership application helped ease some regulations related to civil society in the 1980s, which enhanced the growth of the civil society sector in Turkey.[17] Furthermore, the EU demands help these organizations to convince the resistant audience to implement the reforms and acts as an anchor of the reforms while pushing for more implementation and the NGOs assist with norm internalization. Hence, the EU's impact has been both direct and indirect and both as a trigger and an anchor.

In 2009, women's organizations criticized the lack of implementation and applied it to all, former and current, governments. Many believed that the legislative changes would bring about a change in attitudes and mentality but that did not happen – data show that uniform implementation across the country is problematic and slow. Turkish politicians lack political will and often refer to the legal changes as sufficient to bring about a real change – just like before they referred to the reforms of the early Republic as sufficient in securing gender equality (Pope 2004). Genel and Karaosmanoglu (2006) argue that "many women are far from confident that the Turkish state is genuinely committed to protecting women from discrimination and abuse." The European Policy Action Center on Violence against Women (EPACVAW) stated that in Turkey "acceptance of for example honor killings in local communities is stronger than the normative value of new laws introduced" (2009). Especially monitoring lags behind.

In Turkey, a survey conducted in 2007 indicated that one out of three women experienced domestic violence, 81 percent of women sometimes or always asked their spouse's permission to travel outside of the town, 61 percent to go shopping, 68 percent to visit relatives, and 59 percent to visit a neighbor (Altınay and Arat 2009). So while women's awareness is rising, a majority of them cannot live according to these rules. The same survey, however, reported that more women demanded equality in gender relations and a majority of women did not see any justification for domestic violence. Also, there has been a declining trend of forced or even arranged marriages. The 2008 World Public Opinion survey on equal rights for women showed that 80 percent of Turks saw it as very important that women had full right to equality with men (USA 77, UK 89, France 75 percent) and 60 percent was convinced that during their lifetime women received more rights and the same number indicated that the government should do more for women's rights (World Public Opinion 2008). The campaigns since the 1980s and the EU pressure, both direct and indirect, contributed to these changes in attitudes. The progress has been slow but encouraging.

Turkish women generally support EU membership hoping that the process will bring them more rights and freedoms and more equality in society. The EU law with respect to gender equality and the EU demands coincide with the demands of the feminist movement in Turkey that has been working with transnational groups such as the European Women's League (EWL). Also the Network Women in Development Europe (WIDE), which engages in cooperation between EU MS

and CCs has been very active in Turkey. Another example of international cooperation is a project – organized by Turkish Kadir Has University and the Austrian high
schools' Women's Platform – called "I Want to Work," which addressed the issue
of female employment.[18] These are excellent examples of civil society dialogue,
which is crucial for further improvements in this field because simple transposition
of European law into the Turkish legislation is not sufficient to guarantee gender
equality.

The level of gender equality in the ECECs is much higher than in Turkey but
many problems persist there too. They compare well with the EU average regarding women's employment levels and pay gap, but women face cultural prejudices,
stereotypes, and lack of political will to be more engaged in promoting women's
rights. Compared to the other ECECs, the women's employment rate is particularly
low in Poland. Occupational segregation persists and economic insecurity of the
transition period was a principally worrying problem. Kwak and Pascall (2009)
also note that while the countries' public supports the combination of family and
career lives, they do not encourage division of responsibilities in the household and
family between men and women. They note that these ideas only slowly penetrate
the average person's life.

Women in the ECECs are also underrepresented in the political bodies on both
national and regional levels. Kwak and Pascall (2009: 20) even claim that "democratization . . . has not been shared by women" due to their low participation in
politics. The most serious problems, however, include domestic violence, rape,
trafficking in women, and prostitution caused by adverse economic conditions. A
related concern is that the societies fail to address it as a serious issue and there is a
lack of a comprehensive approach on the side of their governments. Social education programs and information campaigns are not conducted on a more systematic
level. Thus, while the legal situation improved, it still remains a considerable social
problem. Challenging is also the fact that, to a large extent, public debate is absent
on gender equality.

The role of the NGOs seems to be crucial for the promotion of gender equality norms and values. The accession process empowered the civil society, which
has been much more visible in Turkey than in the ECECs but that is caused also
by their elevated level of activity throughout the 1990s. The EU has also helped
these organizations through funding and providing expertise through the twinning
projects and participation of the women's NGOs in the transnational networks. In
Turkey, the EU has for example set up a Civil Society Development Programme and
between November 2006 and 2007, the EU provided more than two million euro
to the Bridges of Knowledge Programme. Altogether, 27 projects were conducted
within this scheme.[19]

While there have been many positive changes on the legal ground, de facto observance of gender equality principles is lagging behind. It could be argued that the lax
attention the EU paid to gender equality might be one of the causes why so many
issues were left unresolved. In the ECECs, the reform process placed gender equality relatively low on the agenda but even in Turkey the problem started to receive
more attention only rather recently. The political representatives in both the ECECs

and Turkey support gender equality on paper and in their speeches but less on the ground giving it only marginal attention despite the criticism from the various civil society groups. While the causes lie predominantly with the domestic environments, the EU failed to push the countries towards more change because although, in social dialogue, they supported higher involvement of women, they applied weak monitoring mechanisms in ensuring implementation. It paid too much attention to the legal and institutional changes whereas the monitoring of implementation lagged behind. Gender equality still has not become a widely adopted political norm and those campaigning for it are often exposed to mockery. In Turkey the issue is – unlike in the ECECs – a political *and* cultural problem, which Öniş and Yılmaz (2009: 21) call "deeply embedded problem of gender inequality" and as such change and improvement will be even more difficult to sustain.

Corruption

Another example is the issue of corruption, which brought only limited results in both the ECECs and Turkey. The fight against corruption embodies one of the key problems of democracy consolidation and in new democracies represents "a more pervasive threat to the rule of law than . . . political repression" (Rose and Shin 2001: 341). It is a "social, economic and cultural phenomenon" (Kaldor and Vejvoda 1997: 74) that requires a change in behavior. The perception of widespread corruption mainly among the elites undermines the public's trust in politicians, thus, also the legitimacy of the political system and the civil service. Szymanski (2006a: 252) notes that it led, in both Poland and Turkey, to a "lack of confidence in politicians" and the same could be said about the Czech Republic, Hungary, and Slovakia. The issue of corruption received a lot of attention in the EU and in the CCs but few truly tangible results could be observed for it is deeply rooted in their institutional systems where a link between politics and business exists, strengthened by privatization and past legacies. All the countries adopted international instruments to fight corruption but it has not led to a true behavioral change.

Appel (2001: 547) remarks that "corruption is an enormous barrier to the process of democratization." Przeworksi (in Appel 2001) links it to the issue of citizenship for corruption does not allow equal treatment of all citizens and as such undermines democratic consolidation. Corruption in the political circles in both the ECECs and Turkey might represent the reason why the anti-corruption legislative measures took so long to be put into place and even longer to be implemented. Corruption does not avoid established democracies but the results differ. In the ECECs and Turkey, citizens believe that corruption is wrong but the legislation and its enforcement are weak, punishments are not severe and often do not reach the top circles.

The EU does not have any binding *acquis* as regards corruption and relies on soft laws such as international agreements and measures covered by the Justice and Home Affairs pillar. The Commission frequently identified corruption as a key problem for all ECECs and it represented one of the key concerns throughout the monitoring period. Its focus on this issue is logical because it affects not only the democratic values and the functioning of the democratic regime but also the implementation of the *acquis* and using the EU funds. Its efforts were, however, undermined by the fact that the EU does not have a comprehensive anti-corruption framework. The 1997 Reports did not even include a specific sub-chapter for anti-corruption measures (even though corruption was mentioned in the general evaluation in the report for Hungary). It was introduced a year later – corruption was labeled a "serious problem" in the Czech report, Hungary was said to be "confronted with corruption problems," for Poland it highlighted the "need to intensify the fight against corruption," and for Slovakia it stated that there was "no major improvement" in fighting against corruption. For all ECECs, the 1998, 2000, 2001, and 2002 reports included fighting against corruption among the key priorities to be addressed.

The 2000 Enlargement Strategy Paper stated that "the continued prevalence of corruption gives cause for concern." More specifically, the 2001 report on Slovakia and Poland said that corruption was a serious cause of concern, for Hungary that it "remains a problem" and for the Czech Republic that "corruption and economic crime remain a serious cause for concern." In 2002, it was a "cause for concern" in Hungary and a "cause for serious concern" in the other three ECECs. The 2003 comprehensive monitoring reports, the last ones for the ECECs, identified corruption as a "cause for concern" in the Czech Republic, and a "serious problem" in Hungary. The Polish 2003 report said that "very little progress" could be observed, and in Slovakia it stated that "there is a continuously high public and professional perception of widespread corruption." The Commission's evaluations – while praising the efforts and steps undertaken – focused mainly on identifying the core problems underlying corruption, listing the measures adopted in that year without any specific recommendations on how to accelerate the efforts.

The 1998 Turkey report marked as one of the key reasons for corruption the absence of public funding for political parties, connections between the state and organized crime, and the situation in the judiciary including low salaries, an issue often mentioned also with the ECECs. The issue was repeatedly labeled a "serious problem." The 2006, 2007, and 2008 reports called corruption "widespread." While indicating the positive developments and the rising salience of the issue in the media, the Commission continually stated that the progress had been "limited."

The elites often delay anti-corruption measures because they benefit from corruption the most. As a result, in the ECECs and Turkey they avoided politicization of corruption and thereby excluded it from the public debate. If major corruption cases surfaced, they would not be labeled as a wide-ranging problem, but rather issues of individuals, or the elites would blame their opponents for using corruption in the domestic political battles, i.e. constructing "fake" corruption cases.[20] Many cases were discovered only accidentally or because of disagreements between those sharing the benefits. Political salience remained low and the occurrence of corruption seemed to increase as a result of the political and economic reforms related to the processes of democratization and liberalization. It worsened after the negotiations started, which could be partially attributed to the relatively frequent occurrence of corrupt practices in using the pre-accession funds.[21] Despite the Commission's reports dedicating increased amount of space to the fight against corruption and for all concerned countries identifying them as key priorities, we saw that apart from legal measures Europeanization had only limited impact in terms of combating corruption.

Fighting corruption is related to the issue of the reform of the judiciary[22] and requires the development of a new, democratic, political culture and a respect for law. Here, the EU's promotion of discourse through transnational networks and socialization within judicial cooperation seems to be particularly important, together with the role of other institutions such as the Council of Europe. It also requires the emergence of an active civil society that would "force accountability upon its elected officials" (Appel 2001: 553). Furthermore, the media need to expose the corruption allegations and hold the responsible authorities accountable to raise public awareness and expose the problem of systemic corruption so that they push it higher up on the political agenda. We saw similar developments in the Czech Republic and Slovakia when the latter was much more successful in reducing corruption levels and the negative perceptions of the public.

Civil society should work to expose and prevent corruption and increase transparency of the political system and the economy, but so far it has been able to turn the problem into an important political issue on a much more limited level than the women's rights organizations with gender equality. Its failure could be attributed to a wide range of factors. Corruption involves informal rules of conduct, which are difficult to target and hard to reach and the enforcement of new rules is hindered by the political and economic elites that benefit from the current system and are closed to external pressures. In the case of the ECECs, the weakness of the state during the transition period allowed corruption to flourish. In Turkey, the insufficient anti-corruption controls, lack of transparency and weak legal sanctions were often seen as major obstacles to eradicating corrupt behavior among the political and administrative elites.

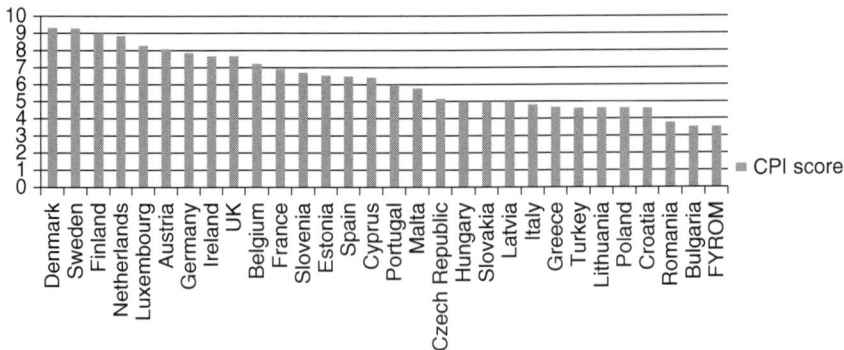

Figure 3.1 Transparency International 2008 Corruption Perceptions Index (CPI)[1]

Source: Transparency International 2008

[1] A country or territory's CPI Score indicates the degree of public sector corruption as perceived by business people and country analysts, and ranges between 10 (highly clean) and 0 (highly corrupt)

Turkey and the ECECs have comparable levels of corruption (see Figure 3.1). The EU Monitoring and Advocacy Program (EUMAP) reports came to the conclusion that the EU had a very positive impact on the anti-corruption legal framework in the CCs but it could have been more efficient if the EU was more coherent and consistent. Beblavý and Beblavá (2009) argue, based on the example of Slovakia, that the accession process had a very positive impact because it excluded the more corruption-prone actors from government while it was later the public that demanded strong anti-corruption legal instruments that was a crucial driver of reform. Thus, they argue that it was the combination of public pressure and the EU demands (and fiscal needs) that drove the changes and that the motivation of the elites was beyond simply pleasing the EU even though conditionality and the reports were also significant factors in this process. They, however, conclude that the EU's effect after accession is more problematic (see Figure 3.2). The Turkish example shows that some legal and institutional changes were put in place in response to EU pressure such as the Public Procurement Authority (KIK) but their effect is limited – KIK, for instance, cannot manage public procurement because the government included a clause in every new law on corruption that states "This law is exempt from the provisions of the public procurement law" (Yavuz 2008).

In both cases, gender equality and corruption, the EU served as a driver and anchor of reform but failed to ensure that the changes would be embedded in the CCs' societies. Deeper socialization and support of the civil society groups that would with the EU's help learn how to drive and then take over the wheel from the EU conditionality demands are essential. EU projects serve a very positive function in this respect. The work of the Economic and Social Committee and its joint consultative committee with Turkey (and Croatia) is, for example, important in strengthening social dialogue and exchanging experiences. Still, the pre-accession financial aid for Turkey has been low, relative to the ECECs. In the 2000 to 2006 financial period, the Czech Republic received €17 per capita and Turkey €2.7. Even

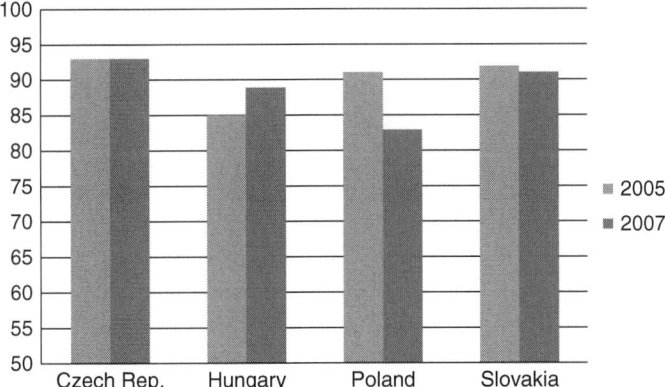

Figure 3.2 Perception of Corruption in National Institutions in 2005 and 2007

Source: European Commission 2008e.

though it increased in the next period – between 2007 and 2009, Turkey received €22.4 per capita, in the same period Croatia received €97.5 per capita, approximately the same amount as the third CC, Former Yugoslav Republic of Macedonia (FYROM). It seems that the EU was particularly successful with helping the countries to introduce legal provisions but lagged behind in monitoring of the implementation process, which the elites often used or even abused. There seems to be a positive learning curve as before the negotiations with Turkey started, the Commission stated that implementation would be closely scrutinized. Even though it does not seem to be always the case, it should be seen as a positive step by those dedicated to the reform process.

Conclusion

The promise of EU membership must be credible and substantial but that does not constitute a sufficient condition for securing successful Europeanization and democratization. As the EU accession process involves very little actual negotiation and often threatens to undermine the political power of the elites, it is naïve to believe that the prospect of accession represents such an appealing vision that the CCs will conform to all EU requirements and demands. Norm internalization is a crucial prerequisite for implementation and stability of the democratization process ensuring that the future MS had passed the point of no return, i.e. became credible partners. The EU needs to be very consistent in monitoring the CC but also needs to ensure that the information collected is correct and objective.

The cases of the ECECs and Turkey both show a combination of "logic of consequences" and "logic of appropriateness". In some instances and to some degree, the CCs were reacting to the prospect of membership and merely fulfilled the EU requirements. Still, it was in numerous cases accompanied by demands prevailing in the domestic environment. Where the latter existed, the nature of the reforms and their implementation seem to be much more durable than in the case of the former. Concurrently, the countries and their political elites had to take into account the cost of compliance and non-compliance both in terms of their country's EU membership and their domestic and potentially also international political power. The level of Europeanization's impact on domestic policies was often underestimated by the political elites in the initial stages of the accession process. Even though the civil society in these countries is often portrayed as weak – and in comparison with many advanced democratic countries is – it has played a vital role in the process. In Turkey, many scholars believe that the NGOs provided fundamental source of pressure on the government to introduce important, especially political, reforms. Not only increase in number but mainly activism of groups such as women's organizations have been impressive. Again, where such development could be observed, the success of the reform tended to be higher. Still, the resources of the NGOs in both ECECs and Turkey are limited.

The adoption and internalization of European norms and values requires a change in attitudes, mentalities, and identities, which is a very protracted and painful process. In order to adopt the EU rules, the state and the society need to be positively inclined to change, i.e. the West must become a matter of identity and not choice (Topidi 2009). We could argue with Pridham that learning from the EU's shortcomings in the case of ECECs and from their experience, EU and Turkey (and the other CCs) have the opportunity to avoid certain past mistakes. Turkey needs to learn from the ECECs experience that human rights and democracy are not negotiable. Furthermore, it needs strong supporter(s) in the EU that will help it improve its image in the MS, which are becoming more vocal in the enlargement process and emphasize various elements of democratization. Some accentuate Turkish relations with neighbors, some gender relations and the civilian control of the military, others the Kurdish issue and economic rights. This decreasing transparency of the process highlights the need to find strong allies in the EU. It would be wrong, however, to focus on large countries only as even fairly small countries can become important and outspoken advocates of Turkish membership.[23]

The image of a country is a significant factor because when mentioning its name, a certain mental picture is produced. The ECECs and Turkey were both believed to be chronic perpetrators of human rights violations with highly underdeveloped civic culture. The countries of Eastern Europe traditionally had the image of "economic backwardness, lack of innovative spirit, tyrannical preponderance of the religious element, state despotism and lack of civil consciousness" (Okey 1992: 107), which was in more modern terms of the 1990s translated into "a region of abandoned children, street beggars and tuberculosis patients that may spread its social diseases westwards" (Manning 2004: 229). Turkey has a much bigger "image problem" either stemming from the Ottoman past, where the Turk was seen as "the savage, debauched and bloodthirsty infidel, unredeemed by moral feeling, unrestrained by law and untouched by artistic refinement" (Yapp 1992: 148) or in a more modern form seen and portrayed as corrupt, worshiping Atatürk, tolerating honor killings and forced marriages, slaughtering ethnic minorities, too Muslim, or too secular, thus, incompatible with the "West."[24]

The EU should avoid any "rhetorical traps" (Tocci 2007) and politicization of conditionality, which undermines its credibility, one of the key elements for conditionality to work.[25] It must fully acknowledge Turkey's legitimate position as a speaker and actor in the game, one worth talking and listening to. Only then will Turkey fully engage in the debate and the communication will become meaningful. The example of Slovakia shows that extreme measures should be taken only with respect to the most vital issues, where the situation is deteriorating and where harsh criticism and firm EU positions can empower the opposition and make the public demand change. For the Turkish public, politicization is, together with the open-endedness, the most disturbing factor in the accession negotiations (Aydin and Esen 2007). Many Turks claim that based on previous experience, the EU might not keep its promises (Eylemer and Taş 2007). Also, the problems mentioned in the Commission's Reports should not overshadow the questions raised by the civil society. In addition, the Commission should develop and nurture dialogue with the many NGOs so that some important issues do not go ignored but also to understand all the implications, causes, and consequences of Europeanization for the domestic situation. The Commission should avoid silencing them through demanding its conditions to be met before the demands of the Turkish society. At best, they will coincide and reinforce each other.

With the rising heterogeneity of the EU MS, the EU and the CC must share some vision of a common European identity. The countries need to agree on some basic level of values, norms, beliefs, and political culture. Turkey needs to openly declare democracy and human rights as inherent to its values and implement policies that would support this without demanding any more exceptions due to the country's "special status" that requires "special treatment" with some modified democratic model or that it should be treated differently than other countries because as some like to argue it is bigger, has higher Gross Domestic Product (GDP), a strong cultural background, and an imperial past.[26]

Turkey might be a distinctive case but that should not be confused with different. Karen Fogg might have been right to say "you can't treat Turkey like Slovakia" (in Matthews 2002) in the sense of learning how to communicate with Turkey but that does not mean that special conditions should apply. They would benefit neither Turkey, nor the EU. Turkey needs to become a functional democracy, not a democracy of appearances, introduce not inchmeal but far-flung reforms. This to a large extent concerns observance and protection of human rights. The Commission considers political conditions and human rights as mutually reinforcing and closely interrelated and highlights the notion of universality and indivisibility of human rights. The Turkish understanding of human rights needs to change – while in the ECECs the dominance of social and economic rights had to be balanced with individual and political rights, in Turkey a revision of the state standing above the individual and their rights must be corrected. As Olli Rehn once said, Turkey must embrace these values "in all walks of life." Furthermore, Turkey cannot consider these issues as domestic in nature and as interference with internal affairs (Eylemer and Taş 2007). People are slowly learning that they have the right to have rights (Arendt 1951).

Turkey also needs to realize that it is not being treated dramatically differently from the previous CCs and should not use it as an excuse to delay reforms and alienate its allies. This is often based on lack of knowledge about the Eastern enlargement and failing to follow the debate in the CCs and MS as closely as they follow in their own – this also explains why many Turkish elites believed that Turkey was more democratic than the ECECs (Eylemer and Taş 2007) and thus strongly resisted their accession before Turkey's. It should follow the logic of some supporters of accession in Turkey, who believe that once Turkey meets the Copenhagen criteria, it will be virtually impossible for the EU and its MS to deny it membership. If Turkey did not consider the Copenhagen criteria very important until the 1997 Council, it should have long before understood that failure to meet them is *the* major threat to Turkish EU accession. The Turkish society needs democratic reforms that must be accompanied by a fundamental change in norms and values of the ruling elites that represent an immense obstacle to further democratization. The deep traditional division between state and government must be abolished for the interests of the state cannot overrule the interests of the citizens and the ruling elites must be held accountable for their actions.

The debate must not be conducted based on "if Turkey joins" but "when" and "how". This will provide sufficient political and public support to the reformers and also make it clear in Europe that this issue is not subject to discussion. In the end, political representation in Europe changes and by the time Turkey signs the accession treaty, Europe will have quite a different political constellation. The government should behave as if there was no doubt about future accession as the newly appointed foreign minister, Ahmet Davutoğlu, said in May 2009:

> The bringing of new alternatives onto the agenda is both the violation of the principle of pacta sunt servanda and is also composed of nothing but a mental exercise which has no use at all . . . We should all . . . agree that now Turkey's EU process is a one-way process which keeps driving via negotiations. It has no turning back.
>
> (*Today's Zaman* 2009c)

Similarly, the Turkish president Abdullah Gül reacted to the remarks made by Nicolas Sarkozy and Angela Merkel about not supporting Turkish full membership by saying, "What is binding for us is the legal situation . . . Various politicians come and go; they say things on different occasions . . .] but we will not be bothered" (Alpay 2009: 15). It, however, works both ways. Just as the European governments become sometimes more and sometimes less supportive of EU enlargement and Turkey, so can the Turkish governments change – the pro-reformers can be replaced with a less reform inclined actors and vice versa. The Turkish public has on several occasions reacted to the developments in the reform process and demanded more changes and it is important that no matter the political situation in Turkey, the elites and the public remain generally open to EU influence and conditionality demands. Many issues at stake can undergo only an evolutionary and not revolutionary change and the EU should be there to help frame them. If Turkey can turn into a "good European," who promotes the values of European integration, its foreign policy goal will be achieved more easily than if it plays the playground bully game. For Turkish democratization to continue, the EU accession process is vital. There are far too many veto players in Turkey, which endangers the process in the absence of an external force. Thus, it is also an obligation for the EU to ensure that maximum is done to achieve the ultimate goal of democratic Turkey.

Notes

1 There is, however, no specific EU definition of what constitutes a consolidated democracy, i.e. the state of affairs each CC needs to meet to become an MS.
2 The list of conditions that define consolidated democracies is very long and we choose not to address them individually but rather focus on the trends and the outcomes of the EU-CC relationship.
3 The revolutions in the ECECs were directly linked to the rising domestic pressure from the social groups that demanded the communist regimes to respect human rights. Similarly in Turkey, various groups started to demand that it improve its human rights record, to grant its citizens democratic rights and liberties. Thus, transnationalization of democracy was a crucial factor in the democratization of these countries where in

the former it contributed to the fall of the communist regimes and in the latter led to expansion of democratic norms. However, it was the 1999 Helsinki decision that empowered many of the pro-reform groups in Turkey and strengthened their position.

4 Uğur (2001) identified the Turkish state's control over and suppression of civil society as one of the important factors that hindered democratization while the economic liberalization was obstructed by the close relations between the state and several powerful business interest organizations. Collectivism and homogenization represent shared elements of the ECEC's and Turkey's experience – the survival of either ideology was the key interest of the state. Due to the suppression of domestic opposition, it was often the external forces that demanded changes and put pressure on both the ECECs and Turkey to respect human rights.

5 The largest confederation of Turkish NGOs is TÜSEV. For a brief overview of the major Turkish NGOs, see Kamp 2009.

6 It would be wrong to associate Europeanization with the EU only as it is affected by a complex institutional architecture of post-World War II Europe. In areas such as minority rights or gender equality, the OSCE or Council of Europe has played a very important complementary role and the EU has often relied on them too.

7 Recently, Egemen Bağış said: "Even if there was no such negotiation process, Turkey should have done these structural reforms and legal arrangements for high quality state service, for increased democratic standards and for peace and welfare of our own citizens" (*Today's Zaman* 2009).

8 It is common that the supporting words are immediately coupled with statements that make membership questionable. Some believe that it has been a deliberate move to push Turkey away.

9 Yapp (1992: 149) shows how deeply rooted these notions are. Despite the little contact the sixteenth-century Europeans had with the Ottoman Empire, they not only saw the Ottoman women as slaves but also as vicious and dissolute.

10 For a study on her mixed record in accentuating the women's situation in Turkey, see Arat 1998.

11 Karat was established in 1997 and has four main strategies: advocacy, monitoring, capacity building, and building alliances. It has both collective and individual membership. It unites member organizations from Albania (3), Armenia (2), Azerbaijan (1), Belarus (3), Bosnia and Herzegovina (1), Bulgaria (3), Croatia (1), Czech Republic (3), Estonia (1), Georgia (2), Hungary (1), Kyrgyzstan (2), Latvia (1), Lithuania (1), Macedonia (5), Moldova (3), Montenegro (1), Poland (3), Romania (6), Russia (4), Serbia (4), Slovakia (2), Ukraine (2). Individual members also include Germany and Slovenia. More on www.karat.org/.

12 Ottoman women were aware of the women's movement in the West and started to demand more rights, especially in the areas of education, employment, and political participation.

13 Equality in marriage included women's right to an equal share in goods and property accrued during their marriage, men were no longer "head of the family," the couple could jointly decide where they would live, men and women would share the financial responsibility for the family, both men and women would be able to represent the family in legal matters, the obligation of the spouse to get permission before choosing a job was abolished, etc. For the full list, see http://www.byegm.gov.tr/on-sayfa/new-civil-code.htm.

14 The EU average of women's participation in the labor market is 57 percent and only 24 percent in Turkey. Also only 18 percent of Turkish women aged 18–24 attend educational institutions as compared to the EU average of 61 percent.

15 According to TÜSIAD, 14 percent of self-employed workers are women compared to 7 percent in Germany. However, this does not mean that the women actually run or work in the business because at times the husbands simply use the woman's name. More reliable data refer to other positions such as academicians (36 percent), architects (33

percent), lawyers (29 percent), economists (32 percent), and top and middle managers (21 percent) (EurActiv 2006).

16 26 NGOs united under the Women's Platform on the Turkish Penal Code and lobbied the government and the parliament to guarantee gender equality. They also organized a campaign called Reform of the Turkish Penal Code from a Gender Perspective.

17 Some argue that as the capacity of the state drops, the need for other forms of governance increases, which might empower civil society (Grote 2009) – the development of civil society in Turkey was reacting to the weakness of the state following the 1980 coup.

18 The project offers around 20 internships for female students with large business companies in Istanbul.

19 For more, see http://www.avrupa.info.tr/AB_Mali_Destegi/AB_Program_Bilgileri,Pro gramprojemerge.html?Mode = 4&Pid = 16

20 In 1997, all relevant Czech political parties were facing allegations of corrupt practices. Also, all Turkish governments and relevant political parties have faced serious corruption claims. Corrupt practices brought down the 2001 government when president Ahmet Necdet Sezer admonished the Prime Minister Bülent Ecevit for tolerating corruption among his ministers and obstructing investigations. A more recent example was the investigation of the German-based Lighthouse Foundation (Deniz Feneri) on fraud allegations. The organization was accused of sending US$26 million from charity collections to conservative companies in Turkey. Some media implicated the Prime Minister Erdoğan and his party and government in the case, which sparked a harsh argument between the Prime Minister and the media, especially the Doğan Yayin Holding. In summer 2008, Kemal Kılıçdaroğlu, the deputy chairman of the Republican People's Party (CHP), accused Şaban Dişli, the deputy chairman of the ruling Justice and Development Party (AKP), of US$1 million worth of corruption (Yavuz 2008). The clash of the two major political parties turned the case into a political battle.

21 In 2001, the EU for example stopped the pre-accession aid to Slovakia on allegations of misuse of the funds and asked the government to investigate the alleged corruption there.

22 The reform of the judiciary in democratizing societies helps to legitimize the reform process. For an analysis of the post-communist judicial reforms and their connection with Europeanization, see Piana 2009, who provides yet another example of how similar past, structures, and recent histories can lead to very different results. She argues that the EU was not able to converge domestic reforms in the countries because of the path dependence effect.

23 Several small and medium size EU MS have articulated their official support for the Turkish EU membership. In May 2009, the Portuguese president Cavaco Silva said "Europe needs Turkey" (Balci 2009). Similarly, the Finnish foreign minister, Alexander Stubb, stated in May 2009 that he and the Finnish government support the Turkish EU bid (Bozkurt 2009b). Carl Bildt, the Swedish PM, recently declared his country's support for Turkish membership (*Today's Zaman* 2009c: 4). Also Spain and the ECECs have repeatedly voiced their support – for the analysis of the ECECs' official positions, see chapter 7 in this volume.

24 On the development of the images of Turkey and Turks in Europe, see Yapp 1992.

25 Former Commissioner for Enlargement, Günter Verheugen said that one of the reasons for the reform process in Turkey slowing down in the previous years was caused by the EU itself and its MS who failed to introduce an "open, reliable and consistent line for its drive to the EU." (*Today's Zaman* 2009d).

26 See Oğütçü 2009.

4 How far away from politics of fear? Turkey in the EU accession process[1]

Rabia Karakaya Polat

Introduction

"Fear Not!" starts the Turkish national anthem. The anthem was written following World War I after which the country came to the brink of partition by the Allied Powers. Fear was a suitable theme for the anthem considering the magnitude of the threat against the nation. However, fear is a theme that still runs deep in the nation's psychology. There are both external and internal "enemies" to be afraid of. What is called "Sèvres syndrome,"[2] for example, puts a shadow on debates about EU membership by fuelling Euroscepticism and a language of "external powers" (*dış mihraklar*) constantly working against Turkey. Likewise, "internal enemies" of the state are defined as those who want to disintegrate the country (Kurdish separatists) and those who challenge the state's secular identity (reactionary Islam).

In fact, Kurdish separatism and reactionary Islam (*irtica*) were included in April 1997 in the *National Security Policy Document* as the most important national security threats. The Office of the Chief of Staff declared that "internal threats against the territorial integrity of the country and the founding principles of the republic became graver than external threats" (Bilgin 2005: 188). This was a very clear example of "securitization" of domestic political issues. In short, the political culture in Turkey is to a large extent influenced by what we can call the politics of fear. Some political issues, such as minority rights, have been defined almost as taboo and considered to be beyond political discussion. Issues of "normal" politics have often been framed and dramatized as "security" challenges to the state. This has constrained the development of free and open discussions on controversial issues. The existence of such a political culture has affected not only Turkey's domestic politics but also its foreign policy (Aras and Polat 2008).

Since the beginning of this decade, however, there has been a remarkable change towards a more participatory and democratic political culture under which some controversial issues, such as the rights of minority groups and the definition of national security, started to be discussed more openly. This change can best be explained by two parallel and interrelated processes of desecuritization and EU membership negotiations. The accession process has affected domestic politics mostly as a result of changing domestic opportunity structures and through the appropriation of European values and norms. The changing opportunity structures have to some extent diminished the role of the civilian-military bureaucracy and societal actors which were largely excluded from policy making processes became more prominent.

In this new context, civil societal actors started to internalize values and norms associated with democracy and with a more pluralist political culture. The parallel process of desecuritization has meanwhile led to partial normalization of formerly securitized issues, where a number of security matters have been redefined as issues of regular politics. With the desecuritization process at work, independent and critical voices are heard more often on sensitive questions such as wearing headscarves at universities, rights of minority groups, and Turkey's relations with its neighbors.

The process of desecuritization has certain limitations stemming from political culture, external factors, and changing domestic circumstances. An important securitizing actor, the military, enjoys a high level of political power and support from different segments of Turkish society (TEPAV 2009) and is likely to continue to play an important role in identifying national security matters and possibly shaping domestic politics. Retired army generals frequently oppose demands for further democratization, which also implies limiting the power of the army, using the argument of Turkey's "sensitive" geopolitical location that allegedly provides the army with a unique role in domestic and international politics.[3] Moreover, issues such as minority rights still have the potential to be framed as existential threats to the Turkish state.

In short, although the political culture in Turkey has started to escape from the confines of securitization, the securitization process is far from complete. On the contrary, it is arguable that these two processes – securitization and desecuritization – compete with each other. While certain securitizing actors continue to exploit the prevailing political culture by reproducing a language of internal and external threats, other actors struggle to transfer these "threats" into the confines of normal politics. The main argument of this chapter is that the EU membership bid plays a key role in putting an end to these competing processes of securitization and desecuritization. As Turkey approaches the EU, securitizing actors lose ground and the country moves away from the politics of fear. However, with the slowdown in the accession process, the feeling of being left-behind fuels the language of "us" and "them" and paranoia-driven politics. Furthermore, the EU accession process influences not only Turkish political institutions and policies but also its political culture. A supplementary argument is that while the EU is relatively successful in inducing formal change, i.e. legislation, its influence on changing values and norms is limited.

The chapter first discusses the concept of securitization and explains why it is a key concept for understanding the political culture in Turkey. Second, it demonstrates the signs of desecuritization since 1999 together with the acceleration in the EU membership process. Finally, it assesses the limitations of the desecuritization process in Turkey and suggests explanations as to why the process is not complete.

The process of securitization

Securitization theorists do not define security as an objective and material condition. Rather, from their perspective security is seen as a "speech act," which implies that "something is a security problem when the elites declare it to be so" (Wæver 1995). Issues become "securitized" through speech acts, which not only describe extant security problems but also create them by presenting them as such. Labeling something a "security issue" allows the actor to claim the need for the use of extraordinary means, emergency measures, and other actions outside the regular boundaries of political procedure.

Far from being objectively defined concepts, discourses of security are "rather the products of historical structures and processes, of struggles for power within the state, of conflicts between the societal groupings that inhabit states and the interests that besiege them" (Lipschutz 1995: 8). At this point, it is necessary to touch upon the link between securitization and domestic power-domination games. Not all political actors are in a position to securitize issues as they like. Securitization is structured by differential capacity of actors to make socially effective claims about threats (Williams 2003: 514). Therefore, this is a field of struggle in which the securitizing actors point at a security issue to secure the support of society for a certain policy or course of action. In this struggle, public officials are in an advantageous position to securitize an issue because they hold influential positions in the security field and have privileged access to information sources including the mass media. The media itself may also act as a securitizer.

What kind of actors can fulfill this role? This largely depends on institutional and cultural contexts. The securitizing actor should have social capital and should be in a position of authority (Wæver 2000: 253). In the case of Turkey, the civilian and military bureaucracy traditionally has had the authority and credibility to make successful securitizing moves. The authority position of these actors was further enhanced by their acts of securitization (Lipschutz 1995: 8). From this perspective, established definition of national security in Turkey is not a purely objective and neutral one. It is rather a successfully securitized collection of state-centric notions of security. Looking through these lenses, how can we understand the process through which political issues are securitized in Turkey? This process can be analyzed by considering its three dimensions. First, there is a need to understand how securitization moves are received by the audience. Second, we need to examine the ways in which the information sources are controlled and/or manipulated by the securitizing actors. Finally, it is necessary to look at the ways in which the discourses of identity interact with discourses of security.

Successful securitization is structured by the forms in which securitization claims can be made in order to be recognized and accepted as convincing by the relative audience (Williams 2003: 514). Psycho-cultural orientation of the audience is important. When the securitizing actor attempts to frame an issue as a security question, this needs to resonate with the audience. Reception from the audience also depends on the linguistic ability of the securitizer. The audience looks for "emotional intensity and logical rigor" (Balzacq 2005: 191) in deciding whether there is a security threat or not. The success of any attempt to securitize an issue is contingent upon the existence of an audience that accepts this claim and grants the actor a right to violate rules that otherwise would bind (Wæver 2000: 251).

In Turkey, the military does not have difficulty in convincing the public since it enjoys high degree of trust and respect among the general public.[4] The existence of a robust civil society can be expected to act against this kind of excessive securitization. However, in certain circumstances issues can be dramatized to such a level that the voices of civil society can also be seen as threats to the state. In other cases, civil society can be mobilized by the securitizers against the supposed/perceived threats. Hence, societal actors may be unable or unwilling to stand against securitization moves (Polat 2009: 133).

The securitization process is enhanced by information control, media manipulation, and more direct forms of repression. Towards the end of 1990s, the Turkish military as one of the most successful securitizing actors developed the practice of directly addressing high level officials, academics, and leading journalists on significant policy issues (Taşpinar 2007). These experts themselves became part of the securitization process through their security analyses informed by the military because they used the same language and logic, which transformed them from observers of a certain policy to its advocates (Eriksson 1999). By issuing press releases and making public statements, the military not only announces its own position regarding certain domestic and foreign policy issues, but more importantly manages to portray certain political issues as imperative security matters. Finally, security discourses are being built around discourses of "self" and the "other." Turkey has been delineating the European "self" versus the Middle Eastern "other" as part of its modernization project and in its attempt to find a place in the Western civilization (Helvacioglu 1996).

Issues of identity are represented with certain images. In foreign policy, the images of veiled women in black and bearded men with traditional clothes in Iran, for example, are often presented in the Turkish media as the images of the "other" posing an existential threat to "our" Western identity and secular regime. In domestic politics the veiling issue is rarely discussed within the framework of individual choice and religious freedom. Rather, veiling is securitized as an existential threat to the state's Western and secular identity. Although securitization theory emphasizes the significance of speech, images and visual imagery are important in securitizing certain issues (Williams 2003).

What is said up to this point does not mean that any issue can be securitized at any time. When the times are critical enough or when exploitable historical references exist, the securitizer has a better chance to convince the audience about the existence of a real threat. Therefore, although security is understood as a "speech act," this does not mean that it emerges out of nothing. In most cases, the securitizing actors frame and dramatize as security issues present *political* problems. The more "evidence" the securitizers can find (a controversial statement from a minority group's representative, memories of foreign occupation, a hostile statement from a neighboring country), the more likely they are to succeed in securitizing. This kind of evidence or context makes the masses ripe for persuasion (Balzacq

2005: 183). One of the highly securitized issues in Turkey is minority rights, espe-cially of the Kurdish population. This is not surprising considering that histori-cal memories of ethnic minorities rebelling against the Ottoman Empire, usually with the encouragement of the West, are still alive.[5] Also, the Kurdish secessionist violence makes it more difficult to focus on the discussion about their rights and freedoms. Some other highly securitized issues are property rights of foreigners, activities of missionaries in Turkey, religious minorities as well as foreign policy discourses on Cyprus and the EU.

As mentioned earlier, the securitization process should be analyzed in conjunc-tion with an analysis of power-domination games in national politics. This game is played between emerging social and political forces that are seeking more influence via the ruling Justice and Development Party (AKP) and the military and civilian bureaucratic elites that have historically been the driving force of Turkish mod-ernization and westernization. The frequently used Şerif Mardin's (1973) center-periphery framework of Turkish politics analysis is particularly useful at this point. It describes Turkish politics as being built around a strong center that is dominated by the civil/military bureaucratic elite and a heterogeneous periphery composed of farmers, the peasantry, and small business owners that is often hostile to the mod-ernizing/westernizing efforts of the center. The civil/military elite have controlled state institutions and the economy since the inception of the Republic in 1923. More recently the rise of a new Muslim bourgeoisie has started to challenge the *status quo* by pressing for greater political and economic rights and freedoms. Another challenge from the periphery has been the demand for more rights and freedoms for the Kurds. Facing these challenges from the periphery, the center started to resort to the securitization of issues such as the lifting of the headscarf ban in universities or minority language broadcasting.

The mistrust between the civil/military bureaucratic elite and the politicians representing the periphery has been part of the Turkish state tradition and political culture. The bureaucratic/military elite's presentation of political issues as existential threats has hindered the emergence of a healthy debate within the public sphere. Every so often, the masses start to fear that the secular character of the state is under threat and are mobilized through street protests to protect its character.[6] At other times, Turkish intellectual life is constrained by nationalist discourses that inhibit open discussion on minority and human rights (Oran, in Düzel 2007). The same approach is also reflected in a number of foreign policy issues, such as the Cyprus question, where the securitizers achieved high levels of public support by delegitimizing any opposition to the official policy line (Kaliber 2005). The "mobilization potential" (Wæver 1995: 63) of securitizing such sen-sitive issues constitutes a barrier against further democratization of Turkey and prevents it from solving its preponderant foreign policy problems. In short, securi-tization polarizes the society; it leads to an erosion of human and minority rights; it slows down the democratization process; and it jeopardizes Turkey's relations with the EU.

The processes of desecuritization and the EU accession process

Despite the significant role of the civilian-military bureaucracy in Turkey's domestic and foreign policy agenda (Cizre-Sakallioglu 1997) and the successful securitization of major political issues, Turkey has been undergoing a period of desecuritization since the beginning of this decade. We conceptualize desecuritization as a process, where issues are moving from "the 'security' agenda and back into the realm of public political discourse and 'normal' political dispute and accommodation" (Williams 2003: 523). This became possible after Abdullah Öcalan, the leader of the Kurdistan Workers Party (PKK) was captured in February 1999, which injected Turkey's state and security elite with confidence. The arrest of Öcalan brought the PKK's violent activities to a sudden halt and enabled discussions on the political aspects of the problem. In addition, the decision of the Helsinki EU Summit in 1999 to give Turkey an official status of an EU candidate country created a political climate that triggered an economic and political reform process. Collectively, these developments prepared a more relaxed environment, in which a public debate on Turkey's prevailing issues as well as its national security understanding could flourish. The more recent retreat in these fields, i.e. the slow-down in Turkey's EU accession process and an increase in ethnic/separatist terror, has demonstrated the fragility of the desecuritization process.

An important parallel development, which resulted from the increased political confidence, has been the opening up of a debate on the established definition of national security (Aras and Polat 2008), which is beginning to be debated by a broader segment of the society and with increasing input from civilians. Formerly dramatized issues that were isolated from an open and rational public debate have started to be discussed within the realm of standard politics. A significant desecuritization move has been the removal of the ban on education and broadcasting in languages other than Turkish (read Kurdish), which was previously perceived as a threat to national identity. Granting this basic right to the Kurdish minority had not been viewed from the perspective of basic rights and freedoms but through security lenses.

Taking the desecuritization of this issue further, Third Sector Foundation of Turkey (TÜSIAD), a prominent business interest group, published a democratization report in January 2007, in which Kurdish language is suggested to be taught in state schools as an elective course (TÜSIAD 2007). Although the nationalist circles criticized the report, there has been an open and fruitful democratic discussion on the issues raised in the report. The ban on publications in Kurdish was also removed, which was followed by flourishing of newspapers, books, and magazines published in Kurdish. In 2009, the government launched the first public Kurdish-language television channel, TRT-6, to broadcast 24 hours a day. On the same day, Prime Minister Recep Tayyip Erdoğan became the first Turkish leader to speak Kurdish publicly when he said in Kurdish, "May TRT-6 be beneficial."

In this process of desecuritization, we have also witnessed the breaking up of the bureaucratic isolation of foreign policy issues as demands to repoliticize and desecuritize became more articulate. The military has become less visible in public discourse on foreign policy in the 2000s (Aydinli, Özcan and Akyaz 2006).[7] The AKP government has avoided further securitization of issues such as Cyprus and minority rights by seeking a solution-oriented policy.[8] A new generation of research centers prioritizes desecuritization and societal construction of foreign policy in Turkey. For example, several think-tanks and civil society organizations with different research agendas strongly favor increasing civilian involvement in the foreign policy making process and its democratization.[9]

Civil society groups' opposition to official policies started to be tolerated, which eventually led to more open debates on formerly dramatized and depoliticized foreign-policy issues. For example in December 2006, members of a foreign policy program of TESEV visited Armenia to work for the normalization of relations between the two countries.[10] In May 2009, members of academia, and the media and civil society from the two countries met in Istanbul at a workshop organized by Foundation for Political, Economic and Social Research (SETA).[11] Such an opening up started to introduce new perceptions and attitudes towards regions in Turkey's neighborhood. Fear of external threats has also been minimized thanks to initiatives such as the Civil Society Development Program (CSDP) of the EU. Civil society organizations in Turkey benefiting from this program have been influential in the rapprochement between Greece and Turkey (Rumelili 2005).

The desecuritization process in Turkey was enhanced by the negotiation process with the EU within the framework of EU conditionality, which is a major catalyst of democratic reforms in the candidate countries (Grabbe 2002). The European accession process has affected Turkish domestic politics and political culture in two ways. First, it reshaped the domestic opportunity structure by reducing the role of the civilian-military bureaucracy and by empowering the political elite and societal actors. Second, within this process we have witnessed the adoption of new laws as well as appropriation of new values and norms. As a result of changing opportunity structures, the role of the civilian-military bureaucracy to a certain extent diminished while societal actors, which were previously excluded from the policy making processes, have enhanced their position.

With regard to the emergence of a new opportunity structure, it is essential to explore the contentious issue of the civil-military relations in Turkey. The Turkish military is an important player in Turkish politics with both formal and informal authority. The army directly intervened in politics through *coup d'états* or memorandums to government in the years 1960, 1971, 1980, 1997, and 2007.[12] The army also partakes in policy making through the National Security Council (MGK). It is also a major securitizer of political issues and this role of a securitizer (through speech acts) is particularly significant from the perspective of this chapter and the securitization theory in general.

The EU accession process diminished some powers of the military while forcing the army to face a dilemma. EU membership is desirable for the army because it is the ultimate reward of the Turkey's westernization project, which has been driven by the civilian/military bureaucracy since the beginning of the twentieth century. At the same time, the accession process requires cutting back of some of the military's power. The EU's request for reforms that would increase civilian control over the military did not represent a major problem because the prospect of EU membership constituted a basis for a "grand consensus" between the divided elites of Turkey (Aydinli, Özcan and Akyaz 2006). Several reforms were implemented in this field since 1999, such as shifting the balance of power in the MGK in favor of civilians, the appointment of a civilian secretary-general for the MGK and reducing its role to an advisory body, the removal of military representatives from the Council of Higher Education and the High Board of Radio and Television, and bringing the Turkish Armed Forces under the judicial control of the Court of Accounts. All these reforms changed the domestic opportunity structure by empowering the political elite vis-à-vis the military bureaucracy. They also facilitated a decline in the military's role in the securitization of political issues at the domestic or international level.

A less powerful military may not automatically bring desecuritization. However, the fact that the army, as one of the biggest securitizers, started to lose its power is in itself important for the process of desecuritization. A recent police investigation and court case dubbed as *Ergenekon* revealed the extent of the power of securitizers which goes beyond the military. The existence of an underground organization called *Ergenekon* was disclosed in 2007 after the discovery of some weaponry in the house of an army officer in Istanbul. As the investigation continued, the evidence revealed a wide network of people including members of the armed forces, police officers, civilian officials, academics, businessmen, trade unionists, and journalists.

Its aim was to create conditions for a military coup to topple the AKP government and to stop the EU accession process. The indictment suggests that this organization was responsible for many political murders including that of a senior judge in 2006 and a Turkish-Armenian journalist Hrant Dink in 2007. The case has already divided the nation between those, who believe that it is the state's sincere effort to dispatch an illegal group, and those, who suggest that this is an operation sponsored by the government to intimidate the opposition (Mahçupyan 2009). The *Ergenekon* case is yet another demonstration of how highly securitized politics has been in Turkey. Several EU officials have already declared their support for the investigation and its exposure is likely to accelerate Turkey's bid for EU membership because it will help the state to clear itself from such illegal formations.

The EU accession process affects the domestic opportunity structures also through empowering societal actors. The Turkish civil society has been blossoming in parallel with the diminishing power of the military. The number of civil society organizations has risen significantly since the 1980s and this increase in the amount of voluntary organizations, associations, unions, chambers, and the like was not only a change in quantity. According to Göle (2000), there was a move towards a more pluralist understanding of democracy since the 1980s, which paved the way for the emergence of new social movements such as environmentalist and feminist groups as well as new issue-based civil associations.

The real turning point in Turkey's civil society matters was, however, the decision of the Helsinki EU Summit in 1999, which incited a wave of political reforms that sparked off civil society. Since then, various harmonization packages and constitutional amendments made their way through the Turkish National Assembly. Laws were amended, including the Law on Associations, the Press Law, the Law on Meetings and Demonstrations, and the Law on Foundations. The 2004 Law on Associations, for example, reduces the possibility of state interference in non-governmental organizations' (NGOs') activities, removes restrictions on their contact with foreign NGOs, and allows them to work with more overtly political organizations (Kubicek 2005). These reforms enabled civil society organizations' to enter into politics, which in turn widened the limits of "normal" politics and narrowed the boundaries of security dominated realms. The civilian forces' push for influencing policy making has been also visible in Turkey's foreign policy, especially in its relations with the EU. Some civil society organizations such as the Economic Development Foundation (IKV) have actively supported the membership process.

The EU membership process changed the domestic opportunity structure and became an external influence on the power-domination game between the civilian/military and the political elite as well as between the state actors and societal actors. The army as a major securitizer became less powerful, which is expected to support the desecuritization process. The increased powers of the civil societal actors in the policy making process should also contribute to the desecuritization process. It is possible to argue that in this new context the values and norms associated with democracy and a more pluralist political culture became more internalized by the civil societal actors and the political elite.

The limits of the desecuritization process

As discussed earlier, the two groups empowered by the EU accession process have been the new political elite representing the demands of the periphery vis-à-vis the civilian-military bureaucracy/center and the civil societal actors vis-à-vis the state. Does this automatically bring desecuritization? Can we say that the desecuritization process in Turkey is complete? The answer to both questions is no. Taking the army's securitizing role as an example, we observe that despite all the decrease in its formal power the army still acts as a major securitizer.[13] What is even more significant is that the audience (general public) is still ready to "buy" its securitizing moves. The agenda of desecuritization is not completely internalized by the civil society. In fact, some civil society organizations joined the army in protesting against a supposed Islamic threat as well as heavily criticizing (if not totally rejecting) Turkey's relations with the USA and the EU.[14]

In 2008, the desecuritizing moves of the governing AKP almost resulted in the closure of the party. In the general elections of 2007, the party increased its vote share to 47 percent, the largest share that any political party received in decades. After obtaining such strong mandate, the AKP attempted to make an amendment in the constitution that would allow wearing headscarves at universities. The Republican People's Party (CHP) took the issue to the Constitutional Court which subsequently decided against the amendment, i.e. the securitization moves of the CHP and the Constitutional Court hampered the normalization of the headscarf issue. Taking the securitizing moves to a further point, the state prosecutor filed a case with the

Constitutional Court for the closure of the AKP on the grounds that it had become a "focal point of anti-secular activities." A case was opened against the AKP with a 162-page indictment accusing the party and its leaders of violating the principle of secularism as defined in the Turkish constitution. The chief prosecutor asked for 71 AKP party members and the President to be banned from politics.

More than four months after the opening of the case, the Constitutional Court decided not to close the party or ban its members from politics. Although six out of eleven members of the Court were in favor of closure, this did not suffice since a qualified majority of seven members was needed to dissolve a political party. However, ten out of eleven judges still found the party a "focal point of anti-secular activities" and decided to fine it by depriving it of half of its state funds. Only the president of the Court voted against the indictment altogether and asked for legal reforms that would make party closure much more difficult. The AKP escaped by inches from being sent to Turkey's graveyard of political parties closed as a result of military interventions or decisions by the Constitutional Court (Polat 2009: 143). Another closure case filed with the Constitutional Court is against the pro-Kurdish Democratic Society Party (DTP). The case was brought up by the state prosecutor on the grounds that the DTP had not renounced the PKK as a terrorist organization. As these cases demonstrate, securitization of the headscarf (and political Islam in general) and the Kurdish issue continue to dominate the political agenda in Turkey.

Despite all the reforms that have been initiated since 1999 to increase the standard of democracy in Turkey, there are various problems with their implementation. It is still widespread, for example, to conflate the issue of Kurdish rights with ethnic/separatist terror, which introduces the element of fear to any debate on this matter. This brings us to the second impact of the EU membership process on political culture in Turkey: the appropriation of new values and norms. The Turkish National Assembly passed many laws introducing major constitutional changes and seven harmonization packages in the period of 2001 to 2004. The concepts of human rights and minority rights gradually entered the political lexicon.

Despite all these developments, values and norms associated with democracy and with a pluralist political culture such as protection of human rights including minority rights, religious freedom, and the rule of law have not become part of the Turkish political culture yet. In short, the significant harmonization in the area of law (formal institutions) did not eventuate into a sufficiently profound change in values and norms.[15] A Turkish judge in the European Court of Human Rights (ECHR) suggests that despite the recent reforms related to the EU accession process the interpretation of "rights" is very narrow in Turkey. As a result, Turkey comes second only to Russia in terms of number of cases brought against the Turkish state in the ECHR (Zaman 2009).

Why is the desecuritization process not progressing as fast as it should? We suggest two complementary explanations. First, the relations with the EU and specific domestic developments shape the progress of desecuritization. Second, the norms and values associated with desecuritization have not been fully internalized. While the reform process introduced legislation favoring desecuritization, its effect on the

Turkish political culture has been rather limited. We will now explore each of the two dynamics in more detail.

We have seen that when the accession process accelerates, Turkey moves away from the politics of fear since the securitizing actors lose ground. On the other hand, when the process slows down and the possibility of full membership seems more distant, a feeling of being left-behind develops. This fuels the language of "us" and "them" and paranoia-driven politics and enhances the vicious circle of securitization. The most radical moves towards desecuritization coincided with positive progress in the accession process. The slow-down following the commencement of the negotiations, coupled with confusing messages from the EU, the failure of the Annan Plan, and the hostility of the new leaders in Germany and France to Turkey's membership prospects enhanced the discourse of double standards (the EU does not treat Turkey as the other candidates) and feeling of encirclement and distrust.

At the domestic level, the increase in the Kurdish separatist violence, the perception that neither the USA nor the EU supports Turkey's fight against terrorism, the developments regarding the securitized election of a new president, and finally the closure case against the AKP added insult to injury. The distrust towards Europe feeds distrust to local elements. Kurds, pious Muslims, and non-Muslims are perceived and portrayed as potential threats connected to foreign peril. Even the AKP government, which had contributed a lot to the desecuritization process, became a securitizer of various issues before the July 2007 general election with the aim of not missing the nationalist votes.

The EU seems to be relatively successful in promoting change in formal institutions while its influence on political culture is limited. Despite the various harmonization packages that introduced new laws, the political culture in Turkey has not been synchronized with that of the EU. Yılmaz (2004: 7) suggests that "the basic concept underlying political culture of Western Europe following World War II was, without a doubt, the concept of 'rights' or human rights." Political culture in Turkey, however, is still very much state-centric. Saving and protecting the state is the most prominent element of political culture. "Rights" can be securitized and perceived as a disguise for some hidden agenda, i.e. separatist intentions. Despite the introduction of various laws, there is still a lack of social consensus among the civilian-military bureaucracy, the political elite, and the civil society on the values associated with democracy and a more pluralist political culture. This can be partly explained by the difficulties in introducing a top-down change to a society. Formal changes have to be supported by an enhancement in democratic discourses. The media could play a vital role in boosting the discourse while a reform of the educational system would serve more long-term goals because apart from formal changes, new values and attitudes need be emphasized from early childhood socialization. There have already been voices demanding the rewriting of history textbooks without security language (Tuncer 2007; Karabat 2009a). Another positive step would be the abolition or at least reform of the compulsory national security courses in high schools, which are often taught by active or retired army officers.

Conclusion

Political culture in Turkey is to a large extent influenced by what we can call the "politics of fear." Certain political issues are often perceived and dramatized as "security" matters and considered as beyond political discussion. This has constrained the development of free and open discussions on controversial issues until the beginning of this decade which is witnessing a significant period of desecuritization. Securitization and desecuritization are competing processes championed by different actors in different institutional settings. While certain securitizing actors continue to exploit prevailing political culture by reproducing internal and external threats through speech acts, other actors struggle to reframe these "threats" as political/policy issues.

The EU membership has a key role in putting an end to these competing processes of securitization and desecuritization. As Turkey's membership process accelerates, Turkey moves away from politics of fear since the securitizing actors lose ground as well as prestige and power. As the membership process slows down and the possibility of full membership seems distant, however, a feeling of being left-behind quickly brings back paranoia-driven politics not only towards the EU but also towards its own citizens. This becomes a vicious circle. Rejection from the EU feeds more securitization and more securitization moves Turkey further away from the EU. As a result, securitization continues to polarize the society, leading to erosion of human and minority rights, slowing down the democratization process and putting relations with the EU at further risk.

It seems that the security-speak around saving and protecting the state from external and internal "enemies" is an important part of political culture in Turkey. Although the EU has been successful in inducing formal change, i.e. legislation, its influence on political culture through changing values and norms has so far been limited. Despite the introduction of various laws, a lack of social consensus between the civilian-military bureaucracy, the political elite, and the civil society on the values of democracy and a more pluralist political culture persists. This chapter suggests that these formal changes need to be supported by more democratic discourses in media and education. Some steps to be taken could be the rewriting of history textbooks without a security language and the abolishing or the reform of the compulsory national security courses in high schools. The EU accession talks and especially the revival of the previous level of advancement could hereafter reduce the role of the civilian-military bureaucracy as well as of the so-called "deep state" and provide a window of opportunity for further desecuritization. In fact, the accession process has already become an anchor for recent reforms which would prepare the ground for a more pluralist and democratic political culture in Turkey.

Notes

1 The chapter was concluded in May 2009. All the information reflects the situation before their date.
2 The defunct Treaty of Sèvres included the partitioning of the Ottoman Empire between the Allied powers after World War I. Sèvres syndrome refers to the prevailing influence

of this event on the inheritor of the Empire, the Turkish Republic. Many analysts suggest that the fear of losing territory still haunts some of the elite and public opinion in Turkey (Karaosmanoğlu 2000). Sèvres syndrome also refers to the conviction that external world is trying to weaken and divide Turkey in cooperation with their internal collaborators (Mufti 1998).

3 It is very common in Turkish media to invite retired generals to comment on domestic and foreign policy issues. These generals often use this opportunity for securitizing various issues and asking for more strict measures on security matters. The most recent example is the attitude of these people towards Kurdish terror and the situation in Northern Iraq after US occupation.

4 A public opinion poll asked 2040 individuals in 25 different cities about their trust in different institutions in 2000, 2004, and 2008. The army precedes all others as the number one trusted institution in this opinion poll (TEPAV 2009). This finding is repeated consistently in various other surveys.

5 Hakan Yılmaz (2006) developed the concept of Tanzimat Syndrome to explain this. Tanzimat reforms in the Ottoman Empire brought new citizenship rights and some privileges to the non-Muslim subjects of the empire in the hope of preventing the dissolution of the empire in the face of nationalist movements and of stopping European powers from interfering in its internal affairs. The next few decades witnessed nationalist independence movements which resulted in loss of a huge territory. Yılmaz (2006) argues that this historical record taught the Ottomans and the subsequent Turkish elite two lessons: giving rights and freedoms to a people would not make them more loyal and that the real intention of European powers in demanding more respect for human rights is actually to weaken and divide the country.

6 In April 2007, hundreds of thousands staged huge demonstrations in major cities of Turkey to protest against the government, which they claimed had a hidden agenda of establishing Islamic rule in the country. In all demonstrations crowds chanted "Turkey is secular; it will remain secular." The protests followed a row between the military/ bureaucratic and political elite over the election of a new president. The government nominated the Foreign Affairs Minister, Abdullah Gül, for the presidential election. The fact that his wife wears a headscarf was perceived by the Turkish army, which sees itself as the guardian of the secular republic, as an existential threat.

7 A notable exception to this is the army's position about a military campaign in Northern Iraq to fight against Kurdish terrorism. The Chief of Staff and various retired generals frequently appear in the media to declare their position on this issue.

8 Turkey's current Prime Minister, Recep Tayyip Erdoğan, supported the Annan Plan as a radical move of departure from traditional Cyprus policy and on several occasions declared his aim to solve this problem within the framework of the United Nations. Even before the vote of Annan Plan, he pointed out that: "I am not in favor of continuation of last 30–40 years' policy in Cyprus. Politics is an art of creating solutions instead of problems. We will do our utmost to this end." See Anatolia News Agency (2003). In addition, Mehmet Ali Şahin, state minister of AKP government underlined the need to extend greater freedom to the foundations of the minorities in Turkey, which takes care of many social needs of the minorities ranging from construction of religious sites to schooling. See Akyol 2007.

9 Examples are Liberal Thinking Society, Turkish-Asian Center for Strategic Studies and Foundation for Political, Economic and Social Research.

10 Turkish Economic and Social Studies Foundation (TESEV) is an independent think-tank carrying out research in the fields of democratization, good governance, and foreign policy. For the purpose and conclusions of the visit to Armenia, see "The Normalization of Turkish-Armenian Relations," available at www.tesev.org.tr/eng/events/armeniasre-port.pdf. For more information on the Turkish-Armenian Citizens Mutual Perception and Dialogue Project, see Kentel and Poghosyan 2006.

11 SETA is a non-profit research institute carrying out research activities on current

political, economic, and social issues with a view towards providing policy recommendations.

12 On 27 April 2007, the army's general staff posted a memorandum on its website blaming the government for having a hidden Islamic agenda and not doing enough to prevent the supposed rise of the Islamic threat. Although not much debated, the military also emphasized the ethnic separatist threat and said "the army will be against those who oppose the Kemalist motto – Happy is he who calls himself a Turk." The army has raised its concerns before about the rise of terror in the country's southeast region and recommended the government launch a military campaign in Northern Iraq. Hence, once again, the military emphasized its position towards the twin enemies of the Republic – political Islam and Kurdish separatism – through a direct intervention to the government and civil politics.

13 The most recent examples include the army's intervention in the election of a new president and Turkey's policy towards Northern Iraq.

14 A notable slogan of the street protests in April 2007 was "Neither the EU nor the USA: Fully independent Turkey!"

15 In saying that, one should not ignore the appropriation of these values at least by some civil society groups who also protested the latest memorandum of the military. Some examples are The Young Civilians (*Genç Siviller*), The Liberal Office (*Liberal Ofis*), and The Movement for Political Horizon (*Siyasal Ufuk Hareketi*).

5 The Cyprus question in Turkey-EU relations

Ahmet Sözen

Introduction

The accession of Cyprus to the European Union (EU) has made the issue of Cyprus very visible, especially as it is tied to Turkey's EU membership bid. Turkish accession to the EU would solve the problem, but the Greek Cypriot controlled government of Cyprus has interfered with Turkish negotiations from the moment they were opened and, especially under President Papadopoulos, has used its position as an EU member state as a means of leverage. However, the Cyprus question should not be seen as an original EU problem, or as a unique matter of Turkey's accession to the EU. The EU's involvement in the Cyprus issue in the 1990s and more intensively in 2000s before the run up to the 2004 referenda on the UN peace plan (known as the Annan Plan) was widely expected to foster the Europeanization of the island in terms of spreading European rules, norms, and values, and hence, through the normative power of the EU, facilitating the solution of the more-than-half-a-century-old Cyprus problem.

In this particular issue, the "world views" of the individual actors seemed to clash, i.e. those of the two communities, Greek and Turkish Cypriots, those of the two motherlands, Greece and Turkey, and the EU. The two sides' varying reaction to the referendum can be seen as a calculated decision on their respective parts. The Greek Cypriot side failed to agree to the unification of the island within the provisions of the Annan plan because, having been promised EU membership anyway, they had nothing to lose. The positive outcome of the referendum in the Turkish Cypriot community could be perceived as a calculated attempt to join the EU. This has often been the dominant explanation of the result.

We wish to explore the less tangible aspects of the Cyprus question. A historical overview of the conflict will show us the extent to which "speech acts" have affected outcomes, how they have been used by the various actors to manipulate results, and how often friendly statements hid ungenial intentions, which influenced the development of the prevailing norms and values. Turkish Cypriots did not only calculate the costs and benefits of the plan. The positive result of the referendum also reflected a shift in policy orientation as a result of a new, modified social reality.[1] The tying of the Cyprus problem to the Turkish membership bid added a new dimension to the problem, where the Turkish side reacted and was forced to react to the developments on the island and to the EU's andits member states' statements on the issue. While the ECECs have not been very vocal in this respect, they have supported the reunification of the island and repeatedly wished to "reward" the Turkish Cypriot community for its goodwill.

We start with a brief summary of the inter-communal negotiations in Cyprus. Here special attention is paid to the most important turning points in the negotiations in order to understand the evolution of the Cyprus problem as it stands today. Then, the EU's involvement both directly and through its normative power is evaluated through illustrative examples. In the light of both the past and the current negotiation processes, we conclude the chapter by laying out probable future scenarios for Cyprus.

An overview of important turning points in the inter-communal negotiations, 1963–2002

In order to comprehend the positions of the two conflicting sides in Cyprus today and to be able to speculate on the probability of a solution to the Cyprus problem in the future, one has to have an in-depth understanding of the evolution of the Cyprus peace negotiations in the nearly five decades that have passed, by focusing on the important turning-points that created the widely agreed upon parameters of a solution in Cyprus.[2]

For the major powers, the Cyprus problem during the Cold War was by and large seen as a dangerous dispute that must be contained at all costs, because it had the potential to poison relations between Turkey and Greece, two North Atlantic Treaty Organization (NATO) allies, which was not tolerable during the Cold War. In that regard, the major powers in NATO, such as the USA and the UK, encouraged both Turkey and Greece to exercise restraint after the December 1963 ethnic clashes in Cyprus and attempted to solve the problem before it escalated into an armed clash between Turkey and Greece. Meanwhile the major powers tried to control the political violence on the island.

The main objective of the mediation efforts in Cyprus during 1963–68 was to prevent the emergence of an armed clash between Turkey and Greece. Key NATO players believed that a conflict between Greece and Turkey would definitely weaken the southern wing of NATO, which was considered as a strategic necessity for the Western alliance.[3] However, the mediation attempts during 1963–67 brought no breakthrough in terms of a solution to the Cyprus problem. The two communities within Cyprus were not even invited to most of the negotiations that took place among the big powers and the two motherlands, Greece and Turkey. In that regard, reaching a solution to the Cyprus problem was a secondary issue which was obscured by the *grand* objectives and interests of the great powers of primarily preventing a war between two NATO members, Greece and Turkey.[4]

In 1968, finally the representatives of the two communities started to meet in order reach a solution to the Cyprus problem. This phase of "inter-communal" talks between the Turkish and Greek Cypriot communities continued on and off until the Greek-engineered *coup d'état* of 15 July 1974 that aimed to unite the island with Greece (Enosis) and the successive Turkish military operation on 20 July 1974. The main objective of the inter-communal talks was to come up with a solution to the constitutional problem on the basis of an independent and integral republic. Turkish Cypriots were trying to maintain regional autonomy in their enclaves, while the Greek Cypriots were trying to maintain total control of the government and force a *de facto* creation of a unitary state. However, the maximalist position taken by the Greek Cypriot president, Archbishop Makarios, coupled with the different approaches taken by the two negotiating parties played a great role in the failure of the inter-communal talks. The Turkish Cypriot side was supporting a "total package" approach where an agreement should be reached on all issues before it was signed. On the other hand, the Greek Cypriot side insisted on a "piecemeal" approach where issues were to be taken separately and agreed upon without any relation to other issues.

In 1977, the meeting between the Greek Cypriot leader, Archbishop Makarios, and the Turkish Cypriot leader, Rauf Denktaş, resulted in the emergence of the basic principles of a solution in Cyprus known as The Four Guidelines (Sec. General S/12723. 1977), which became the reference point for the future proposals and documents prepared by the UN and other actors of the international community. The guidelines posited the following objectives:

1.   An independent, non-aligned, bi-communal federal Republic.
2.   The territory under the administration of each community should be discussed in the light of economic viability and productivity and land ownership.
3.   Questions of principles like freedom of movement, freedom of settlement, the right of property and other specific matters are open for discussion taking into consideration the fundamental basis for a bicommunal federal system and certain practical difficulties, which may arise for the Turkish community.
4.   The powers and the functions of the central federal government will be such as to safeguard the unity of the country, having regard to the bi-communal character of the state.

(Sec. General S/13369. 1979)

After the death of Archbishop Makarios in 1977, Rauf Denktaş and the new leader of the Greek Cypriot community, Spyros Kyprianou, held negotiations in 1979 under the auspices of UN Secretary General Kurt Waldheim. The talks produced a Ten-Point Agreement confirming the Four Guidelines of the Makarios-Denktaş summit (1977) and continued to be the basis for future negotiations, with the addition of the following important points:

1.   The talks will deal with all territorial and constitutional aspects.
2.   Priority will be given to reaching an agreement on the settlement of Varosha[5] under UN auspices simultaneously with the beginning of the consideration by the interlocutors of the constitutional and territorial aspects of a comprehensive settlement. After agreement on Varosha has been reached it

will be implemented without awaiting the outcome of the discussion on other aspects of the Cyprus problem.

3. The demilitarization of the Republic of Cyprus is envisaged, and matters relating thereto will be discussed.

4. The independence, sovereignty, territorial integrity and non-alignment of the Republic should be adequately guaranteed against union in whole or in part with any other country and against any form of partition or secession.

(Sec. General S/13369. 1979)

As an integral part to the Four Guidelines, the Ten-Point Agreement became the reference point and building block of future UN proposals and documents on the Cyprus issue. Today, the parameters for a future Cyprus settlement, such as bi-zonality with regard to the territorial aspects and bi-communality with regard to the constitutional aspects and the political equality of the two communities, based on the two Summit agreements are the only criteria that at least on paper the two sides declared to have agreed upon.

The period between 1984 and 1986 marks a new phase in the Cyprus negotiations where the UN abandoned the "mini-package" approaches in favor of a comprehensive solution. The UN Secretary General Pérez de Cuéllar aimed to formulate a comprehensive approach for the inter-communal negotiations, based on the 1977 and 1979 Summit Agreements. Pérez de Cuéllar, having been the UN special representative for Cyprus before (October 1975 – December 1977), was much more familiar with the Cyprus problem than the representatives of the other third parties. Pérez de Cuéllar's comprehensive approach was received with more enthusiasm by the Turkish Cypriot side than the Greek Cypriot side. The comprehensive approach of the UN coincided with the Turkish side's traditional policy, which favored a total package rather than the piecemeal approach to inter-communal negotiations.[6]

Pérez de Cuéllar prepared a Draft Framework Agreement in 1984, which he later modified several times according to the results of the Proximity Talks (1984). The Draft Framework Agreement called for the following:

1. Federal republic that would include two federated States.

2. That the official languages of the federal republic would be Greek and Turkish.

3. The legislature of the federal republic would be composed of two chambers: a lower chamber with a 70–30 Greek Cypriot and Turkish Cypriot representation and an upper chamber with a 50–50 representation.

4. That the federal republic would be a presidential system where the president would be a Greek Cypriot and the vice-president a Turkish Cypriot, where they separately or conjointly had the right to veto any law or administrative decision.

5. That the council of ministers would be composed of Greek Cypriot and Turkish Cypriot ministers on a 7 to 3 ratio.

(Tamkoç 1988: 123–24)

Rauf Denktaş accepted the final Draft Framework Agreement while Spyros Kyprianou rejected the whole draft after consultation with Greece. Pérez de Cuéllar said that he did not intend to accept counterproposals and called on the Greek Cypriot side to reconsider. The Greek Cypriot side demanded as a response the withdrawal of Turkish troops from Cyprus; unrestricted implementation of the three freedoms (freedom of movement, freedom of settlement, and the right to own property); and effective international guarantees for the implementation of a solution as preconditions to any settlement. Kyprianou also accused the Turkish side of changing the demographic characteristics of the population and that the Turkish "settlers" should leave the island prior to a settlement. The inter-communal talks came to a halt after 1986 due to the presidential elections in the Greek Cypriot community in February 1988. Kyprianou lost the elections and Georgios Vassiliou became the next Greek Cypriot President.

George Vassiliou continued to follow the traditional Greek Cypriot policy despite his initial assurances of a flexible and more realistic approach. At this time, Denktaş started to put forward new concepts, such as separate sovereignty for each community, which was inconsistent with the UN Security Council resolutions and the 1977 and 1979 Summits that he himself had approved. The UN Security Council resolutions made no provisions for separate sovereignty for each community. The sovereignty was shared by the two communities.

Meanwhile, the end of the Cold War led to dramatic changes globally. The gaining of full sovereignty of several states away from Russian influence in Central and Eastern Europe, as well as the emergence of new sovereign states in the former Soviet Union, and the disintegration of former federations, such as Yugoslavia and Czechoslovakia, encouraged Denktaş to claim "self-determination" for the Turkish Cypriot *people* which would give them separate sovereignty. Hence, they would be entitled to an independent, sovereign state which would automatically mean the recognition of the Turkish Republic of Northern Cyprus (TRNC). However, the UN was not interested in involving new concepts which were considered inconsistent with the previously agreed upon parameters – as set out in the 1977 and 1979 high-level agreements. Thus, the UN protected and stuck to the previously agreed upon concepts and principles and so, in their perspective, preventing novel concepts and driving the prospective negotiations into an irreversible impasse.

As a result of the extensive negotiations between Vasiliou and Denktaş, the UN Secretary General Boutros Boutros-Ghali put forth the Set of Ideas in August 1992. It was the most detailed plan till then The report of the Secretary General to the Security Council on 21 August 1992, included, in addition to the Set of Ideas, a map with respect to the territorial adjustments. In October 1992, the two leaders came together in New York to discuss the Set of Ideas. While in the UN New York headquarters, the two sides came very close to an agreement. However, the opportunity was lost when Boutros-Ghali allowed the two leaders to return home for consultation. Because, once home and away from the pressure of the UN, the two leaders changed their views and rejected the proposal. The two leaders indicated that the Set of Ideas could not be accepted unconditionally. By 1993, the

UN was getting fed up with the intransigence of the two communities in reaching an agreement.

One of the most, if not the most, significant outcome of the Cyprus negotiations was the explicit acceptance by the UN and many third parties that there was a big gap of trust between the two communities. The Secretary General in paragraph 63 of his 19 November 1992 report to the Security Council (Sec. General S/24830. 1992) makes that point very clear:

> It appears from the recent joint meetings that there is a deep crisis of confidence between the two sides. It is difficult to envisage any successful outcome to the talks for as long as this situation prevails. There can be no doubt but that the prospects for progress would be greatly enhanced if a number of confidence building measures were adopted by each side.

In an effort to remedy the lack of trust issue, on 24 November 1992 the UN Secretary General produced a series of confidence-building measures (CBMs) for the two communities. These measures were supposed to narrow the big gap of trust between the two sides, so that they would be able to reach an overall agreement more easily. The leaders of the two communities in 1993 started to discuss 15 CBMs proposed by the UN Secretary General (S/26026. 1993), which ranged from expert cooperation on water shortage to environmental and health issues; from opening the Nicosia Airport under the UN administration to opening the closed area of Varosha under the UN administration as a free zone where goods and services could enter and exit freely.

As with previous negotiations, the result of these negotiations on CBMs proved futile. This was mainly due to the UN Secretary General Boutros-Ghali's lack of skill in securing the signature of the two community leaders, and at least in part, to the high politicization of the CBMs by both communities' leaderships. In reality, they were basically humanitarian, social, and economic measures intended to establish trust between the two communities.[7] To make a bad situation worse, the European Court of Justice (ECJ) issued a decision in 1994 that banned TRNC exports to the UK markets.[8] This greatly poisoned the atmosphere in which the UN tried to create trust between the two communities.

The most important contacts between the leaders of the two sides during the second half of the 1990s took place in 1997. The new UN Secretary General, Kofi Annan, tried to bring a new dynamism to the Cyprus negotiations. The Greek Cypriot leader Glafkos Clerides and the Turkish Cypriot leader Rauf Denktaş met for face-to-face talks in July 1997 in New York and August of 1997 in Geneva. Prior to these meetings, the two Cypriot leaders had not met for nearly four years. The Turkish Cypriot side was busy collecting precedents of failed federations in the post-Cold War era in order to build up its policy of two-state solution, while the Greek Cypriot side was busy furthering its application in 1990 to the European Community.

However, the 1997 negotiations took place at a time when the EU decided to open accession negotiations with the Greek Cypriot Republic of Cyprus on behalf of the whole island during its 1997 Luxembourg Summit, which complicated an already complex problem. Hence, the EU's Luxembourg Summit led to a freeze in the very limited relations between the EU officials and the Turkish Cypriot authorities, as well as big tensions between Turkey and the EU, where the EU, in addition to its Cyprus decision, failed to include Turkey as a candidate for EU membership.

On 3 December 1999, the two sides in Cyprus met reluctantly. The Turkish Cypriot side, with encouragement from Turkey, tried to promote the confederation thesis that it had adopted after the Luxembourg Summit. Denktaş was particularly angry that Turkey accepted the conditions put forth in the EU Helsinki Summit declaration.[9] However, he unwillingly remained at the negotiation table due to Turkey's pressure in order not to spoil the positive atmosphere that the announcement of the candidacy of Turkey to the EU at the Helsinki Summit created.

However, when the UN Secretary General announced his *non-paper* to the two sides in 2000, Denktaş declared that there was no reason to remain at the negotiation table, since the *non-paper* had excluded the Turkish Cypriot side's confederation thesis, and as a result he walked out of the negotiations. Denktaş' deed was also a part of the Turkish reaction to the Accession Partnership document that the EU had prepared for Turkey. His reaction was backed by the Turkish National Security Council.[10] In other words, the National Security Council, which found the EU's demands on Turkey regarding domestic reforms as well as flexibility on the Cyprus issue unacceptable, supported Denktaş' leaving the negotiation table.

The emergence of the UN Comprehensive Solution Plan – the Annan Plan

After an unexpected invitation by Denktaş in December 2001, Clerides had occasion to dine with him twice, once at Denktaş' and once at his house. After such a "goodwill gesture" from both sides, the two leaders decided to open face-to-face talks under the auspices of the UN. Although the two sides had not engaged in a real give-and-take bargaining, the pressing EU enlargement calendar pushed the UN to put a comprehensive solution plan in front of the two sides in November 2002. This plan, also known as the Annan Plan, was the most comprehensive and detailed plan on the Cyprus issue that has ever been put on the negotiation table.

This plan internalized all the important milestones, principles, and the agreements previously reached by the two sides. For example, the principles agreed upon by the two sides in the 1977 and 1979 high-level agreements, the Cuéllar's Draft Framework Agreement, and the fundamental principles of the Boutros-Ghali's Set of Ideas became the backbone of the Annan plan. In other words, it filled in the gaps and put flesh and bone to the aforementioned "framework" agreements. The plan was modified twice, in December 2002 and February 2003, in order to incorporate the demands of the two sides in the negotiations. However, the two sides failed to reach an agreement at The Hague meeting in March 2003.

The parliamentary election results in the TRNC in December 2003, where the pro-solution and pro-EU, long-time opposition Republican Turkish Party (CTP) won the election, revealed that the Turkish Cypriots demanded a carefully negotiated solution before Cyprus could become a member of the EU on 1 May 2004. Such a demand gave legitimate encouragement to the ruling AKP government in Turkey, who wanted to open Turkey's accession talks with the EU in 2005, to come up with a new initiative in order to restart the Cyprus negotiations. Hence, after intense diplomatic engagement with the UN, USA, and EU, both the Turkish and Turkish Cypriot sides convinced the UN Secretary General that they had the necessary political will to resume the Cyprus negotiations and finalize them by 1 May 2004.

Kofi Annan invited the two Cypriot communities' representatives, together with Turkey and Greece to New York in February 2004 in order to give their final decision on whether they accepted his conditions for the resumption of the Cyprus negotiations or not. The two Cypriot sides, due to intense pressure from their respective motherlands, the UN, USA, and the EU, reluctantly agreed on the conditions of the UN Secretary General for the resumption of the Cyprus negotiations.

According to the UN Secretary General's conditions, the two Cypriot sides would negotiate under the UN auspices until March 21. If they could not resolve their differences, Turkey and Greece would join them to try and reach a resolution during 22–29 March. If there were unresolved issues after 29 March, the UN would arbitrate to solve them. Finally, the two sides agreed on putting the final plan to the simultaneous and separate referenda for the Greek Cypriots and the Turkish Cypriots on 24 April 2004.

After the negotiations (February and March 2004) between the two Cypriot sides, the two motherlands, Turkey and Greece, joined the negotiation process in Bürgenstock (Switzerland) in late March. At the end of the Bürgenstock negotiations, the final plan – known as the 5th Annan Plan – was drawn up by the UN. This plan was put to simultaneous and separate referenda for the Greek and Turkish Cypriots on 24 April 2004, less than a week before the EU enlargement on 1 May 2004.

So far, the Annan Plan has been the most comprehensive and the most detailed solution plan on the Cyprus issue. It called for the creation of a bi-zonal loose federation consisting of a Turkish Cypriot (constituent) state and a Greek Cypriot (constituent) state. If one closely analyzes the history of the Cyprus negotiations, one can see that the Annan Plan was a natural end product that evolved from the important milestones, principles, and the agreements that the two sides had during the past four decades of negotiations.

The Annan Plan tried to bridge the gap between the two competing and maximalist positions of the disputed sides (see Appendix for the official positions of the two disputed sides on the important issues). The plan cannot be called ideal because it did not cater to either side's demands completely. Instead, it was a feasible plan that forced the two sides to make compromises in order to secure their fundamental needs. The functionality and the durability of the plan depended on the future membership of Turkey to the EU because once Turkey became a full member of the EU, most of the current sticking issues, such as restrictions on residency, property ownership and the issue of security and guarantorship that the two sides face today at the negotiation table would be, according to the UN peace plan, irrelevant.

The separate referenda were held on 24 April 2004. The plan was rejected by 76 percent of the Greek Cypriots while 65 percent of Turkish Cypriots supported it. This result shocked the UN, USA, and EU. The expectation of the international community was that both disputed parties would show a genuine political will, adopt a visionary attitude, and acknowledge and respect the equality and the distinct identity of each other. Such a solution in Cyprus would have created a very valuable precedent for the other ongoing conflict situations in the world. Furthermore, as of 1 May 2004, the Greek Cypriot–dominated Republic of Cyprus became a member of the EU, while the cooperative side – Turkish Cypriots in North Cyprus – was left outside the EU.

The Greek Cypriot leader, Tassos Papadopoulos, who asked the Greek Cypriots to give a "resounding NO" to the Annan Plan during the referenda, had been a widely accepted ultra-nationalist who had no intention or motivation to accept a solution based on power sharing with the Turkish Cypriots.[11] At the same time, a majority of Greek Cypriots opposed the Plan and he insisted on saying that he did not shape their opinion but merely reflected it (Ker-Lindsay 2007). Alvaro De Soto, the previous UN representative to Cyprus, also noted that the Greek Cypriot economic wealth and their EU membership left them with no motivation to accept a compromised solution such as the Annan Plan.[12] Even the former Greek Cypriot foreign minister, Nikos Rolandis (1978–83),[13] indicated that the Greek Cypriot political leadership under Tassos Papadopoulos was not interested in a solution in Cyprus.[14]

Papadopoulos' intention was to buy time and use the EU membership of his country as leverage in order to get concessions from Turkey, which was aspiring to become an EU member. Hence, Papadopoulos was not in a hurry. He preached that he wanted a "functional," "European" solution and that he was opposed to "suffocating deadlines" and "third party interventions/arbitration."[15] He used positive but vague language to make the international community believe that he was open to a solution while playing for time. When the international pressure built up to restart the Cyprus peace talks partly due to the pro-solution stance of the Turkish and the Turkish Cypriot sides, Papadopoulos tried to suffocate the process in working groups and technical committees. This time, language was to serve a different function – to turn the efforts of searching for a viable solution into a neverending talk shop. It clearly indicates how language can be used to sabotage a negotiation process – when hiding the lack of will to find a solution behind a rhetoric structured so that the other side cannot deliver the proclaimed goals.

The UN, in order to be seen as if it was doing something in Cyprus, went along with Papadopoulos and proposed a new process in Cyprus based on the establishment of working groups to deal with the substantive issues of the Cyprus problem and the establishment of technical committees to deal with daily problems in Cyprus. This is also known as the 8 July Process (2006) or Gambari Process, because on 8 July 2006, the UN Secretary General's Special Adviser Ibrahim Gambari managed to bring the presidents Mehmet Ali Talat[16] and Papadopoulos together where they, at least on paper, agreed to establish a number of working groups and a number of technical committees in order to prepare the groundwork for negotiations on the leadership level. Though Talat's and Papadopoulos' advisers met more than two dozen times during 2006 and 2007, they could not even reach a consensus on the number and names of the working groups and technical committees. This was precisely what Tassos Papadopoulos had in mind – slowly suffocating the process. However, both domestically as well as in the international community, Papadopoulos and hence, the Greek Cypriot side lost ground and credibility.

Tassos Papadopoulos lost the presidential election in February 2008 and Dimitris Christofias, the head of the communist Progressive Party of Working People (AKEL) became the new Greek Cypriot leader. Christofias immediately started a "damage control" policy whereby he tried to mend the tarnished image of the Greek Cypriot side on the international platforms due to Papadopoulos' intransigent and uncompromising policies on the Cyprus issue. Christofias accepted his "comrade" Talat's open invitation and the two met on 21 March 2008 where they decided to ask their respective advisers to set up a number of working groups and technical committees together with their agenda and to use their results three months from then to start talks under the auspices of the UN Secretary General.

In late July the working groups finalized their results and presented their reports on the areas of convergence and divergence of the positions of the two sides to the two leaders. On 3 September 2008, the two leaders started full-fledged negotiations on the six substantive issues on which the working groups had prepared the ground.[17] Though there is no agreed upon timetable, it is widely expected that the negotiations would be concluded in 2010 and that if everything goes smoothly, the agreement would be put to simultaneous and separate referenda on the two parts of the island some time in 2010 or 2011.

What has the EU been doing?

Many observers in the 1990s and early 2000s believed that the prospect of EU membership would have played an important facilitating role for the solution of the Cyprus problem. Many believed that the values, norms, and rules that the EU is based on would have been a great incentive for the two conflicting sides in Cyprus to solve the conflict, unite the island, and join the EU as a unified federal state. There was a great truth and wisdom in this, had the EU played its cards correctly. However, that is exactly what the EU had not done. Some scholars warned the EU not to put the cart in front of the horse in dealing with the Cyprus issue – in other words demand the unification of the island in a federal state before granting it full EU membership. The opposite happened because the EU accepted a divided island into the Union and suspended the *acquis* in one part of it.[18]

After the rejection of the UN comprehensive solution plan by the Greek Cypriots, the EU has despite minor steps done very little in contributing a solution to the Cyprus problem on the ground. The EU Council decided on 26 April 2004, two days after the failure of the referenda, to lift the embargo on Turkish Cypriots who voted in favor of the unification plan of the UN and to bring Turkish Cypriots closer to the Union. Hence, the Commission prepared two draft regulations – a direct trade regulation and a financial aid regulation of €259 million. However, the two regulations were boycotted in the EU Council by the Greek Cypriot – dominated Republic of Cyprus.

Subsequently, the Commission presented the two regulations to the Council as two separate documents in 2006. The Council passed the financial aid regulation by a qualified majority vote after some modifications demanded by the Greek Cypriot side such as using the financial aid only on "original" Turkish Cypriot property, which pretty much diluted the original proposal. It became operational three years after the proposal entered the Council agenda. Since the direct trade regulation requires unanimity, it is still blocked in the EU Council by the Greek Cypriot Republic of Cyprus. This created a lot of mistrust and loss of faith in the EU institutions among the Turkish Cypriots, who now consider the EU to be an unreliable actor, who failed to deliver its promises. It has also increased tensions in the EU relations with Turkey, which has been disappointed with the developments.

Although there had been a pro-Annan Plan and pro-EU governments of CTP in power in Northern Cyprus during the years 2003 to 2009[19] aspiring to cooperate with the EU institutions in line with the EU Council decision on 26 April 2004 to integrate with the EU, the EU failed to reciprocate and reward the Turkish Cypriots' desire to integrate with the EU. In other words, the EU failed to reciprocate the determination of the Turkish Cypriots to be voluntarily influenced by the normative power of the EU. Instead, the EU continued to operate based on Protocol 10 to the Treaty of Accession (2003)[20] that provides for the suspension of the *acquis* in Northern Cyprus on the basis of a lack of a "a comprehensive settlement of the Cyprus problem," which makes it "necessary to provide for the suspension of the application of the *acquis* in those areas of the Republic of Cyprus in which the Government of the Republic of Cyprus does not exercise effective control." The suspension can be removed by the Council's unanimous decision.

Thus, the EU treats Northern Cyprus, its governmental and state authorities, and consequently all Turkish Cypriots as part of the Republic of Cyprus, where in fact the Turkish Cypriots have been absent since 1963. The EU tied itself to the definition and the legal framework in Protocol 10 and failed to come up with a novel approach for bringing the Turkish Cypriots closer to the Union. The return of the right-wing, nationalist, old-guard, pro-*status quo* National Unity Party (UBP) to power in the April 2009 general election in Northern Cyprus can be partly explained by the fact that many Turkish Cypriots who had been frustrated by the EU's failure to deliver its promises voted against the CTP that symbolized the attachment to EU norms and values.

In addition, the failure of the EU to deal with the two conflicting sides on equal footing, led the Greek Cypriot side to hijack the discourse of the negotiations. After the rejection of the Annan Plan and the membership of the Republic of Cyprus in the EU, the Greek Cypriot side talked about a "European" solution (during Papadopoulos' term) and/or that the solution should be in line with "EU norms" and "EU values." Many believe that the Greek Cypriot side hides behind "EU norms" and "EU values," while its true intentions are to dilute and render meaningless, if not erase, the previously agreed upon UN parameters such as bizonality and bicommunality and restricted freedoms of settlement and property ownership, political equality of the two communities, and the Treaty of Guarantee. In that respect, the Greek Cypriot leadership put forth such EU norms and values as the implementation of "four freedoms" and inapplicability of permanent derogations, as prerequisites of a solution in Cyprus, whereby they could bypass the previously agreed upon UN parameters mentioned earlier. The Greek Cypriot government and people are aware that the situation is advantageous – they solely represent the island and they can use the EU membership aspirations of Turkey to get maximum concessions – and as Ker-Lindsay claims (2007), to take their revenge on Turkey for the 1974 invasion.

With regard to the direct contribution to the Cyprus peace negotiations, the EU has been rather timid since the 2004 referenda. The reasons for the EU's disengagement with the Cyprus peace negotiations can be explained by and large in three parts. First, the EU's direct and active involvement during the 2004 referenda and its clear support for the UN peace plan was presented by Tassos Papadopoulos to the Greek Cypriots as an "imposition by the imperialists"[21] on the Cypriots. Hence, the EU does not want to experience a similar situation again. Second, the EU has many other important and pressing issues, such as the Lisbon Treaty, global financial crisis, and so forth that pushes the Cyprus problem to the bottom of their agenda. This is coupled with the fact that, except for Greece and the UK, the EU member states know very little about the Cyprus problem which decreases their interest in the Cyprus issue. When examining the programs of the EU presidencies, Cyprus appears at the bottom of the Union's agenda. Thus, the Cyprus discourse is in the EU and a majority of the member states very limited and some would even argue non-existent.

This is for the most part also true for the Central and Eastern European countries (CEECs) and the Baltic States. Even though the Cyprus problem does not stand high on East Central European Countries' (ECECs') agenda, they have at times made statements on the issue and shown interest in finding a settlement. It is not without interest that in 2005, a Polish diplomat Zbigniew Wlosowicz was the UN Special Representative for Cyprus and the Head of the UN Peacekeeping Mission in Cyprus (UNFICYP). Hungarian and Slovak soldiers were members of the UNFICYP in 2008. Even more importantly, Czechoslovakia hosted bicommunal dialogues since 1989, which was after the break-up of the country taken up by the Slovak diplomacy within the "good services" approach. The meetings are attended by Greek and Turkish Cypriot leaders of their respective political parties and under the auspices of the Slovak foreign ministry.[22]

The countries also expressed their concern with the failed referendum in 2004. Mr Eörsi, Rapporteur of the Political Affairs Committee of the Council of Europe, reacted to the situation on 29 April 2004 by saying:

> It is obvious that the Turkish Cypriot community has a deep desire to come closer to European structures . . . the Turkish Cypriot people in the northern part of the island cannot be punished for the negative vote in the other part. If the Turkish Cypriot people wish to become part of Europe, we must consider what we can do about it. First, we must stop denying them the opportunity of participating in European debates. We can call on international organisations, which have the responsibility to consider whether the isolation policy is good or whether it punishes Turkish Cypriots . . . We propose that we invite members of the Turkish Cypriot community to take part in European debates. Is that such a bad punishment in respect of the Greek Cypriots? I do not think so.
> (Parliamentary Assembly Council of Europe 2004)

The Czech foreign ministry issued a declaration as a reaction to the referendum results claiming that both sides and the world should "hope for the re-unification of Cyprus" (MZV ČR 2004) while reflecting on the Republic of Cyprus becoming an EU member state by saying

> Cyprus will become an EU Member State on May 1st, 2004. Turkish Cypriots demonstrated in the referendum their will to re-unity the island and we believe that they should not become hostage of the situation, which will arise after May 1st . . . The Czech Foreign Ministry believes that the EU and the international community will find a way to help Northern Cyprus overcome the economic and social consequences of decades-long international isolation.[23]

These, however, seem to be only reactions to the most pressing issues of the day. Of all the ECECs, Slovakia seems to have the most detailed and structured approach to the Cyprus issue acknowledging that the Turkish accession process gives it a strong European dimension that would affect every EU member state, including Slovakia. Given the 20-year-long active engagement in trying to contribute to the settlement of the problem, Slovakia can play a positive role and Turkey could benefit from a closer cooperation here by reaching out to the other three ECECs.

Third, the Turkish Cypriot (and the Turkish) side does not see the EU as an impartial actor due to the full membership of both Greece and the Greek Cypriot–dominated Republic of Cyprus and their participation in all decision-making bodies in the EU. This concern has been increasingly strengthened by the EU's inability to escape from the myopic legal framework of the statement that the "EU's only interlocutor [in the island] is its member – the 'Republic of Cyprus'" (Protocol 10). The EU's inability to present novel ways of dealing with the two conflicting sides on an equal footing inevitably either ignores the Turkish Cypriot side or places it in a very disadvantageous situation vis-à-vis the Greek Cypriot side on the EU platforms, and in doing so renders itself an inappropriate mediator.

Turkey's EU accession process complicates this situation even further. Many believe that due to the lack of consensus among the EU political elites on Turkey's EU bid, some anti-Turkish EU political elites use Cyprus in trying to derail Turkey's EU bid by adopting a pro-Greek Cypriot stance or by hiding behind Cyprus in the negotiations.[24] Turkey, while supporting a solution of the conflict, on several occasions has protested against the EU using the Cyprus problem as an issue in its accession negotiations. They often blame the EU for importing the problem by accepting the Republic of Cyprus as a full member state and now trying to throw the responsibility on Turkey by tying its accession with the resolution of the conflict.[25] Furthermore, Turkey highlights the failure of the EU to meet its own promises, mainly the regulation on direct trade (see earlier). The fact that some EU member states use Cyprus to hinder the Turkish accession negotiations is no secret and further damages the EU's image and credibility in Turkey.

The Cyprus issue receives a lot of media attention in Turkey and has explosive political potential which forces the government on the defensive. European leaders failed to treat the Turkey-Cyprus issue with the necessary caution, which undermined the credibility of EU's policy not only towards Cyprus but also towards Turkey. As a result, the scepticism towards the EU's true intentions rises, which means that "a settlement in Cyprus would be viewed by Ankara as 'losing Cyprus' rather than sealing a win-win agreement" (Tocci 2003)

Conclusion

It is clear that the Cyprus conflict, though it has become more visible after the island's membership in the EU, as well as it being attached to Turkey's EU accession process, is an old, protracted conflict that has been on the international community's agenda since the 1950s. It is the author's belief that the conflict is approaching its finale. The result of the 2004 referenda showed that the Greek Cypriot side was not ready to share power and accept the political equality of the Turkish Cypriots, but still on 1 May 2004 became under the Republic of Cyprus an EU member state, while the Turkish Cypriot side was left out. In other words, the Greek Cypriots were rewarded with EU membership though they were the intransigent side and the Turkish Cypriots were punished despite their cooperation.

What does the future hold for Cyprus? The 21 March (2008) process that led to the current full-fledged negotiations between Talat and Christofias, seems to be what Alexander Downer, former Foreign Minister of Australia and the current UN Secretary General's Special Adviser for Cyprus, called the "last roll of the dice" in Cyprus.[26] It seems that the international community wants to see one more initiative – the current peace negotiations – after the failure of the 2004 referenda where it was the first time that a comprehensive solution plan had ever been put to referenda in Cyprus. Some observers believe that Talat and Christofias, who once belonged to the same school of thought of socialism/communism and are old friends, are the only two leaders in Cyprus who can solve the Cyprus problem. Some are convinced that their personal trust together with the belief in some shared values can provide a solid basis for an agreement. However, one thing is clear from the track records of the two leaders in the peace negotiations: each is out there defending his own community's needs and interests, and both of them are aware that this time it might indeed be the last roll of the dice.

If the current negotiation process fails, there will be no motivation left for either of the two conflicting side in Cyprus as well as the international community to push for a federal solution for the unification of the two sides. In such a case, even UNFICYP might choose to withdraw from the island. In such a case, the permanent division of the island would become more tangible. It is vital to know which side is responsible for the failure of the negotiations in order to speculate about the future. If it is the Turkish Cypriot side, then the isolation on North Cyprus would continue and the TRNC would go on unrecognized for some time. If it is the Greek Cypriot side, then the door would be open for the TRNC to be *Kosovo-ized* – recognized by a limited number of countries without being a member of the UN. A similar scenario is expected in case the current negotiations actually yield an agreement between the two leaders but get rejected in the referenda. If either of the sides or the Greek Cypriots rejects the agreement in the referenda, *Kosovo-ization* of the TRNC should be expected, whereas if the Turkish Cypriots reject the UN plan, then the TRNC would remain unrecognized for some time.

In case the current negotiations yield an agreement between the two leaders and the referenda are successful on both sides, two possible scenarios can be presented here. The very optimistic scenario is that the two sides have learnt their lessons from the past tragedies and will start to cooperate with one another at least on the very vital issues and will live in a consociational democracy based on power sharing. In other words, the two communities would cooperate on a specific number of issues but would not mix much. By and large, each community would live in its respective constituent state. With respect to the EU's role, the Union could provide a nice umbrella for the cooperation between the two communities as well as for the issues outside of the cooperation pool. A less but still optimistic scenario is that after some time the two sides might decide that cooperation under the federal roof is not so efficient or desirable and that they decide to divorce in a non-violent negotiated solution *á la* Czechoslovakia.

Which future scenario is more probable is very difficult to predict today. However, the challenge we face is not the prediction of a near future arrangement scenario in Cyprus. Cyprus is a member of the EU as a divided island. The problem is that because the EU has been disengaged in the Cyprus issue since the failed referenda in 2004, it is unprepared for any of the scenarios described earlier– just like it was unprepared for the 2004 referenda results that led the EU to allow a divided country to become a member and made the conflict even more complicated. Furthermore, the unsettled dispute threatens to undermine the Turkish accession negotiations because it provides those against the Turkish membership bid with good ammunition.

There are two related explanations for the EU's relative incompetence with respect to the Cyprus problem. First, the EU member states have little knowledge and limited interest in the issue with the exception of Greece and the UK – and now the Republic of Cyprus. The information about the conflict is rarely objective and is often subject to open propaganda. The European public is generally convinced that the entire problem began with the Turkish invasion in 1974. The discourse is, thus, framed by these general beliefs and (mis)perceptions. Furthermore, the UK's strategic interest in keeping its two bases in Cyprus makes it play along with the Republic of Cyprus. Second, the Cyprus card is played by several actors in the Turkish EU negotiations. The ECECs cannot be expected to perceive the Cyprus settlement as vital to their national interests but given their positions in the past, Turkey could use them to counterweigh such forces in the EU and also strive to inform public opinion better about the background of the conflict.

Notes

1 We saw a similar turn in the Greek policy towards Turkey. In the mid-1990s, the new Greek Prime Minister Costas Simitis, decided to reform Greek foreign policy and make it more in line with the that of the EU. Ker-Lindsay (2007) calls this process "Europeanization" of Greek foreign policy. It also meant focusing less on highly political issues and more on low-key dialogue and building of trust, which would later provide solutions to the country's more persistent problems.

2 See Sözen 1998, 1999, and Oberling 1991 for a more detailed account on the history of inter-communal negotiations in Cyprus.

3 The mediation attempts of the great powers were not concentrated on resolving the strife between the communities on the island and did not even involve the communities in question in their discussions. It was very explicitly stated in US President Lyndon B. Johnson's letter to Turkey's Prime Minister Ismet Inönü that the main issue was the relationship between the two NATO allies and the implication of this relationship with regard to the superpower competition of the Cold War: "I must call to your attention, Mr Prime Minister, the obligation of NATO. There can be no question in your mind that a Turkish intervention in Cyprus would lead to a military engagement between Turkish and Greek forces . . . Adhesion to NATO, in its very essence, means that NATO countries will not wage war on each other. Germany and France have buried centuries of animosity and hostility in becoming NATO allies; nothing less can be expected from Greece and Turkey. Furthermore, a military intervention in Cyprus by Turkey could lead to direct involvement by the Soviet Union. I hope you will understand that your NATO allies have not had the chance to consider whether they have an obligation to protect Turkey against the Soviet Union if Turkey takes a step which results in Soviet intervention without the full consent and understanding of its NATO allies" (Stearns 1992: 37).

4 The exclusion of the two communities in the negotiations, as the former US Ambassador to Turkey Parker T. Hart argues, even created suspicion among both the Greek and Turkish Cypriots about the intentions of Greece and Turkey: "When it became apparent that secret talks were being held between Athens and Ankara (1965) at the subministerial level and later at the foreign ministry level, both Greek Cypriots and Turkish Cypriots became disturbed. Not being included, they felt that the two 'mother' countries might be hatching something which would not accord with their vital interests" (Hart 1990: 20).

5 Maraş in Turkish. It is a disputed area and currently under UN control. It had mixed Greek and Turkish population and today is a ghost town where access is not allowed.

6 The Turkish side believed that if they accepted an agreement through a piecemeal approach, then, they would be committed to a negotiation process in which they would have no guarantee of the fulfillment of their interests. Hence, the Turkish side thought

that, if a piecemeal approach was followed, their bargaining power in such a negotiation process would be weakened. For example, they could not give away some of the land in the North as a concession to Greek Cypriot in exchange for constitutional issues. In a piecemeal approach, if the Turkish side made a territorial concession at the beginning, then, they would lose their bargaining power in the constitutional matters. That is why the Turkish side has always preferred a comprehensive or whole-*istic* approach in the inter-communal talks.

7 The author himself was very much involved in the committee studies to prepare recommendations for President Denktaş regarding the negotiations on CBMs. He observed firsthand how the mostly humanitarian elements of the CBMs were politicized by both sides – the acceptance or rejection of any CBM became a political tactic in order to gain bargaining power on the negotiation table. Hence, the CBMs main idea of "building trust" was ignored by both.

8 European Court of Justice, Judgment of the Court, Case C-432/92, 5 July 1994.

9 In order to lift the traditional Greek veto on Turkey's candidacy, Turkey accepted two conditions of the EU: (1) to solve its disputes with Greece through peaceful means, including taking the matters to the ICJ; and (2) to support the efforts of the UN Secretary General and his mission of good offices to solve the Cyprus problem.

10 The National Security Council is responsible for national security policy.

11 Both previous leaders, Clerides and Vassiliou, supported the Annan plan.

12 For more information see NTV 7 March 2005 (www.ntvmsnbc.com/news/312443.asp, accessed 5 December 2009).

13 He was also the minister of commerce, industry, and tourism between 1998 and 2003.

14 *Sunday Mail*, 27 February 2005.

15 See the official press release by the Press and Information Offfice of the Republic of Cyprus at http://www.cyprus.gov.cy/moi/pio/pio.nsf/All/F8A92BF0EC4AC34EC2257 5590027Γ37C?OpenDocument&print, accessed 5 December 2009.

16 Mehmet Ali Talat became the Prime Minister of Northern Cyprus in 2004 and a year later won the presidential election succeeding Rauf Denktaş.

17 The six working groups are: (1) governance and power sharing, (2) property, (3) EU matters, (4) economic and commercial matters, (5) territory, and (6) security and guarantees.

18 See Yeşilada and Sözen (2002).

19 See Çarkoğlu and Sözen (2004) and Sözen (2005a) for the general elections held in December 2003 and in February 2005 in North Cyprus.

20 The Protocol states that the EU will welcome a settlement of the problem "in line with the principles on which the EU is founded" while also saying that the accession of Cyprus to the EU "shall benefit all Cypriot citizens and promote civil peace and reconciliation," which contradicts the actual suspension of the *acquis* and the outcome of the decision to accept divided Cyprus so far.

21 See the text of the TV speech made by Tassos Papadopoulos on 7 April 2004, in *Filelefteros*, 8 April 2004.

22 Based on the history of this dialogue, the Slovak Ambassador calls a meeting every month where issues relevant to both sides are discussed. The results are then presented to the media as joint *communiqué*. More details available on http://www.stcity.sk/index. php/z-domova/2261-mimoriadne-stretnutie-lidrov-cyperskych-politickych-stran-v-bratislave-, accessed on 30 May 2009.

23 Own translation.

24 See Sözen (2005b) for an account on Turkey-EU relations. Some even argue that Greece is pushing Greek Cypriots, a view held by many Turkish commentators but Ker-Lindsay (2007) investigated the indications of Greek attitudes to Turkish accession process and found evidence to the contrary.

25 The Turkish chief negotiator Egemen Bağiş recently stated in an interview for *Today's Zaman* that the motivations of the Greek Cypriots can be tainted by the fact that as an

EU member state and with relatively high per capita income, they do not have many reasons to settle the issue (Doğan 2009b). The Turkish support for the settlement was also highlighted when the newly appointed Turkish foreign minister, Ahmet Davutoğlu chose TRNC as the first foreign visit, one day after he became foreign minister in May 2009. Later that month, Davutoğlu also stated that the EU's pressure to force Turkey to open its ports and airports to Greek Cyprus was not an act of good faith, once more critical of linking the two issues, the Cyprus problem and Turkish accession, together.

26 Downer's speech in the presence of the author in Eastern Mediterranean University, 12 March 2009.

6 The challenge of Euroscepticism in the accession countries

The good, the bad and the shaky EU

Lucie Tunkrová

Introduction

Public opinion plays an increasingly important role in the process of Europeaniza-tion. The debate in the candidate countries (CCs) focuses on the definition of what the EU stands for and what it represents vis-à-vis the nation states. The public tends to support EU membership when the application is submitted, but once relations with the EU become more structured and the country is required to meet specific conditions for membership, the level of support starts to drop and a Eurosceptic discourse emerges. It becomes obvious that membership has not only benefits but also costs and as the more uneasy issues enter the agenda, the debate turns into a "more salient, public and politicized" one (Slomczynski and Shabad 2003: 503).

Hence, as the date of accession approaches, the debate intensifies, often utilized in the domestic political battles, where all sides attempt to win the public's sup-port. Leaving aside the question of the precision of information, it creates three general camps: people who fully support their country's membership perceived as economic, political, or personal benefit; people who articulate lukewarm support and can change camps with respect to the developments in the accession talks; and people who more or less oppose membership based either on claims of losing national identity, independence of policy making, and economic sovereignty or on personal evaluations.

Those, who support EU membership (Eurooptimists), tend to highlight the mate-rial effects such as the single market while those, who oppose it (Eurosceptics), often refer to the more abstract terms such as national sovereignty, national identity, etc. More specific policy issues emerge only in the final stage of the negotiations. The elites and the public increasingly learn that EU membership will bring both benefits and costs but whereas the former are relatively definite, the latter are not, which often leads to a dramatic over-exaggeration of the costs. The most important problem of Euroscepticism in the CCs is the general immaturity of the debate and what Drulák (2001) calls "consensus without discussion."

In both the ECECs and Turkey, membership was commonly presented as a good thing for the country and for the people without any open and broad discussion on the benefits and costs prior to applying for membership. Even during the acces-sion process, the discourse remained largely constrained to secondary issues and often displayed little effort to explain the dynamics of European integration. The widespread consensus did not allow a majority of the elite to express open hostility to EU membership. Thus, the EU debate became part of domestic politics but until the later stage of negotiations when sensitive economic and political questions entered the negotiations, the membership debate remained vague and was utilized by the domestic political actors to undermine their opponents as being either anti-European or "selling" the country to the EU. While understanding the support for EU membership was often seen as normative and the debate focused on the issues of general domestic and foreign policy concerns, genuine matters directly and indirectly connected with EU (non-)membership were to a great extent ignored. Furthermore, the EU by highlighting certain issues modified the domestic debate, which was then mostly conducted within the terms of EU requirements, focusing on certain problems and ignoring others. Also, the discourse depended and reacted to the specific national domestic environments of the individual CCs.

Turkish EU membership is – as was the case with the ECECs – seen by many as an "elite project" (Şenyuva 2006: 21), where the domestic public has often been neglected by both the EU and the domestic elites. As the public lacks the sources of socialization and the objectives of accession/enlargement are not clearly explained to them, the original high support, where "uninformed enthusiasm" turns them into "euronaives" (Riishøj 2004), starts to decline. We could witness this development in the ECECs, when what Harris (1993) described in the early 1990s as "eager anticipation" changed into declining numbers of supporters. Also the Turkish public support started to decrease right after the negotiations had been opened and has been rather volatile ever since, reflecting public perceptions of how the EU-Turkey relations develop. The unstable public support indicates that people tend to frequently change their views based on the discourse/communication problems between the CC and the EU on one hand and the public and their government on the other and reflects a lack of understanding of what the EU is and how it works.

The objective of this chapter is to evaluate the role of Turkish public opinion in the accession process, while also providing links with the development of public opinion in the Central European countries prior to accession, identifying both the universal and conflicting trends. It focuses not only on public opinion but also on the roles of the political parties, the establishment of the integration issue as a cleavage, and the projected developments we might expect.

Conceptualization of Euroscepticism

Candidate countries that are undergoing political and/or economic transformation tend to feature initial high support for EU membership. As the debate becomes more structured, more negative evaluations of the impacts of EU membership and European integration on the domestic polity, politics, and policies emerge. The negative attitudes start to be reflected in the decline in mass public support for EU membership because the "previous, and to some extent romantic and illusory, consensus concerning Europe evaporated" (Kopecky and Mudde 2002: 298). The mass support is, however, not directly translated into negative attitudes but rather into a rising number of undecided, whose positions reflect the perceived outcomes of the negotiations and the ability of the elites to "communicate" accession.

We will be working with the broader concept of Taggart and Szczerbiak's (2002) Euroscepticism, who define it as an "idea of contingent or qualified opposition, as well as . . . outright and unqualified opposition to the process of European integration." Attitudes to EU membership are said to be influenced by a set of three main factors – economic cost/benefit, domestic political views, and identity politics. In the economic framework, positive or negative attitudes to the EU mirror the results of economic reforms related to the preparation for EU membership based on the rational calculation of costs and benefits: in the case of the ECECs the winners of the reform process are more likely to support EU accession than the losers (Gabel and Palmer 1995, in McLaren 2002). Research has also shown that those who support market liberalization tend to support EU membership and vice versa – but it at the same time has indicated relatively large differences between individual countries. An educated opinion based on rational calculation of costs and benefits requires a rather good knowledge of the EU and the ability to forecast future trends and developments. Consequently, it is mostly the *perceived* evaluation of the economic impact that will determine their position.

According to the domestic politics approach, national preferences for political parties are translated into their support for EU membership, i.e. the voters follow the party line. In addition, voters of particular parties support certain values and the adherence to these values is then also reflected in their support for EU membership. This approach to Euroscepticism is ideology-based, thus, it expects that those supporting democratic values will be more pro-European as the EU is fostering democratization. On the contrary, people with xenophobic and anti-democratic attitudes will oppose EU membership. Ideology, however, has not proven to provide a good and stable indicator of Eurooptimist/Eurosceptic party attitudes. Related is another important factor – people who do not believe that the government/state serves their interests and think that the EU can do it better tend to support EU membership, too (Elgün and Tillman 2007). It can, on the other hand, lead to too high expectations as to what the EU can do.

An alternative explanation is based on an institutional approach, which assumes that parties in opposition are more negative about the accession talks than governmental parties, hence, the level of support for EU membership and the accession process reflects party strategy. This variable became more visible with the publication of the first Commission's regular reports in 1997, but Neumayer (2008) shows that the way it was transformed into the domestic debate was very country-specific. The variable's potential strength further increased with the opening of the negotiation talks because the opposition parties could use it to indicate where they believed their governments did not pursue the national interests properly and/or did not implement the required reforms in expected time and form. Some parties become so-called Eurorealists during the accession process, i.e. they support EU membership but oppose the negotiated conditions. They do not wish to oppose EU membership because they want to be seen as "modernizers" and legitimate political subjects but have strategic or ideological reasons for expressing their reservations.

They either try to show that the elites are neglecting or even damaging national interests or – on the contrary – that the opponents are too nationalistic.

Parties are influential in forming public opinion but are not always a reliable factor. Some are divided internally over the issue and at times the party position is quite different from that of its voters. Furthermore, the governments in the CCs often introduce difficult but necessary reforms using the EU as an excuse, which runs the possible danger of alienating the public, who starts to associate the EU with negative impacts on their lives. In general, however, the governmental parties tend to be more open to EU influence and Eurooptimistic than the opposition and we can find examples both in the ECECs and in Turkey – in the Czech Republic, the Civic Democratic Party (ODS) coalition government under Václav Klaus submitted the EU membership application but later adopted many critical positions during the negotiations as an opposition party and was so divided on the issue of accession that it could not present a united position on the accession referendum. In Turkey, Turgut Özal, before becoming Prime Minister, opposed EU membership but then in 1987 his government formally applied for full EU membership and formulated economic policies necessary to become a CC.

The nature of opposition to European integration stems also from identity politics when the public relates the accession process to the threat posed to their country by other cultures, to the survival of the nation state, and to national identity (McLaren 2002; Taggart 1998; de Vreese, Boomgaarden and Semetko 2008). The likelihood of adopting EU rules increases if the state identifies with Europe, its rules, values, and norms. Elgün and Tillman (2007: 397) note that "domestic political attitudes and perceptions of cultural threats are strong predictors of attitudes to EU membership." The salience of this factor increases in countries that have rather short history of independent existence (Czech Republic, Slovakia), have a considerably different cultural background (Turkey), and where significant ethnic minority exists (Turkey, Slovakia) (McLaren 2002; de Master and le Roy 2000). This factor could be traced on various levels and in various discourses in the cases of all ECECs and in Turkey.

Turkish public opinion and the EU[1]

Support for EU membership seems to have three cycles with the CCs: first, high support partially stemming from the lack of knowledge about the EU; second, support falls as people learn more, but the information is rather scattered and often misleading; third, as the citizens learn more about the EU and become more socialized in the process, the support starts to grow again even though it rarely ever reaches the original level.

The Turkish elites have traditionally welcomed the idea of EU membership despite some factors that had the potential to create negative public attitudes such as traditional hostility to Western European states, unfavorable prospects of Turkish membership, and efforts of some political and military circles in Turkey to present EU membership as harmful to the Turkish nation (Uslu et al. 2005). While the public was relatively hostile to EU membership during the Cold War era (Bulbul 2006),

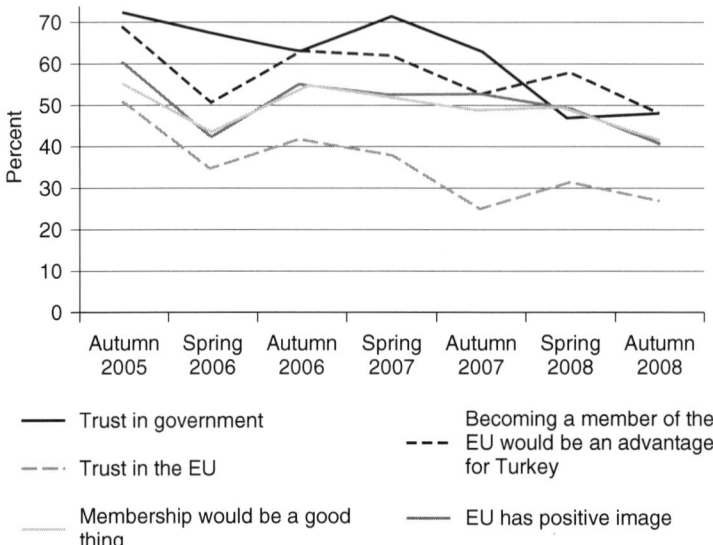

Figure 6.1 Development of Turkish public opinion towards the EU after the decision to open negotiations (Autumn 2005–Autumn 2008)

Sources: European Commission 2005b, 2006c, 2006d, 2006e, 2007a, 2007b, 2008a, 2008b, 2008c.

they became more supportive in the 1990s, the support reaching its highest point in early 2000s but started to decline as soon as the opening date of the negotiations was officially set (see Figure 6.1). As some polls suggest, the Turks were at this point particularly positive about the economic benefits of EU membership and its contribution to the country's democratization even though they were more sceptical about the EU as a politically stabilizing force (Aybar et al. 2007).

In EB 62 from autumn 2004, 62 percent of the Turks believed that EU membership was a good thing (12 percent against and 20 percent undecided), which fell to 59 percent in spring 2005 (EB 63) with 20 percent against and 17 percent undecided and then declined further to 55 percent in autumn 2005 (against 15 percent, undecided 21 percent, EB 64). By spring 2006 it dramatically decreased to 44 percent (25 percent against, 23 percent undecided, EB 65) and then again went up to 54 percent in autumn the same year (EB 66). It stayed at almost the same level in spring 2007, 52 percent (EB 67), and then again declined to 49 percent in fall (EB 68), the same as in spring 2008 (EB 69) but then again fell to 42 percent in autumn 2008 (EB 70). However, the numbers of people who believed that membership would be an advantage has been much higher, even though copying the "membership is a good thing" trends. Just as in the case of the ECECs, there is a large pool of undecided. Also, the opponents could not give any specific reasons for their opposition. These data indicate that the Turkish public is ill-informed about the EU and that their

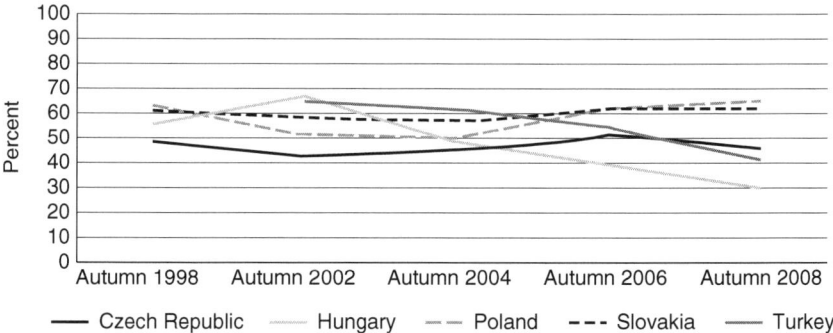

Figure 6.2 European Union membership is/would be a good thing (1998–2008)

Sources: European Commission 2002,[1] 2004c, 2006d, 2006e, 2008c.

[1] The 1998 Eurobarometer asked whether the citizens would vote yes in a referendum. Data on Turkey were not available.

evaluations lack consistency. Lower support levels are prevalent not only among the general public but also the elites (Öniş and Yılmaz 2009) – lower levels of optimism among Turkish intellectuals were first reported in 2002,[2] which Aybar et al. (2007: 340) attribute to their doubt about the effectiveness of "superimposed democratization" or simply their cynicism.

When compared with public opinion in the ECECs, the EB survey in 1990 showed that, "an overwhelming majority was in favor of a general unification of Western Europe, including their respective country." Immediate or speedy (within five years) EU membership supported 62 percent of the inhabitants of Czechoslovakia, 76 percent of Hungary, and 72 percent of Poland. Already at this point, however, the number of undecided citizens was rather high.[3] By the mid-1990s, support for the EU was growing and fewer people were against it but the number of undecided did not decline substantially. After the opening of the negotiations, the highest support for EU membership (see Figure 6.2) was in Slovakia, followed by Hungary, Poland and the Czech Republic. During the negotiations the level of support was falling in all ECECs but Hungary, which was labeled as a country with little signs of Euroscepticism. It later saw a rapid drop in public support between 2002 (67 percent) and 2004 (49 percent) and has been declining ever since. Upon accession the support started to pick up in all ECECs but Hungary. In 2004, 50 percent of Poles and 57 percent of Slovaks believed that membership was a good thing. The lowest support could be found in the Czech Republic but at first sight the Eurosceptic Czech public simultaneously supported deepening of European integration, which indicated the level of confusion in apprehending the concepts and the lack of understanding of the EU in general.

Figure 6.3 indicates that, with the exception of Hungary, the perception of EU membership as beneficial increases after EU accession. This confirms the

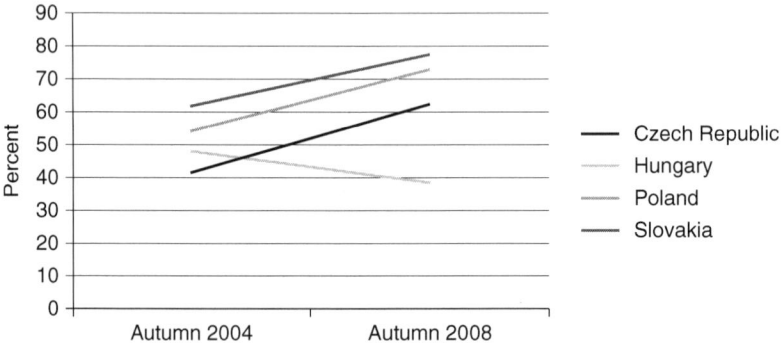

Figure 6.3 EU membership perceived as beneficial (2004–2008)

Sources: European Commission 2004b, 2004c, 2008c.

conclusion of Elgün and Tillman (2007) that while CCs tend to be more focused on less tangible issues such as national sovereignty and identity, the Member States (MS) evaluations tend to be based more on economic factors.

Feeling European (and simultaneously, like nationals of their country) or proud to be European is positively linked with support for EU membership whereas stronger attachment to national identity yields weaker support for the EU.

As Figure 6.4 shows, the Czechs feel less European than the other ECECs. Research has indicated that they feel they do not belong to the West or the East but rather somewhere between the two (Holý 2001 and Klímek 2001, in Vlachová and Řeháková 2009). The Turks feel far less European than the citizens of the ECECs and less than the EU average. What is more problematic is the negative

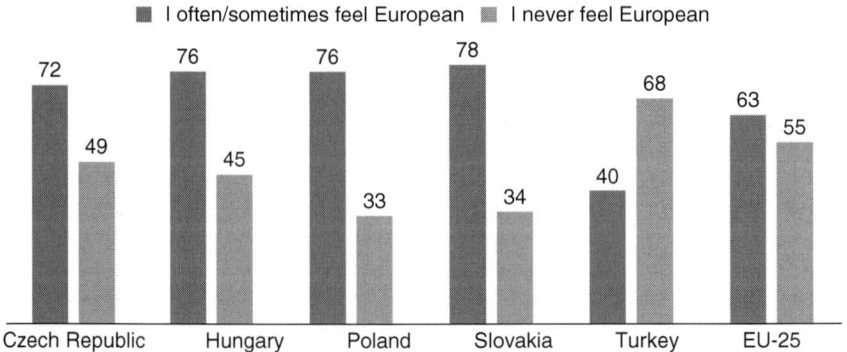

Figure 6.4 Feeling European (2005)

Source: European Commission 2005c.

trend when increasing numbers of Turks claim that they do not feel European – while in autumn 2004, 7 percent said they did not feel European at all and 48 percent said they were proud to be European (EU-25 average was 68 percent), in one year it fell to 40 percent being proud to be European; there was a dramatic increase of those who did not feel European at all to 23 percent; and 30 percent did not feel proud to be European (more people who were not proud to be European could be found in the UK (49 percent), Cyprus (42 percent), Germany (38 percent) and Greece (36 percent)).

Sources of Euroscepticism in Turkey

As we have seen, Euroscepticism has been on the rise in Turkey. This can be attributed partially to the domestic developments in Turkey, partially to the developments in the EU MS, and also to the dynamics of the EU-Turkey relations as the negotiations proceed. It is crucial to understand these developments because "the preferences of the Turkish public . . . constitute the moving force behind Turkey's relations with the European Union" (Çarkoğlu 2003: 171).

The proponents of EU membership in Turkey have traditionally seen it as a key factor in the modernization process following the legacy of Mustafa Kemal, where liberalization and democratization were perceived as an essential means of creating a modern state, a dynamic society, and of establishing ethnic and religious peace and tolerance – just as for the ECECs it was the "return to Europe," in Turkey it was the notion of "becoming of Europe" or "becoming European" (Avci 2006). As Müftüler-Bac (2005: 18) says, "EU membership would finally settle the issue whether Turkey is European or not." For both then, EU membership would serve as a confirmation that their reform processes were successfully completed – in the ECECs the transition to democracy and liberal capitalism, in Turkey the modernization and westernization projects of the republic.

Turkish Eurosceptics support centralist state and emphasize the "unique" position of Turkey. They adopt a state-centric view where the well-being of the society can be achieved even at the expense of the individual and his/her rights; and with respect to economic relations claim that Turkish industry suffers due to high competition from the EU. They also argue that the EU is a Christian club that will not allow a Muslim country in no matter how far the economic and political reforms progress. The last position receives high attention in Turkey and is fueled not only by the statements of some – mainly Christian Democratic – parties in Europe but also by some elements of Europe's debate on Muslim minorities. They also draw attention to Turkish geostrategic importance and suggest that Turkey should not turn a cold shoulder to alternatives such as the USA, the Middle East, or even China and India. In the early 2000s, the major countries that Eurosceptic circles declared as potential allies included Russia and Iran. While many still consider these scenarios irrelevant – Bulbul (2006) showed that for both Justice and Development Party (AKP) and Republican People's Party (CHP) deputies, alternative scenario support is low – they have the potential to become more appealing if the relations with the EU worsen.

Turkish public opinion on EU membership has been shaped mainly by the media. Media extensively affect public opinion and public attitudes (Schuck and de Vreese 2006). The traditional problem of negotiating EU accession is that as long as things go smoothly, it attracts little media attention and the public is kept uninformed. Also, the media frame the issues in the national context, which often strips it of objectivity or the background information. Thus, the public hears about the EU almost only when problems arise, which increases the chances of Euroscepticism because the public starts to perceive the EU as a source of problems. The media vastly contribute to it as they focus on emotional issues and use either very negative or positive quotes (Schuck and de Vreese 2006).

The Turkish media have predominantly paid attention to the way some EU countries, particularly Austria, France, Germany, Italy, and the UK, evaluate the prospects of Turkish membership.[4] In Germany and France but also in Austria, it became part of the domestic political debate, which directly reflects the politicization and ideologization of the enlargement process and has immense potential to become one of the major sources of Turkish Euroscepticism. While German Chancellor, Angela Merkel, and French president, Nicolas Sarkozy, became more vocal about the privileged partnership option for Turkey after the negotiations started, Austria demanded a clause providing for such arrangement during the October 2005 Council meeting.[5] During the 2009 European Parliament (EP) election campaign, both Sarkozy and Merkel mentioned their opposition to Turkey's full membership several times over, and their victory was by media in Turkey – and not only there – attributed to these statements. Also some extreme right wing parties in Europe, who did rather well in the election, declared their opposition to Turkish accession. Turkish newspapers reacted to the election results with headlines such as "EP turned into a minefield" (*Millyet*), "European Left supportive of Turkey melted down" (*Zaman*), or "The number of future Turkish MEPs scares them [the EU]" (*Dünya*).

Öniş and Yılmaz (2009) argue that the negative statements about Turkish prospects of EU membership by some MS led to a "nationalistic backlash" in the country and helped the anti-EU and anti-reform camps while the Turkish media further facilitated this process. They are convinced that this, together with the internal problems of the EU, has had a greatly negative influence on Turkish public opinion. Similarly, Eylemer and Taş (2007) believe that it strengthened the Eurosceptic positions in the country, who claim that the EU is only trying to keep Turkey in its sphere of influence with no intention of securing full membership. Joost Lagendijk said for *Today's Zaman* that he believed the reasons behind the "substantial" fall in support for EU membership in Turkey were the lack of support in some EU MS such as France, which "makes people in Turkey think the whole EU is against Turkey" believing that when France speaks, the EU speaks. The Turks are then convinced that the EU will never accept them no matter how hard they try. The second reason Lagendijk identified was the EU focusing on its own internal problems rather than on enlargement. Lastly, he mentioned the problem of Cyprus, when the EU failed to "deliver on its promises to northern Cyprus" (Doğan 2009d: 6).

As for the European media, the common (mis)representations of the presidential crisis in 2007, the headscarf crisis in 2008, and the statements on Cyprus, Armenia, and the Kurdistan Workers Party (PKK) further worsen the situation because Turkish media often reprint their statements to show how the West is treating Turkey "unfavorably."[6] The lack of consistency in the demands and the different requirements articulated by MS and some EU institutions as if choosing a meal from a restaurant menu prompted the Eurosceptics to argue that despite their efforts to comply with the EU requirements and after "begging at the EU's door" to be admitted, the EU would never accept Turkey as an equal partner.

The Turkish Eurosceptics use all these cards to feed on and fuel the public's fears, prejudices, and insecurities. In 2003 a survey was conducted in Turkey under the all-inclusive title *The Suspicion of Turkey in Europe*, which showed that even in this time when support for membership was high, about a third of respondents believed that the EU was applying double standards to Turkey and almost a half that Turkey will never become a member state (Eylemer and Taş 2007). Part of the fears and doubts is related to religion and culture; some can be accredited to the traditional and widespread suspicion of the real intentions of Westerners with Turkey. Many Turks identify religion as the main building bloc of the EU community spirit (EB 68) and they believe that accepting a large Muslim state would undermine EU's collective identity. A 2009 survey conducted by Bahçeşehir University showed that 72 percent of Turks thought the EU aimed to spread Christianity and 76 percent that it wanted to spread democracy. Also, 76 percent were convinced that Turkey's being a Muslim country negatively influences the EU's attitude towards it (*Hürriyet Daily News* 2009b).

Religious and cultural factors are coupled with the distrust towards the West. A poll conducted by an NGO in July 2005 showed that

> 66 percent of Turks believed "Western countries want to disintegrate Turkey like they disintegrated the Ottoman Empire in the past." According to the same survey, 51 percent of Turks believe that "the reforms required by the EU are similar to those required by the treaty of Sevres which dismembered [the] Ottoman Empire in 1919."
>
> (Gordon and Taspinar 2005)

The 2009 survey indicated that while 57 percent of Turks wanted Turkey to join the EU, 28 percent were convinced that the EU definitely wanted to dismantle Turkey and 48 percent said that dismantlement was among the EU's goals (*Hürriyet Daily News* 2009b). Some Eurosceptics also label the reforms demanded under the Copenhagen criteria as equivalent to the Tanzimat reforms[7] during the late Ottoman times, which aimed at modernization that would prevent the collapse of the Empire. The reforms failed to achieve that goal and some scholars call this the "Tanzimat syndrome."

The ECECs were not spared anti-Western and/or revisionist attitudes either – in Hungary, the chairman of the Hungarian Justice and Life Party equated the EU with the Trianon Treaty and these feelings appeared even after accession as in the June 2009 EP election, Hungarian extremists had in their program not only the abolishment of the Beneš decrees but also the abolition of the Trianon Treaty. In Poland, the leader of the populist Self-Defense, Andrzej Lepper, said that Poland would be a rubbish dump for EU's goods and declared "Yesterday Moscow, tomorrow Brussels" (Szczerbiak, in Kemmerling 2008). Similarly, in the Czech Republic a conservative journal published an article called "Habsburg, Hitler, Moscow, Brussels . . . why can't we rule ourselves?" (Burda 2006). Many believe that the importance the ECECs attached to EU and NATO membership was a reflection of this distrust and doubts about the true "European" interests in the region. On the other hand, other representatives used the argument that if they do not follow Brussels, they will fall into the claws of Moscow – as much as some Turks believe that without Brussels, Turkey will be swallowed by the instability of the Near and Middle East.

A Turkish EU expert, Can Baydarol, notes that the uncertainty of Turkish membership "has created an atmosphere of distrust in the Turkish public against the EU" (Doğan 2009c). The Turkish pro-reform and pro-EU circles also add that such inconsistent policies strengthen the positions of the opponents and allow the government to postpone sensitive reforms.[8] As the declining Turkish support seems to be directly linked to the rise of Turco-phobic sentiments in Europe, the opponents are able to capitalize on the debates in Europe that portray Turkey as a threat to both the European states and the EU and further alienate Turkish public opinion. It is also a problem of the Turkish media, who often fail to recognize the national voices and present it as an EU position. Thus, an MP for the CHP warned in May 2009 that if EU national politicians make statements about Turkey and the prospects of its EU membership, "we should look at their authority" (Alyamaç 2009).

The current Eurosceptic wave is further exacerbated by a range of foreign and domestic policy problems such as the Cyprus issue and the Kurdish question. The EU negotiations touched on many sensitive issues that have high salience in Turkish domestic politics. The drop in support shortly after the negotiations started was partially related to the decision to suspend the negotiations of eight chapters unless Turkey allows Cypriot ships and aircrafts into its harbors and airports, which had rather massive media coverage in Turkey. Prime Minister Recep Tayyip Erdoğan accepted a compromise: Turkey would open its harbors and airports if major economic concessions are provided to Northern Cyprus. The compromise had been heavily criticized by the opposition. The Nationalist Movement Party (MHP) blamed the government for "'selling' Cyprus in order to show the EU what an obedient little child [Turkey] is" (Güsten 2005). In reaction to the rising pressure from the EU to resolve the Cyprus problem and the feeling of frustration, the Turkish public – including some powerful NGOs – was becoming more critical of the EU, some turning Eurosceptic and even anti-European (Bagci 2006). The many elections in Europe and Turkey in 2007 further aggravated the situation.

While the Cyprus issue is related to the Turkey-EU relations, two domestic developments also play a vital role in the public's perceptions of the impact of Europeanization on Turkish society and politics. These are the issues of secularism and the Kurdish question. Islamism and Kurdish nationalism are periphery ideologies that the state has traditionally perceived as forces with a strong potential to undermine the basis of the Turkish Republic. Thus, some fear that democratization and liberalization will empower those groups, who use the rhetoric of reform in order to gain more power vis-à-vis the center. Consequently, the strong opposition to some reforms, for instance allowing official use of languages other than Turkish, became entangled in the debate on the unity of the Turkish state, which still represents a major issue in Turkish politics. For the ultra-nationalists, any concessions to recognizing diversity are seen as a threat to the unity of the Turkish state and nation, and recognition of Kurdish cultural rights as giving in to terrorism (Müftüler-Bac 2005). Öniş and Yılmaz (2009: 2) also highlight the factor of domestic tensions stemming from the need to "balance different components of . . . identity, cultural, geographical, historical, and strategic factors, as well as in struggling to consolidate democracy, while preserving secularism in a predominantly Muslim society."

The religious population in Turkey was traditionally opposed to EU membership but became largely supportive in the late 1990s and early 2000s when they started to realize the reforms would give them more freedom to express their religious beliefs in the highly secular Turkish state. The Kurdish population, often also very religious, is mostly supportive of EU membership, too.[9] It thus, seems, that Euroscepticism is adopted mostly by groups who perceive democratization as a major challenge to their position in the society, i.e. the undemocratic forces – extreme nationalists (Turkey is "being sold" to Europeans), radical Islamists (West as threat to traditional and religious values),[10] and militant Kurds (PKK).[11] On the other hand, the more liberal forces in each "camp" are generally supportive of EU membership even though their preferences and key interests might differ.

Party Euroscepticism

Taggart and Szczerbiak (2002) distinguish between two forms of party Euroscepticism, soft and hard. Hard Euroscepticism is defined by opposition to the project as it exists today. Soft Euroscepticism concerns political parties that lack principal reservations to European integration or EU membership but where concerns exist regarding one or more EU policies or where the understanding of "national interest" is currently in contrast with the EU developments. They are said to be effectively Eurosceptic. In neither the ECECs nor in Turkey can we find a relevant political party that could be labeled a hard Eurosceptic party because they do not express outright opposition to EU membership, which is seen as a key foreign policy goal, but some express dissatisfaction with how the business is conducted. Soft Euroscepticism is then displayed though various platforms, ideological backgrounds, and levels of Europeanization (Tunkrová 2006).

It is often the opposition parties that take on a rhetoric that does not oppose EU membership per se but criticizes the way the negotiations are conducted. That can be related to their party ideology but also, predominantly, to the structure of the domestic political battles and discourse. The asymmetry and democratic deficit of the negotiation process leave little room for domestic debates, which often forces the politicians to move to personal attacks and use emotive language, which in turns pushes the public away from the debate on accession (Sadurski 2004). Şenyuva (2006) notes that the technicality of the accession talks makes many of the issues too complicated for non-expert public to understand and increases the salience of certain sensitive issues in the debate.

Çarkoğlu (2003: 171) argues that as the issues discussed are often very complicated but also very sensitive, "politicians and other opinion leaders simplify and somewhat distort these issues for their convenience and present them for public consideration." He further notes that the less pro-EU inclined elites provide misinformation to the Turkish public, especially on very sensitive issues such as the Kurdish question. It is interesting to note that before 2002, i.e. the emergence of the ruling AKP, every relevant political subject had objections to the accession process and/or the Copenhagen criteria despite the high public support for EU membership. Çarkoğlu argues that this discrepancy between public opinion and party positions was caused by the hierarchical party organization, which was often closed to the influence of the pro-EU groups.

Despite the low sophistication of the EU debate in Turkey, Euroscepticism shows in some political parties. The most vocal relevant political party is the extreme-right MHP. It uses very emotional language to mobilize the public and draw attention to the issues of national sovereignty, land ownership, and the nation state. In 2001, MHP summarized its main arguments against EU membership as opposing the transfer of the parliamentary authority to the EP; deformation of the national character of the economy; violation of national property rights; and fast degeneration of socio-cultural identity (Inaç 2004).

While in government, the party on several occasions restricted the reform proposals and tried to dominate the debate of "protecting" the Turkish interests in the accession debate but failed to express upright opposition to the EU. In 2002, the MHP leader and at that time deputy PM, Devlet Bahçeli, said that the party was not against EU-sponsored democratic reforms but they "should not jeopardize national unity and should not be used as a pretext to extend concessions to Kurdish separatists" (Çevik and Kanli 2002). During the 2007 national election campaign, the MHP election manifesto even called for the end of the negotiations claiming that the EU was blackmailing and bullying Turkey. The party's position on EU membership during the campaign was summarized as "Turkey doesn't need or have to be dragged around the axis of the EU at any costs" (Kurt 2007). We could say that MHP represents mostly ideological type of Euroscepticism with some elements of party strategy.

More recently, the social democrats (CHP) also became more Eurosceptic but this could be understood mainly in terms of the domestic competition for votes. CHP highlights the need to protect national interests and it uses this card against the government party, the AKP, accusing it of betraying the Turkish national interests in issues such as Cyprus or secularism.[12] The party is very critical of the EU's "absorption capacity." CHP party leader, Deniz Baykal, compared the situation to Turkey rescuing "the princess kept as prisoner in a giant's house, which was on the seventh floor of a cave on the highest mountain and get[ting] through all the traps to climb down" (Gülmez 2008: 429). They claim that Turkey receives different treatment, understood as worse treatment, than the previous CCs. In the 2007 national election, CHP welcomed the prospect of EU membership but claimed that "when there is no concrete perspective on this issue [membership] and just opposite conditions are seen, the demands from Brussels are not sensible and conceivable" (*Turkish Daily News* 2007a). The party considered the current negotiation model unacceptable. It demanded a break in the negotiations. Similarly, regarding the Cyprus issue, the party blamed the government for the policy of appeasement with the EU. It claimed a victory by saying that "Thanks to the CHP, the submissive policy of the governing party has not produced any results" (*Turkish Daily News* 2007b).

The CHP's opposition to some reforms proposed by the AKP due to opposition politics resulted in frequent criticism of the party from the EU and the MS, mainly the social democratic parties, which oppose any "privileged partnership" schemes. Meanwhile, CHP has also criticized the government for not implementing the necessary EU reforms and in May 2009, one its members, Kader Sevinç, said that the party's position on EU membership has not changed and that they support it but that there are "few" issues the EU and CHP disagree on, mainly the Cyprus problem, while saying the party "has always supported the government's [AKP] EU efforts" (Alyamaç 2009). Less than a month later, the party criticized the government for not adopting the necessary laws in order to allow the opening of social policy and employment chapters and the Cyprus deadlock, which cause the lack of progress in accession negotiations (Özerkan 2009a). In Bulbul's (2006) comparative survey of AKP and CHP deputies, both parties showed very high levels of support for EU membership (92.5 and 91.91 percent, respectively), even though AKP had more MPs showing unconditional support (29.6 to 13.3 percent) and agreeing with sharing power with international organizations (55.7 to 29.5 percent). It is at times confusing to understand from the statements of the party leader and its members whether CHP supports or opposes Turkish EU membership – according to Gülmez (2008), the party displays elements of soft Euroscepticism partially affected by opposition politics.[13]

Both CHP and MHP have criticized the government for not involving the parliamentary parties in the EU dialogue but when invited to talks about planned reforms in September 2008, CHP and MHP refused to show up. As in the case of some ECECs where the hostility between the main parties has also been very high, the EU reforms often become hostage to political struggles between the political camps and to the inability of the party leaders to overcome their personal malice. Given that the parties are in both cases very hierarchically organized under strong charismatic leadership further exasperates the problem of politics of personalities rather than programs skyjacking the EU issue, the related reforms, and the public opinion. It can also spill over to wider political conflicts. The previous Turkish president, Ahmet Necdet Sezer, vetoed many reform proposals, which was – as is widely believed – related to his bad relationship with the ruling AKP. His 62 vetoes were a record since the times of Mustafa Kemal and included the law on the ombudsman, one constitutional amendment package, a public administration reform supported by the EU, the law on associations, etc. Similarly, Václav Klaus vetoed several laws as both the chairman of the main opposition party and later a president, for example the civil service reform. Just like in the ECECs, there is a lack of consensus on the EU reforms and the Turkish political elites are mainly concerned with power struggle, i.e. short-term interests, which makes it difficult to make big decisions and take necessary steps even between elections.

In Turkey and in the Czech Republic the politics of personalities was also translated into the support for leaders that would show the EU what "crackerjacks we are" – former Czech Prime Minister and current president, Václav Klaus, once said that the EU should be joining the Czech Republic and not the other way round. Prime Minister Erdoğan stated "Turkey is a powerful country that should not act on the basis of what others would say. Instead, they should consider what Turkey would say" (Uslu 2009). Such stances appear among some Turkish intellectuals as well. A former Turkish diplomat Mehmet Oğutçu (2009) wrote for *Today's Zaman* that he would tell those opposed to Turkish accession in the EU that the Turks are not excited about it either, which he claims "serves as a cold shower and strong reminder that Turkey should not be taken for granted and are not clinging to anybody's coattails." This approach runs the danger of alienating the public – as Kaldor and Vejvoda (1997: 71) note, in the "absence of a public sphere, a space for true discussion in a sharply polarized situation, leads often to a political cynicism and apathy."

The supporters' camp comprises mainly of business and liberal circles, most of the Turkish civil society, the Kurdish minority, and moderate Islamist forces. Some of the groups believe that the EU reforms will improve their position in the society; others are convinced that it will make Turkey more stable politically and economically and, thus, increase its power and security. The AKP is largely pro-EU and it declared EU membership a primary goal of its foreign policy (Gülmez 2008).[14] On the other hand, some believe that the party started to follow loose rather than deep Europeanization (Öniş and Yılmaz 2009). Uğur and Yankaya (2008) give two reasons for the slow-down in the reform activity of the AKP since 2004. First, they wanted to address their more religious electorate by, for example, proposing to recriminalize adultery or re-opening the headscarf issue. Second, they tried to face the criticism from the nationalist circles reflected mainly on the Kurdish and Cyprus issues.

The latter could be clearly seen in the 2007 AKP election manifesto, which restated its dedication to the continuation of the accession process that was defined as a process of restructuring in Turkey but held that the Cyprus issue could not serve as a prerequisite in the Turkey-EU relations. Both explanations indicate their relatively short-term orientation within the election cycle. The party could then use the mixed messages coming from the EU and the positions of Germany and France to justify the change in direction even though many other countries expressed their support and the Turkish public remained positive about the benefits of EU membership. It seems, however, that the voters that supported the party in the 2007 national election because of the reform program "punished" the party for the slow-down with less votes in the 2009 local election and forced them to restart (at least rhetorically) the reform process. AKP has always closely followed the directions of public support and its pro-reform turn in 2001 was much affected by a very strict monitoring of public attitudes that were at the time highly supportive of EU membership and pro-EU reforms (Uğur and Yankaya 2008).[15]

Lagendijk partially relates the drop in public support to the domestic politics arguing that as the Turkish politicians did not put the EU in the forefront of their interests, the people started to think that if it was not important for politicians, why it should be for them (Doğan 2009d). By and large, however, the EU debate is very immature and limited and it addresses only specific sensitive issues being for a long time hijacked by the debate on secularism on the one hand and nationalism on the other. While some believe that the EU influence can help in solving these persistent problems, others blame the EU for inappropriate interference with domestic politics. Dümanli (2005) asserts that

> because the opposition has a blurry EU vision, it does not have a basic discourse analysis either . . . If a public opinion poll were conducted today, the public wouldn't know what the opposition is objecting to because it does not concretize its rejections or reflect them on the people.

This is only confirmed in the EB surveys, where those who expressed their opposition to EU membership were not able to provide any reasons for their position.

When compared with the political parties in the ECECs, we find several similarities. The main arguments of the opponents in the Czech Republic were the fear of losing national sovereignty, feeling of being treated as an unequal partner, and – on the side of the right-wing politicians – the socialist policies and practices of the Brussels' bureaucracy. From the relevant parties, it was the right-wing ODS and its former chairman and then president of the country, Václav Klaus, who focused on the rhetoric of defending Czech national interests while emphasizing the economic benefits of EU membership. Their position was much affected by the party's loss of office in 1998 and the lost elections in 2002. Despite the party's official line and the strengthening of the nationalist-populist orientation since the late 1990s, ODS voters displayed very high support for EU membership, a situation similar to what we witness with the CHP. The other Eurosceptic party was the extreme-left Communist party.

Here, relations with MS also played a role. For example, the chairman of the Bavarian Christian Social Union (CSU), Edmund Stoiber, during the election battle stated that the Beneš decrees[16] were incompatible with EU values. He also demanded the abolishment of the decrees as a pre-condition for Czech EU membership and at one point said that the country was not ready for membership, which played into the cards for some Czech Eurosceptics, who claimed that the EU provides Germany with the possibility to exploit the country. Stoiber was later joined by the Hungarian Prime Minister, Viktor Orbán, who said in his election campaign that the abolishment of the Beneš decrees should be a pre-condition for both the Czech Republic and Slovakia (which provided former Prime Minister and opposition leader Vladimír Mečiar with much ammunition for his election campaign). Austria requested the same from the Czechs – together with the demand to close down the Temelín nuclear power plant. This rise of nationalism negatively affected the Czech – and Slovak – attitudes to the EU.

In Poland, the parties were largely supportive of EU membership even though they all proclaimed their goal of defending national interests in the EU. The most critical parties were Self-defense (Samoobrona), a populist party led by Andrzej Lepper, and the extreme-right League of Polish Families (LPR). The former was critical of the EU in specific issues where defending the interests of particular groups was meant to increase its votes. The proliferation of the party anti-EU program took place in the late stages of negotiations, when the most sensitive chapters were open, and as such it could address their specific concerns. We have not reached that moment in Turkey yet but a similar development could be expected.

Another strong element came from some religious circles. Even though the Pope John Paul II supported Polish EU membership, the very conservative Catholic radio station Radio Maryja and the pro-clerical, religious fundamentalist LPR were strongly opposed to it. LPR's arguments were mainly cultural, when it claimed that the EU would destroy "Polish conscience and culture" and that the Poles would disappear in the EU as both a nation and a people. It blamed the EU for embracing abortions and euthanasia. Thus, this party has some parallels with the Turkish religious fundamentalists, who also rely mostly on cultural and anti-modernity arguments. Its position could be – even though on different grounds – also compared to that of the MHP in Turkey in its use of emotional language to mobilize the public and to highlight the issues of national sovereignty, independence, and land ownership.

The two most anti-EU parties in Poland, Self-defense and LPR, were closely related to the peasants in Poland. Given the large share of the agricultural sector in Turkey and the relatively small size of the farms, many of which are family farms, the negotiations of the agricultural chapter will also become very controversial. Two things, however, might weaken this argument – first, the Common Agricultural Policy (CAP) needs substantial reform before Turkey joins the EU; second, with economic development, the number of people employed in agriculture in Turkey will decrease, which will in time wane the polarization of the farmers' attitudes.

Also in Hungary, the negotiations increased the level of party Euroscepticism. The Independent Party of Smallholders, Agrarian Workers and Citizens (FKGP) combining in its program national socialism, anti-cosmopolitanism, and populism (Márkus 1998) labeled the EU as a possible threat to Hungarian national sovereignty and national interests. It became less critical after the negotiations were opened perceiving EU membership as a tool for increasing the country's economic power. The Christian-Democratic People's Party (KDNP) used to be supportive of the EU but its position changed after the lost election in 1998. It asserted that EU membership would mean a loss of Hungarian sovereignty. The most Eurosceptic party was the extreme right, populist, and nationalist Party of Hungarian Justice and Life (MIÉP) that also saw the EU as a threat to Hungarian national sovereignty and asserted that the cost of the EU membership was too high for Hungary. They demanded that Hungary wait for better conditions of membership. In Slovakia, the debate on the issue was very limited because the country was mainly concerned with catching up with its neighbors. There the Eurosceptic parties also focused on the issues of national sovereignty and national identity while mostly supportive of the economic benefits (the extreme-right platform Slovak National Party and the social democratic party Direction [Smer]).

The analysis of the current situation in Turkey and comparison with the ECECs allow us to conclude that as regards the political parties, Euroscepticism is mainly articulated by opposition parties and as such could be in many cases identified as part of the electoral strategy. Also, it is more evident with nationalist populist parties who support EU membership but are critical of many aspects of accession negotiations highlighting the relevance to national identity. So, while the ideological factor plays a role, domestic competition seems to have higher explanatory power. On the other hand, the debate on EU membership remained rather embryonic in the ECECs throughout the accession process and it is still the case in Turkey even though it tends to mature when the more sensitive chapters are opened and with the rapprochement of the accession date.

The issue of EU membership and the EU policies and processes did not develop into a strong party cleavage during the accession negotiations in the ECECs and the same result can be expected in Turkey. Still, the impact of membership affects the development of party positions and voters' attitudes towards the EU, thus, it shapes the possible future European cleavage. Given the meaning of EU membership, it is rather unlikely that a hard Eurosceptic political party would emerge in Turkey, while as the experience with the EU becomes more tangible we can expect changes in the debate where Eurosceptic and Eurooptimist positions become more mature and accommodate the specific issues at stake. Until the more sensitive chapters are open, the debate will focus mostly on the national interests and identity debate. Eurosceptic positions will be found both among left- and right-wing parties and will tend to be stronger in "outsider" parties. As in the ECECs, the issue will become more internalized but it will not *dominate* the political debate except for tense moments such as the ratification of the accession agreement.

In need of a communication strategy

Research has shown that people make decisions about things they do not understand using information regarding something they know well (Martinotti and Stefanizzi, cited in McLaren 2002). The general perception of the EU in Turkey can be summarized by two main positions – everything about the EU is a panacea, which can lead to too high expectations and subsequently disappointment because the EU cannot deliver the imagined goals, or the EU is a source of all evil based on claims that the EU is trying to divide Turkey up. Bahadır Kaleağası, the representative of Turkish Industrialists' and Businessmen's Association (TÜSIAD) in Brussels, commented on the situation saying, "This mentality is unhealthy for Turkish negotiations and can only be solved through educational reform" (Özerkan 2007). The problem of limited knowledge about the issues surrounding EU accession and membership is also reflected by Aybar et al. (2007: 330), who argue that in Turkey "judgments about the pertinent issues are based more on speculation and stereotyping and less on sound knowledge."

It is crucial that the public becomes better informed in order to decrease the appeal of an undemocratic and/or populist propaganda and unrealistic expectations. In Turkey, the accession process affects the redefinition of power in the society, shifting the balance between secularists and Islamists, nationalists and liberals, civilian and military forces, center and periphery (Tocci 2007) and the EU debate has a profound impact on foreign policy issues such as the relations with Armenia, Iran, USA, and Iraq. The situation is much more complicated than was the case with the ECECs, and the EU needs to understand how these various factors interact in order to pursue a successful communication strategy that would sustain public support for the much needed reforms.

The Turkish public feels that they are badly informed about the EU – more than a half believe that it is not easy to find information about the EU (EB 65), i.e. their information is gained through their relation to other events without any substantial knowledge about the institutions and competences of the EU. Furthermore, the objective measurement of their knowledge also shows that it is far below the EU-27 average (EB 70 indicates only 17 percent, less than a half of the EU average). For example, the aforementioned 2009 Bahçeşehir University survey pointed out that one-fourth of Turks did not know if the country was an EU MS or not (*Hürriyet Daily News* 2009b).

The more information people have about the EU, the less threatening it becomes (Inglehart 1970, Janssen 1991, Schuck and de Vreese 2006) and they have fewer tendencies to oppose it based on misperceptions. Without an objective information campaign, the public would not be able to make their own judgment and would have to rely on images as drawn by others only, which could be detrimental to the process of accession. It is not only the government but all representatives of the various sectors of the Turkish society that truly believe in the benefits of EU membership that should explain to the public why to extend their support throughout the accession process.

A successful communication plan needs to include "policy dialogues, jawboning, learning, persuasion and the like" (Checkel 2000). Both the EU and the Turkish government and civil society have to cooperate in changing the image of the EU in Turkey and of Turkey in the EU to a more realistic one. The EU has prepared grants that would improve the knowledge of the EU in Turkey and fight prejudices, doubts, and lack of knowledge in both the EU and Turkey. More projects such as *On the Road*[17] co-financed by the EU's Cultural Bridges program or the EU Quiz National Championship[18] are needed to create higher awareness of the EU and its MS on a less political level.

It is the responsibility of the government but also the civil society to increase the knowledge and actively engage in a dynamic communication strategy. An example of a successful lobbying is the PLATFORM initiative that joins together over 200 NGOs and lobbies for EU membership in Turkey and in the EU MS. The various business chambers have also become more active, namely, the Istanbul Chamber of Commerce (ITO), Union of Chambers and Commodity Exchanges of Turkey (TOBB), TÜSIAD,[19] and the Economic Development Foundation (IKV), which is organizing a series of conferences in both Brussels and Turkey under a campaign called *YES to Turkey*. These civil society groups often bring attention to questions that are deemed extremely sensitive in Turkey such as freedom of speech and demand reforms so that the accession process can continue. For instance ITO, TÜSIAD, and TOBB have all requested the government to abolish the infamous Article 301.

Several of these NGOs are business organizations and some own media groups and as such have a big impact on the formulation of public opinion.[20] Their relationship with the government has, however, not been very strong and never regained the 2004 momentum, when a well-executed communication strategy was put into place. Since the official opening of the negotiations the government has given up much of the originally proposed plans. A more positive signal was the first meeting between the government and the NGOs in March 2009, which aimed at establishing mechanisms to involve the NGOs in the Turkish debate on its EU policies and agendas (*Hürriyet Daily News* 2009c).

Conclusion

The main problem of the EU discussion in Turkey is that it has not matured yet. In all ECECs, the *pro* camp's rhetoric became sophisticated long before that of the *anti* camp, but in many cases the Eurosceptics presented tempting and persuasive arguments by playing the emotional card. The parties' positions also often lacked coherence and consistency and have at times changed from strong support to mild opposition or vice versa. Altogether this contributed to relative instability of public opinion towards the EU and EU membership.

The Turkish case is no different. The Turkish public in its majority wants to see their country closely linked with the West but the elites often exclude them from an open discussion on the costs and benefits of membership. Democracy is about discussion through which the best policy is found and for that, the public must be given an arena for open discourse about the conditions of EU membership. A substantial level of democratization is a pre-condition for such level of dialogue to develop. However, the EU's internal problems and ambiguous attitude to further enlargement (and the strong perception of these) towards CCs makes the public more hesitant to support EU membership and all its conditions than in the past.

The example of the ECECs shows that the support for membership in a CC is not directed solely to the results of accession negotiations or the vague notions of democratization, modernization, and westernization but the realities of daily activities of the EU, including the learning process of the political elites and the public. As mentioned earlier, once the negotiations start, EU membership turns from a "dream into a reality" with all its positive sides and drawbacks. Turks are learning, just like the Czechs, Hungarians, Poles, and Slovaks did before them, that the EU will have an increasing influence on domestic policies and politics even prior to membership. Many do not welcome this idea, especially as they believe that the EU will never accept them as an equal partner, if at all. However, in both cases the close relationship between the reform process and EU membership greatly limits the possibility of the emergence of a hard Eurosceptic force because it would mean an open opposition to the fundamental goals of foreign policy and undermine the process as such.

Many Eurosceptics in Turkey believe that the Western forces want to make Turkey weaker just like some attribute the dissolution of the Ottoman Empire after World War I to them. The effect of the past is clearly present here, as it was in the ECECs, where years under Soviet dominance affected the willingness to transfer decision making to another level and resulted in a less enthusiastic integrationist attitude. It seems that despite their divergent legacies, in both the ECECs and in Turkey, the issues of national sovereignty and identity play an important role in assessing the trends of Euroscepticism. To win public support, the EU accession must be beneficial economically but it should not be seen or interpreted as "hurting the national pride" of the CC. Economic factors set in later as the effects of membership become clearer, which explains why this debate has been largely absent in Turkey so far. Bulbul (2006) showed that AKP deputies considered religious, cultural, and historical reasons the key obstacle to Turkish EU membership while CHP deputies listed economic reasons first, which might reflect their ideological backgrounds. As cultural and party factors are currently the dominant issues of the EU discourse in Turkey, the public debate has so far largely ignored the economic impact of EU accession, which is expected to enter the debate later. With no possibility of a near future EU entry, the cultural opponents have now plenty of space to "operate" the public opinion.

Turkey needs to proceed with the reforms. Presenting the economic benefits of future membership and fortifying the democratization process would strengthen the pro-EU camp and make the accession process more stable and transparent. For most Turks, the EU is mostly about economic welfare but as the economic issues were rarely discussed until now, it might be contributing to the negative trends in public opinion. Moreover, the proposals that Turkey would even as a full EU MS be permanently excluded from some benefits of the single market such as the free movement of labor weakens the pro camp and fuels those groups who claim that the EU does not and never will treat Turkey fairly.

The Turkish supporters of EU accession and the associated reforms are well aware of the need to revive the enthusiasm of the public (Köylü 2009) – at least to some level of the previous support. The decrease in public support does not need to be a permanent trend – Szczerbiak (2001) claimed that Euroscepticism was something like an oxymoron in the Polish environment and Slomczynski and Shabad argued in 2003 that the negative change in public attitudes in Poland was the most striking of all CCs, calling it "dramatic" (503). Time, however, has not only shown that the rapid decrease in Poland was only temporary but also the possibility of high volatility of public support. On the other hand, Hungary, which was first labeled a country with little signs of Euroscepticism has seen a steady decline in public support since 2002.

When linking the support for EU membership and for the reform process, the parties and the public try to evaluate the costs and benefits of accession and of negotiations. The former evaluates how the public would react and how they can maximize the vote, the latter tries to measure the impact on their lives. The rational decision is, however, influenced by many other factors such as speech acts, perceptions, and estimates rather than objective decision because they face the problem of verification. The example of AKP, where proceeding with reforms had little rational obstacles and yet the party chose to step down the efforts, indicates that other variables interfere with the decisions and attitudes.

In the future, it would be very helpful to conduct research on the Turkish media and how they present EU membership, whether as an opportunity or as risk and a threat. This would be particularly useful when the debate becomes more saturated later in the accession negotiations to evaluate how it affects public opinion in Turkey. Also, more sophisticated surveys of public opinion are necessary to allow the researchers to identify the true reasons behind the support or lack of support for EU membership in Turkey and the general trends.

Notes

1 There are various difficulties with measuring the Turkish public attitudes to the EU. For example, in 2009 a survey was published that claimed that 71 percent of Turks support EU membership, which would have been an increase by 29 percent from the autumn 2008 Eurobarometer (EB) survey and the highest support since 2002 (*Today's Zaman* 2009b). For the shortcomings of the various opinion polls on Turkish attitudes to EU membership, see Şenyuva (2006). We choose to use EB surveys in order to be able to compare the results in the ECECs and Turkey. EB data is not fully reliable because the concepts measured can have various meanings in the national contexts but it provides the best available pool of data to compare the five countries in question at the moment.
2 Bulbul (2006) also found that the most Eurosceptic groups among the Justice and Development Party (AKP) and (Republican People's Party) CHP MPs were academicians, teachers, and educators, which he explains by their relatively low exposure to the EU but we find this explanation rather random and not well substantiated.
3 Thirty-nine percent in Czechoslovakia, 17 percent in Hungary, and 20 percent in Poland.
4 The considerably negative public attitude in the Netherlands receives much less attention.
5 The crisis was resolved after intense negotiations with a compromise – privileged partnership was left out and instead a clause on "absorption capacity" was added to the Copenhagen criteria.
6 For example, in autumn 2007, before Turkey launched the campaign in Northern Iraq, *Today's Zaman* printed an article titled "EU says 'terrorists,' European press says 'freedom fighters.'" In June 2009, the media were reporting how some European conservative parties and the extreme right use the issue of Turkish accession in the European Parliament election campaign. They used examples from Austria, Bulgaria, France, Germany, and the Netherlands. The newspapers also report how those who oppose the Armenian lobby get harassed.
7 The period of the Tanzimat reforms that started in the 1830s marked the beginning of the process of adopting European values and principles.
8 Turkish journalist and commentator, Mehmet Ali Birand (2007), argued that the government was playing "victim by pretending to be the government that is prevented by the bad Europeans from doing everything in its power to get Turkey into the EU."
9 Bulbul (2006) found that among CHP and AKP deputies, those who could speak Kurdish displayed 100 percent support for EU membership.
10 Çarkoğlu (2003) found that the only party against EU membership as such was the pro-Islamist Felicity Party (Saadet Partisi), which however has not been in parliament

since its establishment in 2001. Given its low electoral support (in July 2007 national election it was 2.34 percent of the vote) it is very unlikely that it would be able to enter the parliament in the foreseeable future.

11 The PKK was originally supporting the Turkish EU membership process but since 2006 became rather critical thereof. For the analysis of this turn in support, see Uslu 2008.

12 Especially the problem of secularism should be seen as part of a more domestic than European debate for the EU does not have any specific requirements regarding this issue. CHP is blaming AKP for using the EU reforms to undermine secularism.

13 Gülmez also notes that some of the CHP MPs are Eurooptimists. As the party did not strengthen its position in the 2007 election, the Eurosceptic rhetoric might not have been considered successful. However, the 2007 election was in many ways specific, mainly due to the effects of the controversial presidential election of Abdullah Gül earlier that year and the positive economic results on the support of the ruling AKP. The party strengthened its support in the 2009 local elections, which is by many seen as a reaction to the AKP slow-down in implementing the EU reforms rather than to CHP's Euroscepticism.

14 For an analysis on the transformation of the Islamist movement into a pro-European one, see Tanyici 2003.

15 The other two factors they mention were the 1997 "soft coup" and the 1999 Helsinki decision.

16 The decrees were issued by Czechoslovak president Edvard Beneš in 1940–44, 1943–45, and in 1945. The most controversial part deals with the 1945 decree that led to the property confiscation of collaborators and traitors during the Nazi occupation and of ethnic Germans and Hungarians, except for those who themselves suffered under the Nazis. Based on these decrees, Germans and Hungarians were later expelled from the country. The deportations were agreed upon by the Allies at the Potsdam conference in 1945.

17 The *Yollarda – EU literature goes to Turkey/Turkish literature goes to Europe* will be visiting 24 cities throughout Turkey and 8 European cities in 2009 and 2010. More on http://www.goethe.de/ins/tr/lp/prj/cub/enindex.htm

18 It has been organized for students from more than a thousand high schools in 16 Turkish cities since 2007 by the Turkish Ministry of Education, the Commission's Delegation in Turkey and the EU Information Network.

19 For a more detailed account of TÜSIAD activities, see Uğur and Yankaya (2008).

20 The most profound example is the Doğan Yayın Holding that owns the most read newspapers, *Hürriyet*, *Millyet*, and *Radikal*, English written *Hürriyet Daily News*, and TV channels Kanal D, CNNTurk, Star TV, and Ultra Kablo TV.

7 Tug of war or lifelining

Central European views on Turkey's accession to the EU[1]

Armağan Emre Çakir and Angelika Gergelová

Introduction

Absorption capacity is a commonly used concept in discussions about the future enlargement of the European Union (EU). Oli Rehn, European Commissioner responsible for enlargement, defined this concept as the EU's ability to "take in new members while continuing to function effectively" (Rehn 2006). However, nowhere are the criteria of this effectiveness revealed, nor is there a consensus on the components where this effectiveness can be measured. For instance, the European Commission (2004a) divides the concept into the following components: geo-political dimension, economic dimension, internal market and related policies, agriculture, veterinary and phytosanitary issues, fisheries, regional and structural policy, justice and home affairs, and institutional and budgetary aspects. Elsewhere, however, the Commission indicates that "[t]he capacity of the Union to maintain the momentum of European integration as it enlarges has three main components: institutions, common policies, and budget" (European Commission 2006b).

Prior to every enlargement round, "absorption capacity" has been a concern of the EU, although maybe it was not termed as such in each case. For Turkey, this concept has had a special importance since the beginning of Turkey-EU relations as the EU has always been apprehensive of possible problems that could be associated with "absorbing" Turkey. Even as early as the year 1960, only one year after lodging the application for associate membership status and starting the associate membership negotiations with the European Economic Community (EEC), Turkey was told that with the Greek association agreement the EEC had given too many concessions to Greece, and was now cautious towards Turkey considering the problems of the Turkish economy (Birand 1990: 112–16).

Similar concerns were expressed in the Commission's opinion delivered in 1989 on Turkey's request for accession to the Community in 1987:

> Since its third enlargement and the entry into force of the Single Act, the Community has been in a state of flux. It has entered into a new stage in its development which, on account of the importance of the objectives at stake, requires all its energy. Indeed, the success of this stage will make it possible subsequently to achieve European union, the ultimate objective of the Treaties.

> The tasks involved are great and complex . . . This reason alone is sufficient for the Commission to consider that it would be unwise, with regard both to the candidate countries and to the Member States (MS), to envisage the Community becoming involved in new accession negotiations before 1993 at the earliest, except in exceptional circumstances
>
> (European Commission 1989)

The year 2004 was a turning point for Turkey with reference to the absorption capacity of the EU. In this year, first, the EU decided to start the accession negotiations with Turkey. Second, the Treaty Establishing a Constitution for Europe was signed as a comprehensive blueprint for the future of the Union. Third, eight Central and Eastern European countries (CEECs) became members of the EU. This accession was the largest single enlargement in terms of landmass and people increasing the EU's absorption capacity concerns about further enlargement to include Turkey among a handful of other candidates (Bulgaria, Romania, Croatia, and the Republic of Macedonia). This chapter focuses on the period following this turning point. It reflects on how the debate on Turkey's accession in the four East Central European Countries (ECECs) is structured, how the official representatives of these countries frame this debate, and in which contexts the official positions of these countries towards Turkey are shaped.

Methodologically, the chapter focuses on the positions of the official executive representatives of the ECECs, namely, the heads of states, of the governments and, to some extent, of governmental political parties. With a view to trace the discourse and to find out how key executives engage in the debate concerning Turkish accession to the EU, mainly primary sources were analyzed such as official speeches or statements, governmental documents, programs of the political parties, press releases, and unofficial summaries. It was not possible to investigate the same types of documents in all four ECECs, for different actors chose a variety of channels to present their opinions on Turkey as a future member of the EU. Most of the primary sources used were found on the official websites of the heads of states, the governments, or the political parties. Equally important was the media coverage of the topic concerned.

We contacted the presidential and governmental offices or the governments' public relations department in each of the four countries. Consequently, we received documents which the official representatives of the executives considered to be the most important. In the case of the Czech Republic, these were speeches of the president; the Hungarian position was traced especially in press releases and for this chapter Slovakia presented an unofficial summary of the president's position as certain official documents were not accessible to the public.[2] Polish representatives supplied primarily official speeches of the president, press releases of the government, and party programs. Where relevant information was missing, we had to resort to secondary sources.

Apart from the heads of states and the governments, we also focused on governmental (coalition) parties for the purpose of this chapter, as they played a role in the executive. In a few cases, non-governmental political parties were referred to as well, as much as their representatives played an important role in the former government of the country and were influential in the fields of foreign policy or European affairs.

The chapter starts with an evaluation of the general approach of the political elites of the ECECs to Turkey's accession to the EU. It then analyzes this approach in more detail, dividing the concept of absorption capacity into three components – institutional aspects, budgetary/policy aspects, and cultural aspects. In the conclusion, we categorize and evaluate the findings of the arguments of the chapter within the framework of rationalist and constructivist paradigms.

Approach of the elites of the ECECs to Turkish accession

Official representatives of the ECECs frequently indicate that they should promote accession of other EU candidate countries. They believe that as former candidates, who themselves struggled to enter the EU not a long time ago, they should not impede accession of other countries searching for EU membership and fulfilling the Copenhagen criteria. They often refer to solidarity as a key principle of European integration. (Szymanski 2007b; Kaczynski 2007a; Král 2006; Batory 2006). Nonetheless, Turkey is not on their list of priorities; Poland focuses on its Eastern neighbors, especially Ukraine, and the other three countries concentrate primarily on the Western Balkans. Turkey's accession to the EU is usually mentioned as a part of official documents which are primarily dedicated to another issue such as the enlargement process in general, or EU membership prospects of Croatia or Ukraine. The Czech EU Presidency program while mentioning that accession negotiations with Turkey will continue, stated that the Presidency "will do everything to ensure that EU enlargement with . . . [Croatia] takes place as soon as possible," and thus prioritized Croatia over Turkey. Most of the references to Turkey found in the official statements of the governments or the heads of states are limited to general support for further development of close relationships or, in case they are more specific, for Turkey's EU membership.

The Czech president, Václav Klaus, favored the enlargement of the EU in general, saying that "any country, willing to participate in the European integration process, should have a chance to do it, on the condition of fulfilling the agreed-upon political, economic and social criteria." (Klaus 2006a). The Czech government is in favor of Turkey's EU bid, and has a relatively clearer view on Turkey than the governments of the other ECECs. The Czech president supported the opening of accession negotiations with Turkey in 2004 and the Czech EU Presidency program for the period from January to June 2009 included a proposition to open three chapters during its term, although opening two chapters with Turkey in each EU term presidency had become the common practice (Özerkan 2009b).

The former Prime Minister, Mirek Topolánek, officially supported the full membership bid and categorically refused any alternatives offered to Turkey such as privileged partnership, semi-membership, etc. (Vláda České republiky 2008). His main argument was that every country which fulfilled the membership criteria had the right to aspire for full membership in the Union (EurActiv 2008). This position was supported by other members of his government who were responsible for EU affairs or foreign policy of the Czech Republic. The problem of absorption capacity as such was not discussed, while the importance of Turkey as a strategic partner was mentioned quite often; for instance, the former Minister of Foreign Affairs, Karel Schwarzenberg, stressed that Turkey was of strategic importance for the EU and that it should become a member after undertaking the necessary reforms and fulfilling the accession criteria (Euroskop 2009).

The Civic Democratic Party (ODS), which was the main coalition party in the Czech Republic from 2006 to spring 2009, was also supportive of Turkey's accession to the EU. The Green Party, the smallest coalition partner in the Czech government, favored Turkish accession to the EU as well, although their reasoning was different from that of ODS. The Greens preferred deeper political integration potentially resulting in a federation, thus, they were in favor of further enlargement of the EU irrespective of the size of the candidate country, its culture, religion, etc. (see Sychra 2006). Nevertheless, they failed to show why there is a positive link between a federation and further EU enlargement, since federalist tendencies (deepening) are often seen as incompatible with enlargement. They also paid little attention to the Turkish EU membership bid, thus it is not possible to find a more detailed explanation in their official documents or speeches. The only member of the government that was clearly opposed to Turkish full membership in the EU was the Christian Democratic Union – Czechoslovak People's Party (KDU-ČSL).[3] They wanted to promote intensive cooperation and close relations between the EU and Turkey, but they preferred an alternative solution such as privileged partnership (their position was very similar to the one represented by the German CDU/CSU).

In Poland, the president, Lech Kaczyński, is a proponent of Turkish membership in the EU. The same can be said about the cabinets headed by Jarosław Kaczyński and then by his successor Donald Tusk. The official view is based on solidarity with other candidates who are said to have the same right to become members of the Union as the ECECs had. For Polish political elites Turkey's strategic role mainly with respect to energy security is important (Kaczynski 2007a). The opinions of Polish political parties towards the Turkish EU membership bid are not uniform. Civic Platform, Self-defence, the Democratic Left Alliance and Social Democracy of Poland are in favor of Turkish accession, while The League of Polish Families and Law and Justice Party are rather against it (Szymanski 2007b: 556).

The Hungarian view emerged gradually. Before the European Commission recommended in October 2004 to open accession negotiations with Turkey, the government presented no clear position towards Turkish membership, and only declared that no candidate country that met the Copenhagen criteria could be denied membership in the EU (Batory 2006: 5). Among the candidate countries, Croatia or Ukraine, were of particular significance for Hungary and hardly any documents focused specifically on Turkey alone even though Hungary is generally supportive of Turkish accession. On the occasion of the start of the accession talks, the Hungarian Ministry of Foreign Affairs made an official declaration entitled "EU Foreign Ministers' Decision on Croatia and Turkey" which contained the following passage:

The beginning of the talks is an important political message to the Turkish society, and will reinforce the position of the forces, which are committed to the European perspective. It is in our interest for the largest possible part of the Turkish society to support the efforts of the Turkish government for the furthering of profound democratic reforms, and for the taking over and the practical implementation of the *acquis*. We find it important that the negotiating framework emphasizes the necessity to take into consideration the absorption capacity of the EU.

(Ministry of Foreign Affairs of the Republic of Hungary 2005)

Slovakia too highlights the importance of fulfilling the EU requirements. The president of the country, Ivan Gašparovič, acknowledged that accession of any country, geographically located on the European continent, should be subject only to compliance with Copenhagen criteria. Gašparovič is in favor of further enlargement of the EU if the candidate country meets all the criteria but also states that full compliance does not necessarily result in the EU's obligation to accept Turkey as a member (Moravčík 2009). While he articulated Slovakia's support for the Turkish EU membership bid, Slovak representatives raised some concerns regarding the political criteria, including the Cyprus issue, the Turkish-Armenian relationship, and the problem of the so-called Armenian genocide. However, it is the president who represents the official position of Slovakia on the issue of enlargement.

When it comes to evaluating Turkey's accession with reference to the concept of absorption capacity, or to the possible specific effects thereof on the ECECs, official documents and declarations made by political representatives of the ECECs usually lack detailed statements. Nevertheless, some individual arguments can still be found and categorized into three main components:[4] institutional aspects, budgetary/policy aspects, and cultural aspects.

Institutional aspects

The institutional structure of the EU was one of the main concerns of the ECECs during their accession negotiations. Especially the Czech Republic and Hungary refused to accept fewer seats in the European Parliament (EP) and insisted on having 22 seats as the EU-15 MS of approximately the same size – Belgium, Portugal, and Greece. Poland demanded the same number of seats (54) as Spain had, and in the Lisbon Treaty was promised the same right as Germany, France, the UK, Italy, and Spain – to have a permanent Advocate-General in the European Court of Justice. These countries also tried to maximize voting weights in the Council of the EU. This may suggest that being very sensitive about their relative power in European institutions; the Czech Republic, Hungary, Poland, and Slovakia would have worries about Turkey gaining power in the institutions of the EU.

It is difficult to predict the exact number of seats Turkey would receive in the EP after accession to the EU, as well as the voting weight it would be assigned in the Council. However, under the current system of vote distribution, Turkey would receive relatively strong voting power in the EU institutions comparable to the large

MS and disproportionate to its GDP.[5] Interestingly, an examination of the positions of these countries vis-à-vis Turkish EU membership reveals that institutional implications of Turkish membership is not a substantial concern for the ECECs.

The Czech Republic is the only ECEC that has had the experience in the EU Presidency, and, thus played an important role in the Union's external relations. In the country, the president, the government, and political parties forming both the government and the opposition have slightly different approaches towards Turkey's membership from an institutional perspective. The position of President Klaus, concerning Turkish accession to the EU, has been clear and consistent, and always contextualized within the broader *finalité politique* of the EU debate. Klaus is one of the most fervent Czech critics of the Constitutional Treaty and Lisbon Treaty, and frequently comments on the present institutional structure of the EU, and on the direction of European integration, being very negative about further deepening. In this framework, as indicated earlier, Klaus is in favor of Turkey's accession to the EU provided that Turkey complies with all the criteria set in advance.

Among his many arguments presented in favor of Turkish accession, Klaus indicates that he strongly opposes the idea of ever closer union, which he equates with neverending unification, deepening of European integration, and transforming the EU into a federal state (Klaus 2005b). For him, admission of a large country would weaken federalist tendencies. He expects Turkey to suspend the trend towards deepening of European integration. However, he does not clearly distinguish between institutional aspects, such as majority voting or strengthening of supranationalism, and deepening of integration in a more general way, and fails to explain why precisely it would be impossible to move towards political union with Turkey inside the EU.[6]

The right-wing liberal-conservative political representatives of the Czech Republic, especially members of the ODS, to some extent share Klaus's view. Yet, neither the Prime Minister nor other Czech ministers representing the ODS address institutional aspects when it comes to impacts of Turkish membership on the Czech Republic. The same holds true for the Greens and Christian Democrats, the other two governmental parties, who have not raised this question irrespective of whether or not they support Turkey as a future member of the EU.

The position of Polish president Lech Kaczyński is very similar to that of Klaus: "the policy of enlargement – yes; deepening – not necessary" (Szymanski 2007b: 550). Again, it is not certain what exactly Kaczyński means by deepening, for he does not explain his position in more detail – thus we do not know whether this argument concerns primarily EU institutions or, for example, policies of the Union. Elsewhere, institutional questions are not invoked by Polish political elite in this context.

As for Hungary, the Christian democratic Hungarian Democratic Forum (MDF) is the strongest opponent of Turkish membership among parliamentary political parties. Their argument is that when Turkey becomes a full member, it "would become very influential within the EU's decision-making bodies and institutions" (cited in Batory 2006: 9). In other words, the party raises concerns about negative impact of Turkish accession on the position of Hungary in the EU institutions. Other representatives of Hungarian political elites do not seem to address this particular question.

In the case of Slovakia too, institutional problems that may arise in the event of Turkish membership are not considered to be of primary importance. In a report presented to the Slovak Parliament before adopting an official position on the opening of accession negotiations with Turkey, institutional arrangements were mentioned briefly in connection with Turkish national interests which might differ from the rest of the EU and as such may pose some problems during negotiations and decision-making processes after Turkey becomes a member of the Union (*Vláda Slovenskej republiky* 2004). However, the report fails to mention any specific interests or to explain in detail why these interests could lead to a decision-making deadlock.

The discussion earlier suggests that institutional matters are not of immediate concern for the ECECs in the case of Turkish membership to the EU. Detailed arguments have not been developed in this issue. The strongest support for Turkey's gaining influence in the EU institutions comes from the Czech president Klaus in connection with his anti-federalist stance and a negative notice with respect to Turkish influence also appears in some Slovak governmental texts.

Budgetary and policy aspects

There is little dispute that Turkish membership will be costly for the EU. Thus, budgetary and policy aspects are among the main concerns when it comes to impact of Turkish membership on the EU or on individual MS. However, calculating the exact amount of this cost is not an easy task. According to one estimate (Gros 2005: 3), Turkey may receive up to 0.20 percent of the EU's budget.

The ECECs are critical of the preparation procedure of the EU's budget. In 2005, when the UK Presidency presented the proposals for the 2007–13 financial perspective to the General Affairs Council, Poland and the Czech Republic together with the Baltic States and Portugal considered them "unacceptable" and "a giant leap backwards" (EurActiv 2005).[7] Those critical of the Union's budget structure, tend to be more supportive of Turkish accession, for they perceive it as a chance to introduce necessary reforms. Should the current rules be applicable when Turkey enters the EU, the country would be eligible for a significant part of the overall expenditures of the Union. Thus, thorough reforms are unavoidable. This position was, for example, held by the Czech president as well as the Czech government which put the revision of economic and social cohesion policies among the priorities of the Czech EU Presidency.

The ECECs acknowledge that both the EU and Turkey are confronted with major challenges, hence all the parties concerned need to undergo reforms. They highlight the opportunities for economic development in both the EU MS and Turkey. This is confirmed by the analyses of economic consequences of the last two enlargement rounds (2004 and 2007). The ECECs underscore that enlargement had positive impact not only on the newcomers but also on the whole Union. This suggests that the official representatives of these countries are generally rather supportive of

Turkish accession. Thus, the key documents focus mostly on specific opportunities stemming from the integration of a large dynamic market into the EU. The ECECs expect to profit from the growth in trade with Turkey and from investment opportunities (especially in the area of industry, infrastructure, and energy). More detailed analyses of the economic relations between Turkey and the EU can be found in all the ECECs' political communication (e.g. Batory 2006, Král 2006, Szymanski 2006b, *Vláda Slovenskej republiky* 2004).

In March 2009 the Czech EU Presidency organized a conference that aimed at evaluating the five years since the 2004 enlargement. The Czech Prime Minister, Mirek Topolánek, and Deputy Prime Minister responsible for EU affairs, Alexandr Vondra, highlighted the expediency of the last two enlargement rounds for both the old and new members referring to the data from a report drafted by the European Commission (2009), which pointed out that the largest enlargement in the EU's history had been a real economic success. They anticipate that a similar scenario can be expected regarding Turkish accession.

The structure of Turkish economy and the different character of its labor market is another matter that is discussed by the ECECs political representatives. They often highlight that while the Turkish GDP per capita is relatively low,[8] the economic environment is very dynamic and has a great potential stemming from the positive demographic structure.[9] For the ECECs, Turkey's market structure and young population are closely related to the issue of free movement of labor. For them, this is a particularly sensitive topic because they themselves were subject to transitional periods imposed on them by most members of the EU-15. The ECECs representatives consider these measures unsubstantiated.

The Czech Republic attempted to play a more pro-active role when it identified the abolition of all single market barriers as one of the key priorities of the Czech EU Presidency. The Czech representatives suggest (along with the other ECECs) that restricting free movement of labor is not only unfair, but also disadvantageous for the EU as a whole because the benefits for the host country are foregone.[10] The official representatives of the ECECs invoke the same logic when it comes to Turkey. However, some actors in the ECECs such as the Slovak Ministry of Foreign Affairs, claim that proposals for permanent exclusion of Turks from the free movement of labor within the EU or, at least, long-term transitional periods will have to be seriously considered (*Vláda Slovenskej republiky* 2004: 6).

The Common Agricultural Policy (CAP) and Structural Funds seem to be the two areas where the ECECs' official statements emphasize mostly the negative economic consequences of Turkish membership. They reckon that Turkey will be entitled to high financial contributions. The ECECs are net recipients from the EU budget, and are eligible mainly for funds under the Convergence objective of the EU Cohesion Policy. All the regions in the Czech Republic (except for Prague), Slovakia (except for the Bratislavský region), Hungary (except for the Közép-Magyarország region around Budapest) and Poland are covered by the Objective One that was designed for regions with GDP below 75 per cent of the EU average. The ECECs' governments take into account the impact of Turkish accession when assessing the plans to redraft the current redistribution mechanisms. The critical voices argue that should the redistribution mechanisms remain unchanged, the gains of the ECECs, who currently belong to the group of the net recipients from the EU budget, would deteriorate.

For example, the Hungarian critics of Turkish accession emphasize that Turkey is "a large and underdeveloped country, the incorporation of which would put a strain on the current EU budget. Turkey would also increase regional disparities within the EU, it being considerably poorer than any of the new Member States" (Batory 2006: 8). In Slovakia, concerns are raised regarding regional disparities, which some believe would become difficult to eliminate as a result of Turkish accession, and it would become one of the focal challenges for the EU. The government has stated that not only would the ECECs be negatively affected by becoming statistically wealthier but also that special attention must be paid to agriculture claiming that if reforms remain inadequate or are postponed, significant transitional periods for Turkey would have to be applied (*Vláda Slovenskej republiky* 2004: 6). Concurrently, the Slovak government frequently notes that it is very difficult to assess the real impact of Turkey's entry on the EU and individual MS, because both the European policies and the character of Turkish economy might change significantly by the end of the accession negotiations.

All in all, economic concerns do not seem to have played a major role so far in the opinion formation of the ECECs' elites. The debate in Poland and the Czech Republic is rather positive in nature. In Poland, potential negative consequences are sometimes mentioned by those, who try to analyze alternatives to Turkish full membership, but they rarely reach the political level. As far as Slovakia is concerned, arguments regarding economic aspects point to the necessary reforms in both the EU and Turkey, rather than drawing attention to potential economic burdens Turkish membership may bring. Likewise, the Czech Republic is focusing primarily on internal reforms of the EU's policies. Hungarians seem to be the most critical and cautious of Turkish accession on economic grounds emphasizing the potential burden Turkish accession may pose to the budget of the EU.

Cultural aspects

In the ECECs, the discussion of the Turkish EU membership often brings up questions of European identity. This is a very complex concept, the definition of which is beyond the scope of this chapter. The question is whether a common European identity exists, how it is formed and defined, what it is constituted by, and what can be regarded as "European" in the sense of sharing a European identity. Basically, when considering the case of Turkey, two main approaches can be identified: first, there is a political approach in terms of "objective" criteria, among which democracy, the rule of law, and the protection of human rights are the most important ones when it comes to accession of new members to the EU.[11]

This approach is adopted by the official documents of the EU, which can be easily illustrated, for example, in the wording of the preamble to the Treaty Establishing a Constitution for Europe and its successor, the Lisbon Treaty. Though there were heated debates about, for instance, whether or not to refer to God or to Christianity as a source of European heritage, such concepts were not included in the final text. Second, a cultural, more "subjective" approach plays an important role when it comes to the definition of European identity. In the particular case of Turkey this discussion mostly focuses on the religion and modern history of Turkey. While the ECECs' executives generally highlight the salience of the first type of defining European identity, the cultural arguments are also often brought up by individuals and political parties both to support and oppose the Turkish EU bid.

The Czech Christian Democrats consider full membership of Turkey incompatible with the founding principles of the EU (*KDU-ČSL* 2006: 85). For them, European identity is based on the Judeo-Christian foundations, which are irreconcilable with Turkey as a Muslim country. Therefore, the accession of a Muslim country is not acceptable (Král 2006: 13). Almost the same arguments can be found in the statements of the Slovak Christian Democratic Movement (KDH) that opposed the opening of the accession negotiations with Turkey because of its non-European cultural and religious traditions (Hrušovský 2004). In other words, these two parties believe that EU enlargement is conditional on cultural aspects, religion being the most important for them. Both Czech and Slovak Christian Democrats then also refer to the issue of human rights, such as the rights of women and minorities, which falls rather under political, thus more objective or technical conditionality defined by accession criteria.[12] Nationalist politicians in the ECECs also regard Turkey as incompatible with European identity using the cultural approach. The Slovak National Party (SNS) indicates that they strongly oppose Turkish membership in the EU because the country has a very different culture based on Islam. Ján Slota, the head of the party, while making a link between Islam and fundamentalism, labeled Turkey as dangerous for Europe (SNS 2006).

Other decision makers in the ECECs usually present a more tolerant position with regard to cultural and religious diversity. They also use the cultural card but for a different purpose. For Klaus, "Europe" must be clearly distinguished from "the EU." He claims that the former is a continent whose culture and civilization has been influenced by Turks (or, more precisely, by their ancestors), the latter is a "man-made" organization. He puts it as follows:

> Turkey will be in the future entering the EU, not Europe. Turkey will – I hope – get a chance to enter the man-made, time-determined institution, called the European Union. There is no membership in a – for centuries spontaneously evolving, geographically delineated – European continent."
>
> (Klaus 2005a)

He articulates his support for diversity brought by a large, culturally different country and emphasizes the importance of the political definition of European identity, where accession of a candidate country should not be assessed by its culture, religion, or history but by the attitude that "any country, willing to participate in the European integration process, should have a chance to do it, on the condition of fulfilling the agreed-upon political, economic and social criteria" (Klaus 2006a). Some other members of the ODS are also very open to religious diversity. They say that Europe is not based only on Christian values and that Islam played an important role in European history and culture. They refuse the image of the EU as a Christian club (Král 2006: 17) which means that European identity should not be defined on religious grounds while actually using the cultural explanation too.

The Polish president uses the cultural argument but presents an alternative view of it, calling himself "a representative of Europe's indisputably most Catholic – in terms of everyday religious practices – and thus most Christian country" (Kaczynski 2007a). He explains his support for Turkish membership as follows: "we deeply believe that, on the basis of these two religions – provided that one does not adopt a fundamentalist approach – one can find a junction, a link that will allow us to live together within one close-knit union of states" (Kaczynski 2007a). In answering the question whether Turkey is a European country or not, he said:

> Turkey is the link between the East and the West, between Asia and Europe. For ages the history of European nations and Turkey were intertwined. I am profoundly convinced about the significant role of Turkey in the intercultural, religious and civilizational dialog.
>
> (Kaczynski 2007b)

Similar to the Czech conservatives, he highlights the importance of religious and cultural dialogue rather than hostility. Arguments favoring Turkish entrance are often reinforced by others that point to the cultural and religious differences as a source of diversity which can enrich the whole Union. Moreover, they claim that Turkey could play a role of a bridge vis-à-vis the rest of a Muslim world. The accession of a fully democratic Turkey (Král 2009) could be perceived as a clear demonstration that Islam can coexist with liberal democracy and values shared by all Europeans. This is closely connected to security-strategic arguments which are often invoked mainly by those who consider the geopolitical aspects of future enlargement to play a primary role (especially Poland – see e.g. Szymanski 2007b: 555–56) and is not challenged in any of the ECECs.

The political representations sometimes also invoke Turkish potential to stabilize the whole region of the Middle East, strengthen the position of the EU in this area, and they also mention the possible role of EU membership in preventing radical Islamic forces from becoming more influential in Turkey. The particular issue of Muslim radicalism divides them slightly too. While some note that Turkey has been a secular state since 1923, opponents insist that the secular character of the country has been guaranteed by the army, which is far from being democratic or a sign of honest adherence to the values of secularism. Vondra, the former Czech Deputy Prime Minister for European affairs, criticized the statement of the French foreign minister, Bernard Kouchner, who claimed that Turkey was becoming more religious. Vondra said "if you have these concerns, the best way is to engage Turkey, not isolate it" (Bozkurt 2009a) while calling on Turkey to kick-start the reform process.

The parties and representatives who invoke the democratic and political values rather than the cultural ones focus on the need to meet the Copenhagen criteria. As said before, virtually all ECECs officially have repeatedly stated that as long as the country fulfills all the rules, it should be allowed to join the EU. They affirm that Turkey is attached to the values of liberal democracy, fundamental freedoms, and the protection of human rights (see e.g. *Vláda Slovenskej republiky* 2004; Batory 2006). Consequently, it cannot be denied membership once it fully complies with the Copenhagen criteria. In other words, Turkey can become a member of the EU regardless of its culture or religion. This position follows the official line of the EU documents.

An overview of the approaches of the elites of the ECECs to Turkey's accession to the EU suggests that even countries like Poland who emphasize their Christianity most of the time do not see cultural or religious differences as an impediment to Turkey's absorption. They believe that Turkey's inclusion will serve Europe's cultural plurality – read intergovernmentalism in the case of the Czech Republic – and increase intercultural and religious dialogue. There is one significant group in the ECECs more cautious on this issue – Christian Democrat parties, the representatives of which consider European identity to be founded on the Christian value system.

Conclusion

The ECECs seem to be undergoing a transformation not only in their adaptation process to the EU in general, but also, among other things, in the particular framework of the EU's relations with the third countries. Their opinion on Turkey is being formed. For instance, the official Hungarian view on Turkey's accession to the EU was made public only when the Commission recommended in 2004 the opening of accession negotiations with Turkey, and some governments and political parties still have no detailed views on the possible impact of the Turkish accession on the institutional structure of the EU. Turkey starts to appear in the agenda of the elites of the ECECs even though it is below Ukraine and the Western Balkans.

The examination of opinion formation with reference to the concept of absorption capacity in the ECECs' executives yields interesting results. It seems that in most cases for the ECECs values and identity of the EU seem to be more important than material benefits. For example, in evaluating the possible accession of Turkey to the EU, the Ministry of Foreign Affairs of Hungary talked about the reinforcement of the position of the forces which are committed to the European perspective before mentioning the absorption capacity of the Union. However, we can also infer that since these countries are in the process of repositioning themselves with reference to the EU, the definition and identity of the EU in their minds has not been clarified yet. Among these ambivalent views, the conception of the EU by the Czech president Klaus constitutes an exception for it has been persistent. It depicts the European integration broad-mindedly as an economic cooperation project that should be open to all willing to participate as long as they are able to fulfill the political, economic, and social criteria agreed upon in advance.

The ECECs are sometimes also ambivalent about their own identity and interests within the EU. For instance, they identify themselves both with MS as well as with candidate countries such as Turkey. Whilst protecting the interests of the EU on the one hand, they refer, on the other hand, to their own experiences. For example, they object to the restriction on the free movement of labor applied to new members, and in doing so, they try both to protect the interests of the EU (they assert that these restrictions are not to the advantage of the EU) as well as their own interests together with those of the candidates including Turkey (saying that these restrictions are unfair). It also seems that some actors in ECECs have not developed full command on the parameters of European integration. For instance, the Green Party in the Czech Republic favors a federalist EU which might be seen by many as incompatible with its support for further enlargement.

The ECECs inclination towards not impeding the accession of the other countries, which fulfill the Copenhagen criteria, and their reference to solidarity as a key principle of European integration may be attributed to the concept of the "logic of appropriateness." The Copenhagen criteria were originally formulated for the ECECs, and their membership was conditional on the fulfillment of these criteria. Now, these countries consider it improper to invent other conditions for membership to the EU. Elite-level socialization and creation of a common outlook have always been notoriously difficult in the EU. A clear example is the slightly dissident attitudes of some members of the Czech and Polish governments, who oppose the idea of "ever closer union" as they equate this with federalism.

In the particular case of Turkey, the ECECs' elites are more favorable towards Turkish membership than one would expect at first; they do not see Turkey as a potential rival in the EU, or as a country whose membership would bring many problems in the Union. This rather optimistic perspective is based on a combination of rational calculations/expectations and constructions: those who prefer a more intergovernmental Union reckon that Turkey's existence will be an impediment to the federalist tendencies in the EU. On the other hand, few seem to worry about the relative deterioration of their voting power in the European institutions as a result of Turkish accession. Similarly, whilst fearing the possible economic burdens of Turkish membership on the EU budget because Turkey is expected to claim substantial funds from regional and agricultural policies, they also think that Turkey's accession may lead to a revision of these policies, which they have been hoping for. They highlight the strategic benefit of Turkish accession.

In the constructivist dimension, probably because of the fact that their interaction with Turkey has been limited so far, strong common interests, values, or identities have not been formed yet. Yet, being newcomers and subjected to restrictions in the field of free movement of labor, they still see commonalities between themselves and Turkey, and due to the "logic of appropriateness" they prefer not to oppose Turkey's accession. Christian Democrats and nationalists are the staunchest opponents since they identify Turkey as the cultural "other," their discourse draws more on identity issues than institutional or economic concerns. The generally positive attitude will probably persist in the near future. A radical change in this broad elite support for Turkish membership in the ECECs seems to be unlikely in the existing conjuncture. However, once the conditions of Turkish membership become more specific and as the enlargement agenda collides with other policies and interests, they might reevaluate their position.

The official positions of the ECECs towards Turkey give interesting signals that necessitate further and in-depth studies. First of all, the generally favorable attitude may be a source of comfort for Turkey against the negative attitudes from the other MS' public opinion. Second, Turkey may also take the advantage of the transformation in the profile of the votes with positive votes increasing. It can take advantage of this window of opportunity: while the elite and public opinion in these countries is still in the process of formation, Turkey can have a chance to make a positive influence. By establishing contacts at both elite and public levels Turkey can make herself known in these countries, give positive messages, and take other initiatives that would contribute to the construction of a better view of herself. This would serve to develop bilateral relations between Turkey and these countries, and facilitate Turkey's bid for EU membership.

Notes

1 The chapter was concluded on 5 May 2009. All the information reflects the situation before this date.
2 Some arguments about the absorption capacity and Turkey are expected to appear in the new book by the president, Ivan Gašparovič, which was being printed when the chapter was concluded.
3 The Christian Democrats, KDU-ČSL, have been members of all coalition governments in the Czech Republic since 1993, irrespective of which party won elections.
4 These components have been derived from the three components of the European Commission's (2006b) definition of the concept of absorption capacity presented in the Introduction section: institutions, common policies, and budget. In the case of the ECECs two amendments will be necessary on the components in the Commission's definition. First, it may be useful to combine common policies' component and the budget component since these two would refer to the same thing for the ECECs: sharing the material benefits with Turkey. Second, cultural aspects may serve as a fourth component. Though not a part of the official discussions on absorption capacity, in most cases culture is a point of reference when discussing if the EU is "willing" to absorb Turkey. It is understandable that such vague and debatable concepts as "culture" or "religion" are uneasy subjects for official texts of the Commission, and probably for this reason they are omitted, but they occupy an important place in both public and scholarly discussions.
5 For example, among others, Quaisser and Reppegather (2004) predict that if Turkey becomes a member of the EU, it will have 11.2 percent of the seats in Parliament, 7.8 percent of the votes in the Council of Ministers, but will produce only about 14 percent of the GDP of the EU.
6 This is even more interesting because the 2004 "Big Bang" enlargement does not seem to slow down the decision-making process even though it might be one of the leading causes behind the "enlargement fatigue."
7 The reason of the disagreement was the Presidency's proposal to maintain a maximum limit a country could get from structural funds at 4 percent of GDP.
8 The Eurostat-estimated values for 2008 were 83 percent in the Czech Republic, 70 percent in Slovakia, 61.6 percent in Hungary, 55.1 percent in Poland, and 44.2 percent in Turkey of the EU-27 average.

9 The population of the country is very young, which becomes increasingly important for an ageing Europe. Although Turkish demographic evolution has somewhat slowed down recently, it may still be anticipated that the country's population will continue growing in the foreseeable future. According to Eurostat and the United Nations Population Division, the share of population under 14 is between 14 and 15 percent in the ECECs and 27.9 percent in Turkey and the share of population over 65 is between 12 percent (Slovakia) to 16.2 percent (Hungary) while it is only 6.6 percent in Turkey.

10 See Topolánek 2009.

11 The political notion of European identity, pleading objective accession criteria, is also connected with geographical aspects – the question of how to define European borders in geographic terms. However, the concern about Turkey being a part of Europe from a geographical point of view can be recently traced only in Hungary, where opponents of Turkish membership in the EU argue that "only a small part of the country is, geographically-speaking, located on the European continent. A concern in this respect was that the inclusion of Turkey into the EU would create a precedent for (other) non-European countries to seek membership" (Batory 2006: 8). This is a position held by isolated political parties and their representatives and does not reflect the official approach presented by the state.

12 These included democratic deficit, the question of Cyprus, illegal migration, low level of economic development, and others.

8 The support of East Central European countries for Turkey's accession to the European Union

Pavel Šaradín

The accession of Turkey into the European Union (EU) has two basic dimensions. The first is how much the citizens of Turkey want their country to join, and the second, how much support it finds among the citizens of the EU and their political representatives. This question also concerns the East Central European countries (ECECs), yet to a lesser extent than can be seen for example in Germany or Austria. None of the four countries, Czech Republic, Hungary, Poland, and Slovakia, has a large Turkish minority living there, which would create some pressure on the societies to adopt a more specific position. In this chapter we will focus on the question of how the citizens of the four ECECs (also known as the Visegrad countries) view the future membership of Turkey in the EU, including the individual political actors, such as political parties, their representatives as well as several civil society groups. We will be primarily interested in those groupings that have a negative opinion of Turkish membership for the reasoning that those against tend to be more active and articulate, feeling the need to mobilize from early on in order to convince the society of the negatives of Turkish accession to the EU.

There are also naturally more of these negative voices than those who support Turkish membership. This is essentially logical, because Turkey will not become a member of the EU for a while, which lowers the potential for a supportive mobilization of the public, and also because among the candidate countries, Turkey is not the major priority for them – for example the Czechs support EU enlargement but the accession of Croatia is more significant to them than Turkey. In this case it is partly because it is a Slavic country, but also because it is a highly visited holiday destination for the Czechs, thus, the country favors the least complicated access to Croatian territory and other benefits of joined EU membership.

In Table 8.1, we present the support for further enlargement in the ECECs and also how these countries feel about Turkish accession in comparison with EU-25 and Austria before the opening of the negotiations with Turkey in 2005. We choose the specific case of Austria because it is also a Central European country, which except for the Cold War era shared with the ECECs hundreds of years of common history within the Austro-Hungarian monarchy. Table 8.1 indicates that the support for EU enlargement in the ECECs is higher than the EU average and even twice as high as in Austria. Concerning future Turkish membership, the support among the citizens of Austria is minimal, with only 10 percent in favor, while 80 percent

Table 8.1 ECECs' position on further EU enlargement

Member State	Support for EU enlargement	For Turkish membership	Against Turkish membership
Czech Republic	66	37	**51**
Hungary	66	51	**38**
Poland	76	54	**31**
Slovakia	73	37	**50**
Austria	31	10	**80**
EU-25	50	35	**52**

Source: European Commission 2005a

are against. It is also interesting that in Hungary and Poland more than 50 percent support Turkish membership, while in the Czech Republic and Slovakia it is only 37 percent. In these two countries, which up until 1992 formed a common state, the percentage of those for and against is close to the EU-25 figures, whereas in Poland and Hungary the opposition is far weaker and the support much higher.

It is important to note that the public in the ECECs does not consider Turkish EU membership a topical matter and most of the reactions are related only to the fact that in 2005 the EU started accession negotiations with Turkey. The ECECs joined the EU in 2004, and prior to this date, the debates concerning the so-called Turkish question had been rare and focused mainly on the issues of European values and what Europe and Turkey had in common or how different they were from each other. The issues of the European institutions' absorption capacity and the relative high power Turkey would carry there were mostly pushed in the background. The ECECs started to address these problems only after they became EU members. The obvious question related to all these issues is how long the accession talks will last before Turkey fulfills all the criteria. That they are and will be complicated is guaranteed and nothing proved it better than the partial suspension of talks due to lack of agreement on Cyprus only one year after they began (2006). We will not explicitly address this specific aspect and concentrate rather on the trends in the support of Turkish EU accession in the ECECs, which has become a particularly significant discussion after the opening of the negotiations in 2005.

In the text, we also would like to show how the support for Turkish EU membership relates or does not relate to the position of the political parties, movements and initiatives on the scale of Euroscepticism–Eurooptimism. It also is of interest whether these positions have an influence on their opinion regarding the accession of Turkey or not. We are mostly concerned with following what arguments are primarily used against Turkish membership. As previously mentioned, the ECECs do not have any experience in living with a Turkish minority, not even a Muslim minority, as do some countries of Western Europe. The only direct experience is related to the past, as in certain historical periods some of the ECECs had a direct contact with the Turks during the wars between Europe and the predecessor of the Turkish Republic, the Ottoman Empire.

The debates on Turkish EU accession in the ECECs have not been to this point deep, intensive, or systematic. The individual contributions emerged most frequently before the opening of the accession talks with Turkey reacting to the situation, or at a moment when a polemical commentary appeared in several influential media sources, which prompted arguments voicing agreement or disagreement. The framework of these discussions was formed from the differing conceptions of (liberal) ideology, European values, historical experience and the role of religion.

Let us first summarize the main general arguments against Turkish EU membership as heard in many European countries in 2005:

a)   Turkey is a poor country, whose GDP per capita is well below 50 percent of the EU-25 average. Upon accession it would be entitled to a significant amount of resources from structural funds which could meet with a negative reaction from several EU member states. There have also been concerns about the consequences of free movement of labor from a country of 70 million people.
b)   Turkey has a bad human rights record.
c)   Turkey is significantly different from Europe in terms of culture and religion, almost all its territory lies outside of the European continent.
d)   Fear of the strong representation of Turkey in the EU institutions given its population size, especially applied to qualified majority voting.
e)   The Eastern border of Turkey lies in an unstable region, from where immigrants could enter into the EU, for example with criminal or terrorist intentions.

The ECECs were discussing these very same issues as well. For example, the Czech Minister for Regional Development, Petr Gandalovič, argued against the first point saying:

> If Turkey becomes a member of the EU, it will not mean a loss for the Czech Republic regarding the European funds. Until 2013, the amount of financial resources from the EU funds is firmly set. After the year 2013, the Czech Republic should reach the level of 75 percent of the EU GDP, and therefore the EU funding will not be much relevant to us.
>
> (Víšková 2006)

We find occasional criticisms of virtually all the points with the exception of human rights violations. Both those for and against Turkish EU membership raise concerns in this area, which partially stems from the fact that human rights are considered one of the basic European values.

The current debate in the ECECs is closely linked to the opening of the accession talks with Turkey in 2005. We will now look at how the issue was addressed in the individual ECECs and how the arguments have developed since.

Czech Republic

On 9 May 2005 (Europe Day), the European Values association, which is a Czech pro-European non-governmental research and educational agency, began to con-

tact citizens and collect signatures for a petition, which would prevent the opening of EU negotiations with Turkey. The petition was a part of an international
project, *Voice for Europe*, which followed the same objective. The Association had
a similar petition signed already a year earlier against setting the date by which
Turkey would be informed of the accession talks opening (Novinky 2004). They
also organized a demonstration in front of the Turkish Embassy in Prague, which
stressed primarily the violation of human rights and the discrimination against
women in Turkey (BBC 2005). They tried to prevent the start of the accession talks
and claimed that the objective of the demonstration was to "remind" people that
Turkey did not fulfill the candidate country criteria. The former Prime Minister
from the Social Democrats (ČSSD), Miloš Zeman, presented a similar argument at
an independent forum meeting in Žofín (Prague). Evidently inspired by the theories
of Samuel Huntington that the greatest conflict of the twenty-first century would
be the clash between the Euro-American and the Islamic civilizations, he put the
Turkey-EU relations into this perspective and added "We should therefore not strive
for Turkey's accession into the European Union" (Kubeczka 2006).

Various articles presenting diverse perspectives on the issue of Turkey and
Turkish EU accession appeared on the server euRabia.cz, which focuses on the
issues of coexistence between Europe and the Arab world. The goal of the organization that runs the website is to "truthfully inform about the growing danger
represented by the creeping encroachment of Islam onto Europe." The message
to their readers further reads that they want to distance themselves "from racism,
xenophobia, religious and national hatred." For example, Alexander Tomský,
a Czech journalist and publisher, who lived for a long time in the UK, warned
there: "All speculative arguments in support of Turkish EU membership are not
only not valid, but unjustified because the problem of Turkey is not a problem of
Turkey, but a political problem of the state and objectives of the Union" (Tomský
2007).

A former Minister of the Czech government and a top member of the Civic
Democratic Alliance (ODA), which was a junior liberal-conservative government
party between 1992 and 1998, Pavel Bratinka (2005), voiced his dread of Islamist
Turkey on the website of the Civic Institute:

> Let's not forget his [Prime Minister Erdoğan's] threatening and aggressive
> speech addressing the EU, if he dares to reject the opening of the EU acces-
> sion talks in such a way. This is Turkey, which cannot and should not become
> a member of the EU. This Turkey would reject any decision of the Council of
> the EU or the European Parliament or the decision of the European Court of
> Justice that did not relate to their Islamic view of the world of fanaticism or
> religious wars.

Pavel Bratinka, therefore, considers Turkey to be a country in which fanaticism is
predominant, followed by religious wars. A similar opinion is supported by Roman
Joch), member of the Civic Institute. At a seminar of the Center for Economics and
Politics founded by Václav Klaus, he claimed that:

The educated Turkish pro-Western elite does not represent the problem of accepting Turkey into the EU, it is rather the free immigration of its non-Western Islamic citizens, of which a majority have a lukewarm respect for personal freedoms and a minority of which is strongly unfriendly to them. The massive influx of people with these illiberal ideas into Europe would lead to immense unrest, street protests and bloodshed, and the subsequent restrictions of our freedoms.

(Joch 2005)

According to him, the accession of Turkey would lead to the unleashing or strengthening of the civilizational war.

These statements confirm our previous claim that the negative voices in the debate prevail over the positive ones. Such conclusion could be expected as it is much easier to criticize than create something positive. Moreover, rooted in the Czech society is a tendency to overlook Eastern countries, which also relates to Turkey.[1] The East symbolizes imperfection, poverty, and due to this in a certain psychological form, a lack of seriousness, that is, the opposite of the West.

However, some supportive statements appeared too. In the same time period, when these anti-Turkish initiatives were being articulated, others supported Turkey in becoming a full EU member state. Such was the initiative *Turkey in the EU* whose goal was among other things to inform the public about the opinions of public actors on this issue. The initiative explained its establishment in the following manner:

Not long ago we saw billboards declaring a big NO to the accession of Turkey. We will gradually add arguments why we are in favor of accession. The path will be long and difficult. It is easier to create fear than to listen and understand.

(Election archive, Palacky University in Olomouc)

Among the respondents who answered the question of how they perceived Turkish membership in the EU were members of both houses of the parliament from various political parties, but also local representatives.[2] This initiative was, however, more of a momentary project because the website had not updated since the initial few months.

Apart from the initiative just mentioned, *Turkey in the EU*, other positive or more neutral positions could be found. Petr Vaněk (2005) reacted to the criticism of the *Voice for Europe* and wrote in *Literární noviny* that it is possible to hold a number of things against Turkey, but it is not possible to say to Turkey "never" instead of "not now," because it could have an extremely negative impact on the positive trends in the progress made in the Turkish society. The website of the Institute for European Politics, *Europeum*, published an article, in which the author stated:

I am convinced that in the long-run the European Union would not be endangered by the accession of Turkey more than by the recent enlargement to the

East and that the Turkish EU membership could have very positive consequences for both Turkey and the EU and possibly for the whole world.

(Pachta 2004)

The article mentioned a number of reforms that were carried out in Turkey, the improvements in the Turkish economy, and the fact that from an economic standpoint the accession of Turkey would not be a bigger burden for the EU than the membership of Poland (especially in the area of agriculture).

Support for Turkish membership was also articulated by the President, Václav Klaus, and by the Civic Democratic Party (ODS), which he founded in 1991. Klaus's main argument is that after further enlargement the EU would not have the opportunity to deepen politically, which has been his dominant concern for a number of years. In addition to Turkey he also supports the idea of Morocco and Kazakhstan joining the EU. In his speech in Istanbul in May 2005 he argued that if Turkey was not accepted than it would mean the failure of European multiculturalism, of which – as he says – the West likes to speak so much (Klaus 2005c).

Other supportive views mentioned Turkey's membership in NATO, where they claimed the country had unequivocally successful membership record, that is, they related Turkish EU membership to European security.

As mentioned earlier, the so-called Turkish question has played a rather marginal role in the programs of Czech political parties. The main reason is the fact that there is no sizeable Turkish (Muslim) minority living in the Czech Republic, which would influence their programs. Another reason could be the fact that the Czech Republic has been an EU member state for a relatively short period of time. There were only two elections to the European Parliament (2004 and 2009) and the campaigns were dominated by economic issues rather than foreign policy. We could observe a similar development in the parliamentary elections, where the foreign policy themes seem to play a less important role.

The representatives of the Czech political parties express their views on Turkish EU membership only sporadically, or they react to current events, declarations, appeals, and reports. During the visit of the Turkish PM Recep Tayyip Erdoğan to Prague in November 2007, the Czech PM, Mirek Topolánek, unambiguously supported the accession of Turkey into the EU and added that he believed that during the Czech Presidency (2009) the accession talks with Turkey would be very intensive (ČTK 2007). Such is the official standpoint of the Czech government, regardless of the fact that at a minimum one member of the coalition government did not agree with it. In this area, however, Topolánek's government maintained a continuous foreign politics orientation because the previous government with Social Democrats as a senior coalition party[3] supported the opening of the accession talks with Turkey. Let's now look at the positions of selected political parties and their representatives.

The Czech Social Democratic Party (ČSSD) expressed its fundamental position on Turkish EU accession during the aforementioned visit of the Turkish PM Erdoğan to Prague. The chairman of the party, Jiří Paroubek, issued a *communiqué*, in which he stated: "The Czech Social Democratic Party has supported

Turkey's accession to the EU in the past and that position persists" (Kočová 2007). The position of the ČSSD has been consistent; in one of his pre-election interviews in April 2006, Paroubek stated: "I am generally for accession, but it depends on how Turkey develops. If their economy improves, if they move closer to the legislative structure of the EU, if they meet the human rights standards, then it will be good to have such a populous Muslim country on our side" (MF Dnes 2006). Other influential members of the ČSSD, for example MPs Radko Martinek and Zdeněk Koudelka were also positive about Turkish EU membership.[4] On the other hand, in his 2004 EP election campaign, a prominent member of the party, Richard Falbr (2004), took a negative stance towards Turkey's accession when he stated that "Turkey does not belong in Europe." He used arguments such as the trade unions there "meet, choose their leadership, and the Turkish police immediately takes them into prison."[5] The party did not present a united front then because in the very same election campaign Libor Rouček, also a member of ČSSD, supported Turkish membership. Generally speaking, this position seems to be the prevailing one in the party.

The second largest party on the left, the Communist Party of Bohemia and Moravia (KSČM) also supports Turkish membership in the EU. The deputy chairman of the party, Jiří Dolejš, did not see any reason why "we should prevent Turkey from its path to the EU." His colleague, Zuzka Rujbrová, differed only in that she was not sure if there would be a need for a referendum on this issue or not.[6] The Chairman of the Party, Vojtěch Filip (2006), in an attempt of analyze the geopolitical position of Turkey, stated that Turkish EU membership is more of strategic interest to the United States but did not express any specific opinion on its accession.

One of the center parties, The Christian Democratic Union – Czechoslovak People's Party (KDU-ČSL) draws most of its popular support from areas with a large share of pious Catholic population. The party is among the relevant Czech political parties the strongest opponent of Turkish EU membership. The only MP who expressed a different opinion was Jiří Karas, who stated that he was for Turkey's accession to the EU but only under the condition "that Turkey comes to terms with the discrimination of its Christian minority."[7] When the European Commission in 2004 recommended the opening of the accession talks, a Czech MEP, Jan Březina (2004b), believed that in the end the EU summit would decide "objectively" that Turkey did not meet the Copenhagen criteria. Later, after the EP also recommended opening of the talks, Březina, labeled this vote as groundbreaking:

> In the history of the EU, I cannot remember an example when they began negotiating membership with a state, where incidents of torture are not scarce, where the rights of women and minorities are to a large extent violated and where a non-Islamic religion is not even granted its right to exist.
>
> Březina (2004a)

In another article, he attacked the British Conservatives and ODS, by stating that in supporting Turkey they have left the European tradition of defending human rights.

This opinion was shared by other representatives of the KDU-ČSL. In their comments published in the Czech media, they mentioned additional arguments against Turkish accession to the EU. The Christian Democrats resented, for example, the discrimination of Christians in Turkey; they drew attention to the cultural and religious differences; and the fact that Turkey was an Asian country. A good number of influential party members were negative towards Turkish accession, including members of both parliamentary chambers, as well as the youth party associations of the Christian Democrats, who issued a statement in which they warned that "accepting Turkey into the European Union would pose a fundamental danger to its values and cultural integrity" (Čermák n.d.).

The ODS adopted a completely different position from the KDU-ČSL. Their program indicates that they prefer EU enlargement over deepening of European integration process. The ODS is within the parameters of Turkish EU membership interested mainly in economic cooperation, and their long-term chairman, Václav Klaus, always supported Turkish membership. The current chairman of the party, Mirek Topolánek, in connection with his trip to Croatia in March 2005, issued a resolution in which he at the same time mentioned his support for Turkish accession: "ODS supports further enlargement of the European Union, to Croatia and other Balkan states, Turkey and Ukraine. We believe that these countries have the full right to apply for membership in the European Union" (Topolánek 2005).

Another voice of support came from a prominent party member, MEP Jan Zahradil, who was during the 2004–2009 election period a member of the EU-Turkey Joint Parliamentary Committee, and as such could closely follow the events related to Turkey. His reasons for the support of the Turkish EU bid were "strategic, economic, political and cultural." Jan Zahradil (2006) rejected the arguments of the critics and claimed that "Turkey sometimes serves as a scapegoat and as a way [for the EU] to escape its own problems." The Euro-Parliamentary Club of the ODS, presided over by Jan Zahradil during this period, rejected to support the EP's 2006 Progress Report on Turkey. This 16-page document spoke, for example, about the slow pace of reforms in the area of protecting human rights, discrimination of women, freedom of speech, religious freedom, minority rights, the problem of the so-called Armenian genocide, etc. The ODS declarations on this Report stated:

> The formulations and suggestions included in this report are in many respects outside of the general framework of requirements common during the EU accession negotiations and are not related to the current political and economic situation in Turkey.
>
> Furthermore, we cannot accept the manipulation with long past historical events and its use as a political tool in the contemporary context (in relation to the Turkish question of the so-called Armenian genocide during World War I). The Czech Republic has its own very negative experience with attempts to retroactively misuse the past.
>
> Finally, we cannot accept references to the so-called constitutional process of the EU, contained in the text of the Report, which tries to anticipate the

future institutional organization of the EU and revive the EU Constitutional Treaty.

(ODS 2006)

One of the major fellows of the ODS think-tank, CEVRO, Petr Robejšek (2007), answered a survey question regarding Turkey's membership very clearly: "In my opinion, a strong and internally connected EU is not in our national interest. Therefore I welcome everything that would contribute to the disintegration of the EU." This seems to represent the position of several members and supporters of the ODS and explains why they so actively support Turkish accession to the EU, which they frequently connect with the possible paralysis of European political integration in the future.

The smaller political parties have relatively limited possibilities to contribute to the formulation of the country's foreign policy but as members of the government, parliament, or other important institutions, they unquestionably exercise their, albeit restricted, ability to influence public opinion.

Two MEPs, Josef Zieleniec and Tomáš Zatloukal, who were elected on the platform of the Association of Independent Candidates SNK-European Democrats, were very active during the petitions against Turkish accession. Josef Zieleniec was in the 1990s a long-term deputy chairman of ODS and a government minister, MP, and later an independent senator. Both Zieleniec and Zatloukal participated at a meeting under the statue of St. Václav in Prague, one of the symbols of Czech statehood, where they supported the petition, and Zieleniec (2005) stated: "Turkey is not a European country, it has not shared European history and does not have the same approach to politics or to public life." In his speech at a plenary meeting of the EP in October 2007, Zieleniec restated his opposition to Turkey's accession and pointed out that the EU institutions should inform Turkey that the EU does not have a united position about its accession:

> It is a question of our responsibility towards our citizens, and to Turkey, which does not deserve to have the truth hidden from it. I am sure that the Turkish nation would rather prefer a report about the divided opinion to us hiding the reality of the situation, which Europe and our Parliament has long demonstrated.
>
> (Zieleniec 2007)

On the other hand, another MEP elected under the same platform, Jana Hybášková, has very actively supported Turkey's accession. According to her it was important to allow the country to undergo what she calls "Europeanization of its demographics," which would create a strong middle class there. She explicitly stated that it is good to have a "strategic partner *inside*, under our control, in our club and legislature, than *outside of it*" (Kopecká 2005).

In 2006, for the first time in the history of the Czech Republic the Green Party (SZ) was elected to the Parliament. It has acted positively towards Turkish membership because it took the stance that the EU could provide Turkey with the same service it did for the Czech Republic and act as an engine of democratization:

The Green Party supports Turkish accession to the EU but this can happen only on the condition that Turkey democratizes. The EU was also in our case an engine of democratization – and this is why Turkey needs the European perspective.

(Bursík n.d.)

The party highlighted the need to meet all three Copenhagen criteria.

The other minor political actors in the Czech Republic do not present any arguments other than those already mentioned earlier.

Hungary

Even though Hungary, respectively the hereditary Hungarian lands, was throughout its history on several occasions threatened by the Ottoman Empire, the past seems to have zero or very little effect on their present relations. The official Hungarian position is in favour of the Turkish EU bid as is the winner of the 2006 national elections, the Hungarian Socialist Party (MSZP). The second largest party in the Hungarian party system is the liberal-conservative Fidesz, whose attitude towards Turkey is more problematic and divided. The leadership of the party seems to oppose it, while several of the party's members and representatives praise Turkey's democratic efforts. The question is how Fidesz would behave if it were the governing party. Two smaller parliamentary parties are against Turkish accession to the EU, the liberal Alliance of Free Democrats (SZDSZ) and the conservative, Christian-Democratic People's Party (KDNP), although they earlier declared a different standpoint (Batory 2006).

Despite the fact that the government has declared its support, we can say that in comparison to the support of Croatia or Ukraine entering the EU, it is less profound. The former Prime Minister, Ferenc Gyurcsány, during the visit of his Turkish counterpart in Budapest stated that his country could count on Hungarian support. His words were confirmed by the one of the leading politicians of the Socialist party, Szili Katalin (Kossuth Radio 2008). Currently, the Hungarian government is actively cooperating with Turkey; there are now six successful projects in operation in the areas of agriculture, education, and cooperation of local municipalities (Magyar Koztarsasag Nagykovetsege n.d.). The Hungarian government also supports introducing courses of Turkish language.

Even in Hungary the Turkish question from time to time activates some sections of the civil society – as we could observe in virtually all European countries. Despite the fact that they are mostly isolated groupings and initiatives without support of the wider society, they receive a lot of media attention. Among the most active is the Foundation for European Values (Az Európai Értékekért Alapítvány Célja), which is against the Turkey's EU accession primarily due to the different cultural, societal, democratic, and religious traditions.[8] The Voice for Europe (*Hang Európáért*) has also undertaken a number of initiatives – its members participated in demonstrations against the opening of the accession talks with Turkey in Prague, Bratislava, and even in Brussels (Királyi Séta 2005). One of the main criticisms they raised against the Turkish government was the issue of the so-called Armenian genocide, and was followed by a headline: "Turkey's Trianon as the Armenian genocide" (Szigetvári n.d.). This particular issue is addressed by the Christian movement in Hungary, which provides detailed analyses of the "Armenian genocide" on its website portal.jobbik.net.

However, a majority of the time Turkey is criticized for economic reasons or from the perspective of the EU "absorption capacity." They claim that Turkey suffers from vast regional differences; therefore, some of its regions could become a burden for the EU budget, which could be especially detrimental to the interests of the smaller and medium-sized countries of the Eastern enlargement (Szigetvári 2006). Batory (2006) lists among the "anti-Turkish" representatives of the Hungarian civil society the Movement for a Better Hungary (a small extreme-right grouping that demanded that the Hungarian foreign minister vetoed the accession of this "Muslim Asian country" (to no avail); an online group European Women for Liberty that believed that Turkey's (bad) record in promoting gender equality disqualified it for EU membership; and a website Islam in Europe that warned against Turkey by describing it as a nominally secular but in practice Islamic country. Among the most articulate critics of Turkish membership is a political party, Jobbik, which is a far-right Hungarian extremist party, which scored high in the 2009 EP elections, when it received 15 percent of the vote and gained three EP seats. The representatives of Jobbik are outspoken critics of Islam, which they consider to be incompatible with European values (Kárpát 2005). The party has also warned against the population of Turkey and its relatively high birth rate, warning that if Turkey joined the EU, it would become the most populous country there.

Poland

As we have seen in the case of the Czech Republic, many Polish non-governmental organizations became actively involved in the process of discussing Turkey's accession to the EU. In Poland, there was a campaign led by the association Europe of the Future (*Europa Przyszłości*), which was founded in January 2005 in Wrocław, and a year later had 50 members. They began their activities with a street exhibition in Wrocław named *The first Holocaust of the 20th century*. On the panels there were photographs of massacred Armenians who were killed during 1915 to 1918. In May 2005, the Association began a signature campaign, with the goal to organize a petition in Poland against Turkish accession to the EU. The campaign was accompanied by the slogan "Be tolerant, but not naïve." In Poland, an informal association of several organizations who did not want Turkey in the EU was also established under the name Voice for Europe (*Głos dla Europy*). Thus, we could observe a development that took place in several European countries here too. The chairwoman of the association Europa Przyszłości, Joanna Orska, commented on her opposing position to Turkish membership in the following manner: "We see the beginning of negotiations as an irresponsible experiment, whose results the politicians do not even try to predict" (Gazeta Wyborcza 2005).

The framework of the campaign built on the following main predicaments: Turkey is a Trojan horse, the Turkish minority in Western Europe is a so-called "fifth column," and the others are just waiting to get in; it portrayed Turks as dubious relatives; claimed that Turkey would never succumb to the authority of Strasbourg; that Turks persecute the Kurds and did not acknowledge the "Armenian genocide," etc. All these arguments were presented in an article entitled "They Will Be Here any Minute" (Kaźmierczak 2005). Jan Wójcik, an organizer of the petition *Voice for Europe* in Poland presented the initiative in the following manner:

> We are not racists or anti-Islamists, but we remember September 11 or the murder of Theo van Gogh, the Dutch director. At the same time we support democratization of Turkey, yet we have the opinion that for both sides it would be more advantageous to have a privileged partnership with the Union or massive financial support than full membership.

At the same time, there are also those who defend Turkish EU membership. In opposition to the anti-Turkish campaign, the foundations Unia & Polska and Europa21 were established. In addition to the political organizations, there were other platforms which went beyond the narrow framework of politics such as Merhaba[9] and the Association of Polish-Turkish Friendship and Cooperation.[10] Both organizations did not openly express their interest in politics and did not specifically address the integration process – they concentrated, according to their websites, on culture and tourism. Economic cooperation falls under the Platform of Polish-Turkish Association of Business.

One of the most common arguments heard in Poland against Turkey's EU bid is its religion. Poland is a country with one of the highest shares of pious Catholics in Europe. A number of opponents to Turkish accession use the religious card typical of this specific environment. Most often they speak of the danger of Islamization of Europe and the cultural differences. Turkey could in their view act as a foreign element in the EU. They also stress within this framework the problem of human rights violations.

We will now look at the positions of the Polish political parties and their representatives. Poland has very actively supported further enlargement of the European Union and has a fundamental interest in neighboring Ukraine becoming an EU member. The Polish Eastern policy can be perceived as exemplary for two reasons. Poland is a large country in the Central and Eastern European region and has tried to strengthen its role while at the same time has an interest in having a stable neighborhood. Therefore, they support among other things the transformation processes in Ukraine and the democratic opposition in Belarus. Polish politicians know that the Ukrainian path to EU membership will be a very protracted one and they have actively tried to promote discussions on this matter. Several statements on the matter point out that the preference of Ukraine often overshadows the debate on the Turkish accession prospects.

At the end of 2004, the former Minister of Foreign Affairs Włodzimierz Cimoszewicz (SLD) expressed for the Ukrainian information server ProEuropa. info his support for the accession of Ukraine and Turkey into the EU. He, however, especially praised Turkey:

> We support Turkish accession for several reasons which relate to economic development, international security, and cooperation with the Islamic world. We are aware that together with the accession of Turkey we will overstep a certain borderline included in the title of European Community. With Turkey, we will move further. If we are prepared for this, then there can be no doubt that the European states on the European continent have the right to join the EU. These are arguments in favor of Ukraine, which also needs to be supportive of them in order to utilize them.
>
> (ProEuropa.info n.d.)[11]

Polish political representation has been continuously consistent in their stance towards the question of further EU enlargement. At a conference held in May 2006 at the Warsaw Institute for Security Studies, the Minister of Foreign Affairs, Anna Fotyga, supported the accession of the Balkan countries, Ukraine and Turkey to the EU and in the case of Turkey pointed out that it would be a long process for both sides involved (Ministerstwo Spraw Zagranicznych 2006). Other Polish Ministers of Foreign Affairs such as Radoslaw Sikorski (PO) have expressed opinions in the same manner. This trend has been supported by other top political representatives, including the former president Aleksander Kwaśniewski, who in a speech in Cyprus stated:

> I am of the opinion that there is space for Turkey in a united Europe. I am convinced that it is necessary to support the process of democratic and civilizational transformation in this country. It is a great challenge to form EU's relations with Muslim societies, both inside and outside of the Community. It is good that the Union decided to open accession negotiations with Turkey.
>
> (Kwaśniewski 2005)

The rival and successor of Kwaśniewski as President, Lech Kaczyński (PiS), formulated his statement in the same spirit during his visit to Turkey in January 2007. In Ankara, he announced that "Turkey will strengthen uniting Europe." Kaczyński's further statements regarding Turkey's EU membership were also supportive.

Similar to the case of the Czech Republic and Hungary, the Polish politicians opened the question of the human rights record and the historical problem of the "Armenian genocide." An MEP, Konrad Szymański (PiS), not only mentioned that the discussion about the accession of Turkey should not exclude Ukraine, which should be accepted earlier than Turkey, but also referred to some of his doubts primarily concerned with religious faith:

> Personally, I have big doubts about the results of accepting Turkey. In the process of democratization, the Islamic forces could gain a large influence and become an organizational factor for migration to the whole of Europe. I would prefer, if the benefits of accession – related to single market, military and geopolitical – were gained without membership. I am convinced that this is possible.
>
> (PiS 2007)

Another Polish politician, this time a Member of the Parliament, mentioned other unresolved issues that concerned Turkey, primarily freedom of religion, interventions against the Ecumenical Patriarch, delays in the investigation of the murder of Christians in Malatya,[12] and the non-existence of laws on the freedom of assembly. His main aim, however, was to incorporate into the 2008 European Parliament Report on Turkey his proposal, which stated the following:

> The EP calls on the Turkish government and leaders of the Turkish public opinion to provide for a greater openness in the Turkish-Armenian reconciliation process and especially to acknowledge the historical responsibility of the Turkish state for the Armenian genocide in 1915–17.
>
> (Szymański 2008)

Another PiS MP, Michał Kamiński (2009), was especially critical: "I still have great doubts about the European aspirations of Turkey. I am concerned primarily about the growing infiltration of Turkish politics with radical Islamic elements." His party colleague, Wojciech Girzyński (2008), adopted a different perspective for he saw in Turkish membership a possible future partner to counterbalance Germany: "The tandem of Poland-Turkey is weaker than the agreement of Poland-Turkey-Ukraine, yet it would be possible to change in our favor, and to the detriment of Germany, the power distribution in the European Union." Despite this different attitude, the party is rather negative and its members express many reservations of a religious and cultural nature.

The Polish People's Party (PSL) perceives Turkish and Ukrainian EU accession in essentially positive terms even though at times it expresses fears of a character we saw with PiS. Moreover, their representatives state that the acceptance of both countries would be difficult, as they are large and populous, which would necessitate a reorganization of power distribution in the EU institutions, which could primarily discomfort France and Germany.[13] Also positive were the positions of two other parties, which played an important role in post-1989 Polish politics (even though at different times) – the liberal Civil Platform (PO) and the Democratic Left Alliance (SLD), whose leader's opinions have been mentioned earlier.

Slovakia

Slovakia belongs, together with Poland, to the group of relatively strong Catholic countries. The main political representatives support further EU enlargement and the public opinion takes a similar stance. Slovakia primarily favors the accession of the Balkan countries, especially Croatia and Serbia. Turkey's EU membership is seen in Slovakia as more problematic. Among the political parties, the most anti-Turkish membership is the Christian Democratic Movement (KDH), which "supports the enlargement of the EU to countries that share the common European values" and for Turkey they see privileged partnership as the best possible option. Another party which is against Turkish EU membership is the Slovak National Party (SNS), for whom "the accession of Turkey to the EU is unacceptable," as

Turkey does not fulfill the basic criteria of political and human rights and represents a threat of "Islamization" in the EU.

During the period when Slovakia had only been an EU member state for a few months, the chairman of the right-wing populist SNS, Ján Slota, called for the rejection of Turkish membership. This emerged out of his appeal for a "Europe for Europeans," from which Slota derived the main arguments. We must add that the SNS is built on strong Christian values and Slovak nationalism. For them, Turkey is not European and never will be and it has always been outside of the European cultural framework. In an information packet, which accompanied the "Europe for Europeans" appeal, there were quotes, arguments, and reminders of historical events in the Turkish-European coexistence and clashes. Ján Slota, for example, recalled the words of the then (2004) Cardinal Ratzinger who in 2006 became Pope Benedict XVI, who said:

> Europe is a cultural and not just a geographic concept. It emerged from the Christian formation of the world and the Ottoman Empire was for a majority of time in opposition to it. Turkey has despite its secular Constitution an Islamic basis. Therefore, it is possible for it to bridge Europe and the Arab world. Yet, accepting Turkey into the European Union would be a tremendous mistake.
>
> (SNS 2004)

In any case, the current official position of the Catholic Church to Turkish membership is different. The top representatives have several times announced that they support Turkish accession.

Ján Slota referred to several historical events, yet he mainly mentioned those from the fifteenth to eighteenth centuries, for example the seventeenth-century wars against the Hungarian kingdom, during which the Turks destroyed Western Slovakia. The SNS's main arguments relevant for contemporary Turkey are: Turkey lies on a drug trafficking path, it would become easier to smuggle drugs to the continent; the EU would put a huge burden on the its own agricultural policy; it would change the composition of the EP in favor of Muslims; and it would massively increase immigration to the EU. It is worth mentioning another argument which we have met with only indirectly before (in a remark by the chairman of the Czech Communists) that Turkish membership would increase the influence of the USA in the EU, which the SNS finds absolutely excruciating (SNS 2004).

The official position of the government is, however, supportive of Turkish membership. Prime Minister Robert Fico (Smer) stated in 2006 that Slovakia supported Turkish accession to the EU, and that religious affiliation did not matter (Aktualne. sk 2006). This statement has been repeated several times since then, even when – as we have seen highly critical – SNS became a governmental party after the 2006 parliamentary elections. However, several influential Smer politicians did not adopt the same position as the chairman Robert Fico. For example, in the 2009 EP elections, Monika Beňová (Smer) stated:

Certainly the most ready candidate is Croatia; further activity in this period should focus on the Balkans – Serbia, Bosnia and Herzegovina, and Montenegro. I am not a supporter of Turkish membership in the EU and we should send Turkey an unambiguous signal that we prefer another form of cooperation, for example privileged partnership.

(Marušiak and Godársky 2009)

KDH also takes an unequivocal opposition to Turkish accession. They supported the European Commission's decision to freeze the negotiations of eight chapters with Turkey at the end of 2006.

The fact that Turkey is not adequately prepared for membership in the EU can be seen in its unwillingness to open its airport and ports to Cyprus, and in not recognizing the Republic of Cyprus. Last but not least there are cultural differences, which cannot be overlooked. Turkey was never disqualified on the basis of religious difference as Fico stated, its unwillingness can be seen in the fact that they are not prepared to share the values which are the basis of the EU. KDH supports a model of privileged partnership with Turkey, which could lead to negotiations between the European Union and Turkey.

(KDH 2006)

On the other hand, the party of the Hungarian minority in Slovakia, Hungarian Coalition Party (SMK), has had a positive view of Turkish accession, nevertheless it has always accentuated the necessity of fulfilling the accession criteria.

The civil society initiatives and associations have expressed themselves less often on this topic than in the other ECECs. The right-wing political and social initiative, e-zin Pravé spektrum, whose authors have often held very Eurosceptic positions, published a text in October 2004 called "We Have to Say No to Turkey." Here, again, were repeated arguments of a historical, cultural, and mainly religious nature. There appeared the frequently discussed matters such as the so-called Kurdish question, discrimination of Turkish Christians, as well as economic reasons (the problem of agriculture), which according to the author of the text would mean more money for the Turks, and less money for the Slovaks (Daniška 2004).

The nationalistic organization Slovak Solidarity distributed a poster *No to Turkey in Europe*, and called on their supporters to download it from the web and post it in public areas. Its essence was to admonish the danger of Europe's Islamization.[14] The opposite standpoint was taken up by the Young Social Democrats who supported Turkey's accession and their main argument was that it would diversify Europe and facilitate multiculturalism (MSD 2004).

Conclusion: Eurooptimism/Euroscepticism of the political parties

The political parties, movements and initiatives mentioned here can be categorized by their programs, slogans, mottos, and positions of their individual members into various groupings on the Eurooptimism–Euroscepticism scale. Although a number of very sophisticated typologies could be used, we will present one which is adequate for our purposes. In 2006, we published a text in which we were able to use a very simple typology. We divided the parties into the following: pro-European without exceptions, which support a federal EU; pro-European with exceptions, which support intergovernmental cooperation; and reserved anti-European (Baun *et al.* 2006).

We will use this typology here for both the civic movements and initiatives, and the political parties – with only one exception. The orientation towards the federal model/ intergovernmental cooperation will be applied to political parties only. We will analyze the subjects presented earlier, their position towards the EU, and what their political objectives in relation to the cooperation and the Turkish EU membership are.

As we can see in Table 8.2, in the case of support or opposition to Turkish EU membership, the type of cooperation the actor prefers is irrelevant. The level of Euroscepticism or Eurooptimism therefore is not a significantly determining factor in establishing the stance towards the Turkish EU membership bid.

We have shown in this chapter that the ECECs discuss Turkish membership within the same themes as the other EU member states, or that they address the same concerns. In several cases it is difficult to evaluate the position of the political party because opinions develop over time and the representatives also react to current events. Moreover, individual members can protest against the party resolutions and break the party's unified stance.[15] It is easier to observe coherent opinions in the case of individual initiatives which often emerge for the purpose of opposing Turkish EU membership or to defend it.

It is, however, important to follow the developments in the ECECs as they have a different historical experience with multiculturalism, or more precisely, that there's is not the type of experience that we know from Western Europe. It is naturally the legacy of the decades of communist regimes, where the countries of Central Europe were held in cultural, political, and mainly economic isolation. These relatively poorer and democratizing countries were not very attractive for refugees and immigrants. They are only now slowly learning to live with diversity, with communities that have not historically lived on their territories. It will also be interesting to learn why Hungary and Poland are more accommodating to Turkey than the Czech Republic and Slovakia.

In the future, we can expect that the debate on Turkish accession will intensify. Primarily those in opposition will become louder in expressing their concerns with Turkish accession and they will continue to use and build up on the four themes introduced at the beginning of this chapter.

Notes

1 For the discussion on the formation of Czech identity between East and West, see Vlachová and Řeháková 2009.
2 For more, see http://tureckodoeu.pspace.cz.
3 The party was in government between 1998–2002 (single party minority government) and 2002–2006 (coalition governmenr with Christian Democrats [KDU-ČSL] and the centrist liberal Union of Freedom [US]).

Table 8.2 Political parties, movements, and initiatives and their position to Turkish accession

Party	Country	Position	Objective	Turkey
ČSSD	CZ	Pro-EU without reservations	Federal EU	Support accession
KDU – ČSL	CZ	Pro-EU without reservations	Federal EU	Reject accession
KSČM	CZ	Pro-EU with reservations	Intergovernmental cooperation	Support accession
ODS	CZ	Pro-EU with reservations	Intergovernmental cooperation	Support accession without exceptions
SZ	CZ	Pro-EU without reservations	Federal EU	Support accession
European Values	CZ	Pro-EU without reservations		Reject accession
euRabia	CZ	Pro-EU with reservations		Reject accession
Turecko do EU	CZ	Pro-EU without reservations		Support accession
FIDESZ	HU	Pro-EU with reservations	Intergovernmental cooperation	Reject accession
Jobbik	HU	Reserved anti-EU	Intergovernmental cooperation	Reject accession
KDNP	HU	Pro-EU with reservations	Federal EU	Reject accession
MSZP	HU	Pro-EU without reservations	Federal EU	Support accession
SZDSZ	HU	Pro-EU without reservations	Federal EU	Reject accession
PiS	PL	Pro-EU with reservations	Intergovernmental cooperation	Support accession
PSL	PL	Pro-EU with reservations	Intergovernmental cooperation	Support accession
PO	PL	Pro-EU with reservations	Intergovernmental cooperation	Support accession
SLD	PL	Pro-EU without reservations	Federal EU	Support accession
Europa Przyszłości	PL	Pro-EU without reservations		Reject accession
HZDS	SK	Pro-EU with reservations	Federal EU	Support accession
SDKU	SK	Pro-EU without reservations	Federal EU	Support accession
Smer	SK	Pro-EU without reservations	Federal EU	Support accession
SMK	SK	Pro-EU without reservations	Federal EU	Support accession
SNS	SK	Pro-EU with reservations	Intergovernmental cooperation	Reject accession
Pravé spektrum	SK	Reserved anti-EU		Reject accession

Source: author

4 See http://tureckodoeu.pspace.cz
5 Richard Falbr was between 1994 and 2002 chairman of the Bohemian-Moravian Confederation of Trade Unions.
6 For more, see http://tureckodoeu.pspace.cz
7 For more, see http://tureckodoeu.pspace.cz/?c_id = 89
8 See http://www.euert.hu/htmls/az_alapitvanyrol1.html
9 See http://www.merhaba.mc.ptja.pl/
10 See http://www.spiwpt.republika.pl/turystyka/index.html
11 It is interesting to note that this was said before the Orange Revolution took place in Ukraine.
12 In 2007, three Christians were murdered in the South Eastern Turkish city of Malatya – two were Turkish converts to Christianity and one was a German citizen.
13 For more, see http://www.psl.org.pl/?q = 0&news = 555
14 See http://pospolitost.wordpress.com/2008/05/27/nie-turecku-v-europe/
15 The pressure to follow the party line might increase as the accession conditions for Turkey become clearer and as the accession date draws closer.

9   Conclusion

The new European Union

Pavel Šaradín

The central concern of this book was the accession of Turkey to the European Union. While obviously not the first book dealing with the topic and surely not the last, it is one of the first attempts to explore this issue not only from the European perspective but specifically from a Central European one. The Central European experience differs to some extent from the pan-European or Western European. The East Central European Countries (ECECs) underwent approximately four decades of non-democratic development after World War II. This experience became manifest in their different value framework, including their higher support for further enlargement of the European Union (EU) than we can find in the older EU member states. This attitude partially stems from their "lost Europeaness" when communism caused Europe to be for a long time identified culturally, politically, and geographically with Western Europe only – the Polish writer Andrej Stasiuk talks even today about "second hand" Europe.

On the one hand, there is the long-term and continual cooperation in the West, and on the other, there is the experience with totalitarianism and the expectation of a better future related to the "return to Europe" in the East. A Slovenian sociologist and poet Aleš Debeljak (2004: 109) said that Eastern part of Europe had feelings of "half Europeans." In the ECECs and in virtually all post-communist countries of Eastern Europe, the period of the 1990s was filled with debates about the extent to which they were European, why some things worked better in Western Europe and when and how they were going to overcome "post-communism." They waited for the EU accession date as a confirmation that they finally became (again) true and equal Europeans.

There were various conditions to be met and the accession reports were read with utmost concern. As we have seen, however, the accession conditions had a problem of a discrepancy between rules and practice, which needs to be more explicitly addressed in any current or future accession talks. Spain, Portugal, and Greece were previously admitted to the EC with many shortcomings in their democratic structures with the assumption that these would be addressed later. The current approach is different – it increasingly prefers to allow countries in only after they address their problems. However, as we saw with the so-called Eastern enlargement, the articulated demands and reality often did not match. Thus, the EU has been trying to tighten up the rules ever since, increasingly applying the principle of safeguarding implementation rather than only promises of reforms, i.e. trying to ensure that "irreversible" democratization occurs. In real terms, it means that harmonization of laws is not sufficient without implementation on the ground. This, however, is hard to monitor, thus, the question is to what extent it simply represents just the rhetoric to appease some EU actors, who feel uneasy about further enlargement.

As we have shown in the book, Turkey and Central Europe have many common analogies in the experience with non-democratic regimes. The ideologies of state culture undermined in certain phases of their history the building and formation of democratic culture and institutions. The Turkish-Central European perspective outlined in this volume provides several interesting insights into some problems with applying the conclusions of Europeanization research to newly democratized/ democratizing countries. Combining the two perspectives presented the possibility of opening a number of new angles. The countries of Central Europe are well aware of the fact that they joined a very different EU than the countries before them, largely due to the immense growth in EU legislation and areas of EU competence, of growing political and economic integration. They are also aware of the different impact of EU integration after the introduction of the Copenhagen criteria in 1993. Democratic conditionality has become a key EU accession strategy moving from the originally more procedural condition to provisions of substantive democracy. The last enlargements tested how they work and when they can be effective.

The accession of the former communist countries to the EU was a crucial moment in the continent's history, which symbolically ended the Cold War division of Europe. Accession referenda were held in virtually all candidate countries (CCs) for the first time allowing their citizens to actively and directly participate in the EU accession process. Various arguments for and against EU membership and the Accession Treaty were presented. It was not all that difficult to justify membership for the feeling of belonging to Europe was omnipresent. In addition to perceiving the EU as a successful peace project, Central and Eastern Europeans were supportive of their countries' EU accession because of economic, security, social, cultural, tourist, and other reasons. It was much more difficult to present arguments why not to accede to the EU and these negative voices predominantly emphasized the potential loss of national sovereignty, economic exploitation, and the fear of excessive influence of some countries in the EU, particularly Germany.

Roughly speaking, technical issues prevailed during the accession talks in the ECECs but more recently new venues of interest regarding the EU were opened, such as the issue of European identity. As already stated, in the 1990s the ECECs articulated their belonging to Europe, "confirmed" by their accession to the EU. With the opportunity to increase their power and influence, to co-decide and to bear responsibility for European affairs, they have started to ask more often: what Europe? What is still European and what is not? In the EU-15 as well, we could find expressions of renewed attempts to understand and define the nature of European identity.

Over the past 20 years, numerous accounts have been written about Europe, its building blocks, historical turns, and especially its future. The year 1989 had obviously played a major part in the recent wave of debates over European issues when the two parts of the European continent divided by the Cold War started to reunite and get to know each other. In recent years, the technical, legal, and political aspects of the Lisbon Treaty opened an immense space for another round of debates about the importance of Europe and the EU as such. What is Europe, then?

An American essayist George Steiner (2005) explored Europe in the book *The Idea of Europe*; his effort to understand Europe did not focus on one aspect only but strove for a comprehensive account and he presents five "levels" of Europe. The first three are very inspiring; it is the public space defined by cafés, landscapes shaped and humanized by walking, and cities defined by references to the past, consisting for example of the names of streets or squares. The fourth is very commonly used and referred to; it is the double legacy of Athens and Jerusalem and in a certain sense it relates to the entire Western culture, not only Europe. The fifth level, albeit somewhat disputable, is eschatological. There have been very few attempts such as this one and it has a clear goal viewed through the prism of simple logic: if we expand deliberation of Europe to more than one region, our conclusions may prove to be more trustworthy. Then we can add further definitions and notions which co-define the continent. Let us remember, for example, Kundera's (1993) perception of the novel as a European invention, Miłosz's (1992) book *Native Realm* (*Rodzinna Europa*), or Le Goff's (1990) analysis of medieval Europe.

George Steiner defined his notion of Europe using five levels, five axioms, and numerous examples. We can add more: for example cafés were one of the defining traits of Austro-Hungarian/Central European culture. Where else than in the novels by Joseph Roth do we find a more picturesque description of cafés, which did not differ from one another and which stretched from Lvov through Krakow to Vienna and Trieste? How could Japanese tourists pass Vienna's Café Hawelka when touring European cultural attractions? But it is not necessarily true that the more examples there are, the stronger an axiom. Steiner's claims are different in nature. It will suffice if we realize the contexts of the European foundations he defined.

However, Europe also has its disturbing history, a past that cannot be forgotten and which we have not always managed to come fully to terms with. Steiner primarily mentioned anti-Semitism which had grown in many places in Europe as Christian traditions were developed and enforced. According to him, concentration camps had a long history in Europe dating far back before Nazi Germany. The reminder of these tragic events has a single meaning here: we must not idealize Europe, we must not close our eyes to our own past, hide from memory which has concrete names visible everywhere in the streets.

If Western Europeans were at times uneasy about welcoming back their "lost neighbors," who themselves struggled with defining their precise place within Europe, the Turkish case indicates much stronger traces of both. The experience of the ECECs could help Turkey not only because they have recently passed through the gates of the EU. On the one hand, it was necessary and useful to fulfill the membership criteria and conditions defined by the EU institutions but on the other, the ECECs had to face the stereotypical and even disdainful evaluations by some politicians and some public in EU-15. Central Europe is perhaps more sensitive to some political manifestations than the West, which can help them understand some Turkish specifics even though Turkey has many specific problems that might seem foreign and distant to the ECECs. Still, they all too well understand the problems of overcoming the legacies of the past, how rigid they are, and the hard task of changing people's minds. Moreover, their general tendency to define Europe in less rigid terms within their own identity search, which we can with some overstatement see as "half Europeanism," allows for a relatively smooth incorporation of Turkey into this modified version of "Europeaness."

We have intentionally titled this conclusion "The New European Union." The term "New EU" refers to the changes related to the so-called Eastern enlargement in 2004 but also some institutional reforms such as the increased powers of the European Parliament. Nevertheless, the crucial factor of an even "newer" Europe is still ahead: the accession of Turkey. The ECECs had battled with a large number of issues in their effort to accede to the EU but there were no major doubts in cultural, religious, geographic, or political terms. This is not true for Turkey and its accession will thus be much more difficult for the EU to "swallow." Only when Turkey has acceded will we be able to talk about the truly "new" EU precisely because of the aspects we have just mentioned. The EU has transformative power (Christiansen et al. 1999) not only for the member states and CCs but also for itself – its decisions transform the EU, including enlargement which is one of the more dynamic forces of transformation. While the EU vastly increased its level of institutionalization over the past 20 years, it has also enlarged from 12 member states in 1990 to 27 in 2007. It seemed that deepening and widening are possible at the same time but it came to a halt as both processes are experiencing a "fatigue" these days or something similar to what Václav Havel labeled the disillusioned atmosphere in the late 1990s' Czech society – the EU, its member states, and citizens have a bad mood (*blbá nálada*).

It is not enough to wait until Turkey identifies with Europe and the EU – the Turkish government and the EU must actively contribute to the process, something that was in the previous enlargement rounds neglected and is still causing problems. Some call it communication or information campaign, for others it is merely propaganda. No matter the label, the citizens should be able to identify with certain core values and perceive them as inherently European – and Turkish – to feel part of the project and to feel included to ensure that the reforms become embedded in their minds because as said at the beginning of this volume, the CCs see the EU as a legitimate actor only if the people can identify with it – at least to some extent. If we use the most neutral definition of the EU values defined politically as democracy, human rights, and rule of law, both the EU and the CC must feel strong attachment to it in terms of values – even if its practice is, in both the member states and the CCs, at times strained. We have shown that the process of Europeanization can be successful only if the country sees it as legitimate and the domestic forces strong enough to influence the political (and other) elites are willing to pursue the necessary reforms. So, Europeanization changes the CCs but cannot do so without their active cooperation sustained over time.

This volume addressed not only the problems that the Central European countries had struggled with but the criteria Turkey has managed to meet and where it still lags behind. The future debates will see major shifts in the concept of European identity. Its narrow definition most commonly provided today will no longer be possible. The Eastern enlargement has slowly led to the redefinition of "Europe" and the connection between "us" and "them" will have to undergo another development as a result of Turkey's accession. Let us hope that the successful transformation of Central European countries and their accession to the EU can be inspiring for Turkey although their accession process was much easier than it will be for Turkey. As for Turkey, it is vital that both parts of the continent are equal and share the responsibility for the project called the EU.

Appendix

Table A.1

Issues of Negotiation	Greek (Cypriot) Position	Turkish (Cypriot) Position
POLITICAL SYSTEM	A unitary state structure is preferred. A federation in which the Turkish Cypriot can have "autonomy" is offered. May accept a bi-communal, bi-zonal federation without the equality of the Turkish Cypriot community. However, enormous side payments are needed for the acceptance of a bi-zonal, bi-communal federation in which the two federated states will have political equality.	"Two sovereign states" or a bi-zonal, bi-communal "confederation" of "two sovereign states" is preferred. However, with substantial side payments, a bi-zonal, bi-communal federation with specific political equality for the Turkish Cypriot community may be accepted.
Federal powers	Strong federal (central) system.	Very weak confederal/federal (central) system.
State powers	Very weak and limited powers.	Very strong and extensive powers. Specifically, the states will be sovereign.
Sovereignty	Single sovereignty for the whole island (i.e. for both communities).	Separate sovereignty for each people/nation (community) based on the self-determination right of each community.
Representation	Greek Cypriot President, (maybe) Turkish Cypriot Vice-President (no rotational presidency). Ratio of Greek to Turkish Cypriots in council of ministers, federal	Rotational Presidency; 50:50 Greek and Turkish Cypriot representation in (con)federal institutions.

Issues of Negotiation	Greek (Cypriot) Position	Turkish (Cypriot) Position
	legislature and institutions to be based on population ratio (80:20 Greek to Turkish Cypriot).	
GUARANTORSHIP	A multi-national force, such as NATO, or UN force. No unilateral intervention right for Turkey.	1960 Treaty of Guarantee to remain without any change (unilateral intervention right for Turkey).
THREE FREEDOMS		
Freedom of movement	Absolute freedom.	Freedom with very small restrictions (for former EOKA terrorists, etc.).
Freedom of settlement	Absolute freedom.	Freedom with restrictions (a quota to be imposed so the bi-zonality is respected).
Freedom of property ownership	Absolute freedom.	Strong restrictions, and after a moratorium.
TERRITORIAL ADJUSTMENT	Greek Cypriot State having 80 percent of the land. May go down to around 75 percent.	Turkish Cypriot State to retain 29+ percent of the land.
MILITARY BUILDUP	Demilitarization of the island. A multinational force and lightly armed police force of Cypriots maintaining order.	Separate forces of defense and police for each state. Turkey keeps a contingent on the island for the security of Turkish Cypriots.
DISPLACED PERSONS & PROPERTIES	All displaced persons have the right to return to their properties.	Restricted access to the displaced persons. Compensatory payments for the displaced persons and territorial adjustment to respect the bi-zonality.
SETTLERS/ IMMIGRANTS	All Turkish settlers should go back to mainland Turkey.	All Turkish immigrants should stay in Cyprus.
EU MEMBERSHIP	Strongly supports.	Supports membership only after a final solution, separate referenda for the two communities, and special relations of Cyprus with Turkey (i.e. Turkey having same rights as the other EU members in Cyprus).

Bibliography

Adıvar, H.E. (1924) *Yeni Turan,* Istanbul: İkbal Kitabevi.
—— (1930) *Turkey Faces West. A Turkish View of Recent Changes and Their Origin,* New Haven: Yale University Press.
—— (1935) *Conflict of East and West in Turkey. Extension Lectures Delivered at the Jamia Millia Islamia in 1935,* Lahore: Muhammad Ashraf.
—— (1955) *Türkiye'de Şark, Garp ve Amerikan Tesisleri,* Istanbul: Doğan Kardeş.
—— (2000) *Vurun Kahpeye,* Istanbul: Özgür [1926].
Aktualne.sk (2006) "Fico: Turecko patrí do EÚ, na náboženstve nezáleží." Online. Available HTTP: http://aktualne.centrum.sk/domov/politika/forum.phtml?op=text&id=222372&topic[]=412129,1 (Accessed 1 May 2009)
Akyol, T. (2007) "Azinlik Vakiflari," *Milliyet,* 11 January.
Akyıldız, K. and Karacasu, B. (1999) "Mavi Anadolu: Edebi kanon ve millî kültürün yapılandırılışında Kemalizm ile bir ortaklık denemesi," *Toplum ve Bilim,* 81: 26–43.
Alpay, S. (2009) "Why Does the EU Matter for Turkey?," *Today's Zaman,* 18 May: 15.
Altınay, A.G. and Arat, Y. (2009) *Violence against Women in Turkey. A Nationwide Survey.* Istanbul: Punto. Online. Available HTTP: http://www.kamilpasha.com/wp-content/uploads/2009/04/altinayviolence209.pdf (Accessed 22 May 2009).
Alyamaç, S. (2009) "CHP Committed to the EU, Says Rep," *Hürriyet Daily News,* 28 May. Online. Available HTTP: http://www.hurriyet.com.tr/english/domestic/11740415.asp (Accessed 28 May 2009).
Ananicz, A. (2007) "Conditionality, Impact and Prejudice in EU-Turkey Relations. A View from Poland," in N. Tocci (ed.) *Conditionality, Impact and Prejudice in EU-Turkey Relations,* Roma: Quaderni IAI.
Anatolia News Agency (2003) "Erdoğan Favors Changing Traditional Cyprus Policy," 2 January.
Appel, H. (2001) "Corruption and the Collapse of the Czech Transition Miracle," *East European Politics & Societies* 15(3): 528–53.
Aras, B. and Polat, R.K. (2008) "From Conflict to Cooperation: Desecuritization of Turkey's Relations with Syria and Iran," *Security Dialogue,* 39(5): 475–95.
Arat, Y. (1998) "A Woman Prime Minister in Turkey," *Women & Politics* 19(4): 1–22.
Arendt, H. (1951) *The Origins of Totalitarianism,* New York: Harcourt Brace & Company.
Arikan, H. (2006) *Turkey and the EU: An Awkward Candidate for EU Membership?,* Aldershot: Ashgate.
Arts, W. and Halman, L. (2004). "European Values Changes in the Second Age of Modernity," in W. Arts and L. Halman (eds) *European Values at the Turn of the Millennium,* Leiden: Brill Academic Publishers.

Avci, G. (2006) "Turkey's EU Politics: Consolidating Democracy through Enlargement?," in H. Sjursen (ed.) *Questioning EU Enlargement. Europe in Search of Identity,* London: Routledge.

Aybar, C.B., Mergen, A.E., Perotti, V., and McHardy Reid, D. (2007) "Analysis of Attitudes of Turkish Citizens towards the Effect of European Union Membership on the Economic, Political and Cultural Environment," *Turkish Studies,* 8(3): 329–48.

Aydın, S. (2002) "Cumhuriyet İdeolojik Şekillenmesinde Antropolojinin Rolü: Irkçı Paradigmanın Yükselişi ve Düşüşü," in *Modern Türkiye'de Siyasî Düşünce. Cilt 2: Kemalizm,* Istanbul: İletişim, 344–369.

—— (2003) "30'ların tezlerine geri dönüş: Anadolu'da „proto-Türkler'in yeniden keşfi," *Toplum ve Bilim,* 96: 8–34.

Aydin, M. and Esen, A.T. (2007) "Conditionality, Impact and Prejudice: A Concluding View from Turkey," in N. Tocci (ed.) *Conditionality, Impact and Prejudice in EU-Turkey Relations,* Roma: Quaderni IAI.

Aydinli, E., Özcan, N.A., and Akyaz, D. (2006) "The Turkish Military's March towards Europe," *Foreign Affairs,* 85: 77–90.

Bagci, H. (2006) "Will Turkey's Painful Process Stop?," *The Anatolian,* 19 June.

Balci, K. (2009). "Europe Needs Turkey, Its Enthusiasm," *Today's Zaman,* 11 May.

Balzacq, T. (2005) "The Three Faces of Securitization: Political Agency, Audience and Context," *European Journal of International Relations,* 11(2): 171–201.

Bardi, L., Rhodes, M., and Nello, S.S. (2002) "Enlarging the European Union: Challenges to and from Central and Eastern Europe-Introduction," *International Political Science Review* 23(3): 227–33.

Batory, A. (2006) *The European Future of Turkey and Ukraine: The Policy Debate in Hungary,* Budapest: Center for Policy Studies, Central European University.

Baun, M., Dürr, J., Marek, D., and Šaradín, P. (2006) The Europeanization of Czech Politics: The Political Parties and the EU Referendum,"*Journal of Common Market Studies,* 44(2): 249–80.

Bayramoğlu, A. (2005) "Milli Güvenlik Siyaset Belgesi nedir?," *Yeni Safak,* 29 April.

BBC (2005) "*V Praze se demonstrovalo proti vstupu Turecka do EU,*" 20 June. Online. Available HTTP: http://www.bbc.co.uk/czech/domesticnews/story/2005/06/050620_ cz_eu_turkey_1820.shtml (Accessed 12 September 2007).

Beblavý, M. and Beblavá, E. (2009) "(Anti)corruption in Slovakia and the European Union: Comparison of Pre-Accession and Post Accession Policies and Situation," paper presented at the Enlargement – Five Years After: The State of European Integration and New Challenges for the Discipline, Budapest, May.

Beissinger, M.R. (2008) "A New Look at Ethnicity and Democratization," *Journal of Democracy,* 19(3): 85–97.

Beneš, V. (2006) *Kdo se bojí Turecka v EU?* Online. Available HTTP: http://aktualne. centrum.cz/blogy-a-nazory/clanek.phtml?id=163825 (Accessed 23 March 2009).

Benhabib, S. and Isiksel, T. (2006) "Ancient Battles, New Prejudices, and Future Perspectives: Turkey and the EU," *Constellations* 13(2): 218–33.

Berktay, F. (2004) "La situación de la mujer en Turquía en el marco del proceso de adhesión a la UE," *Revista CIDOB d'Afers Internacionales* 75: 101–109.

Bianet (2009) "How will New Minister of Justice Deal with Article 301?," 7 May. Online. Available HTTP: http://bianet.org/english/freedom-of-expression/114368-how-will- new-minister-of-justice-deal-with-article-301 (Accessed 28 June 2009).

Bilgin, P. (2005) "Turkey's Changing Security Discourses: The Challenge of Globalization," *European Journal of Political Research,* 44(1): 175–201.

Birand, M.A. (1990) *Türkiye'nin Ortak Pazar Macerası: 1959–1990,* İstanbul: Milliyet.
—— (2007) "Erdoğan Watches as EU Sails by," *TDN,* 14 December: 15.
Borragán, N.P.-S. (2002) "Coming to Terms with European Union Lobbying: The Central and Eastern European Experience," in A. Warleigh and J. Fairbrass (eds) *Influence and Interests in the European Union: The New Politics of Persuasion and Advocacy,* London: Europa Publications Limited.
—— (2003) "The Organisation of Business Interests in Central and East European Countries for EU Representation," in J. Greenwood (ed.) *The Challenge of Change in EU Business Associations,* Basingstoke: Palgrave.
—— (2004) "EU Accession and Interest Politics in Central and Eastern Europe," *Perspectives on European Society & Society,* 5(2): 243–72.
—— (2006) "Post-Communist Interest Politics: A Research Agenda," *Perspectives on European Society & Society,* 7(2): 134–54.
Bower, L. (2001) "Women Making Strides," *The Prague Post,* 7 March. Online. Available HTTP: http://www.praguepost.cz/busi030701d.html (Accessed 11 May 2005).
Bozdoğan, S. and Kasaba, R. (1997) "Introduction", in S. Bozdoğan and R. Kasaba (eds) *Rethinking Modernity and National Identity in Turkey,* Seattle/London: University of Washington Press.
Bozkurt, A. (2009a) "Czech Deputy PM Says Turkey Key to Natural Gas," *Today's Zaman,* 25 April: 17.
—— (2009b) "Finnish FM: Turkey Is Not Breaking Away from Europe," *Today's Zaman,* 9 May: 4.
Bratinka, P. (2005) "Do Evropy chtějí tři Turecka, *"Občanský Institut.* Online. Available HTTP: http://www.obcinst.cz/cs/Do-Evropy-chteji-tri-Turecka-c832/ (Accessed 15 November 2007).
Březina, J. (2004a) "Nebezpečný sen liberálů a socialistů," *KDU-ČSL.* Online. Available HTTP: http://www.kdu.cz/default.asp?page=311&idr=10324&IDCl=13084 (Accessed 7 November 2007).
—— (2004b) "Turecko přes růžové brýle," *KDU-ČSL.* Online. Available HTTP: http://www.kdu.cz/default.asp?page=311&idr=10324&IDCl=12782 (Accessed 7 November 2007).
Bulbul, K. (2006) "Turkey and the EU: A Survey on Turkish MPs' EU Vision," *Alternatives: Turkish Journal of International Relations,* 5(3): 32–60.
Burda, A. (2006). "Habsburk, Hitler, Moskva, Brusel . . . Proč si neumíme vládnout sami?" ePortál, 2 February. Online. Available HTTP: http://www.eportal.cz/Articles/611-habsburk-hitler-moskva-brusel-proc-si-neumime-vladnout-sami-.aspx (Accessed 10 April 2009).
Bursík, M. (n.d.) "Tak tedy: jaká to bude politika," *Strana Zelených.* Online. Available HTTP: http://www.zeleni.cz/106/clanek/tak-tedy-jaka-to-bude-politika/ (Accessed 14 October 2007).
Çarkoğlu, A. (2003). "Who Wants Full Membership? Characteristics of Turkish Public Support for EU Membership," *Turkish Studies,* 4(2): 171–94.
Çarkoğlu, A. and Sözen, A. (2004) "Turkish Cypriot General Elections of December 2003: An Appraisal," *South European Society & Politics,* 9: 122–36.
Casanova, J. (2006) "The Long, Difficult, and Tortuous Journey of Turkey into Europe and the Dilemmas of European Civilization," *Constellations,* 13(2): 234–47.
Çelik, N.B. (1999) "Söylem Kuramları, Hegemonya Kavramı ve Kemalizm," *Doğu Batı,* 8: 27–39.
Čermák, D. (n.d.) "Tisková zpráva," *KDU-ČSL.* Online. Available HTTP: http://www.kdu.cz/default.asp?page=311&IDCl=12739&ID=135 (Accessed 14 October 2007).

Cevik, I. and Kanli, Y. (2002) "Bahceli Says Reforms Subject to Impact on National Unity," *TDN,* 26 January. Online. Available HTTP: http://arama.hurriyet.com.tr/arsivnews. aspx?id=-527357 (Accessed 15 April 2005).

Checkel, J.T. (1999) "Social Construction and Integration," *Journal of European Public Policy*, 6(4): 545–60.

—— (2000) "Compliance and Conditionality," *ARENA Working Papers,* WP 00/18. Online. Available HTTP: http://www.arena.uio.no/publications/wp00_18.htm (Accessed 17 June 2008).

Chen, X. (2002) *Occidentalism. A Theory of Counter-Discourse in Post-Mao China,* Lanham/Boulder/New York/Oxford: Rowman and Littlefield.

Chiva, C. (2006) "Ethnic Minority Rights in Central and Eastern Europe: The Case of the Hungarian 'Status Law,'" *Government and Opposition* 41(3): 401–21.

Christiansen, T., Jørgensen, K.E., and Wiener, A. (1999) "The Social Construction of Europe," *Journal of European Public Policy*, 6(4): 528–44.

Cizre-Sakallioglu, U. (1997) "The Anatomy of the Turkish Military's Political Autonomy," *Comparative Politics,* 29(4): 151–65.

Copeaux, E. (1998) *Tarih Ders Kitaplarında (1931–1993) Türk Tarih Tezinden Türk-İslam Sentezine*, Istanbul: Tarih Vakfı Yayınları.

Cordell, C. (2000) *Politics of Ethnicity in Central Europe*, New York: Palgrave.

Council of the European Union (2009) "European Council 11 and 12 December 2008. Presidency Conclusions." Online. Available HTTP: http://www.consilium.europa.eu/ ueDocs/cms_Data/docs/pressData/en/ec/104692.pdf (Accessed 13 March 2009).

ČTK (2007) "Premiér Topolánek podpořil snahu Turecka o vstup do EU." Online. Available HTTP: http://ib.ctk.cz/infobanka/ (Accessed 16 November 2007).

—— (2009) "Schwarzenberg podpořil vstup Turecka do EU," Online. Available HTTP. (Accessed 30 April 2009).

Dagi, I.D. (2001) "Human Rights, Democratization and the European Community in Turkish Politics: The Özal Years, 1983–87," *Middle Eastern Studies* 37(1): 17–40.

Daniška, J. (2004) "Turecku treba povedať NIE," *Pravé Spektrum – politicko-spoločenský e-zin.* Online. Available HTTP: http://www.prave-spektrum.sk/print.php?208 (Accessed 3 June 2009).

Dartan, M. and Hatipoglu, E. (2006) "The Future of Turkey-European Union Relations: Post-December 2004," in N. Neuwahl and H. Kabaalioglu (eds) *European Union and Turkey: Reflections on the Prospects for Membership*, Ankara: TOBB.

Debeljak, A. (2004) *Evropa brez Evropejcev*, Ljubljana: Sophia.

de Master, S. and le Roy, M.K. (2000) "Xenophobia and the European Union," *Comparative Politics*, 32: 419–36.

de Ridder, E. (2008) "EU Democracy Promotion in the Czech Republic and Slovakia: the Power of the National Government," paper submitted for the 58th UK Political Studies Association Conference, Swansea, April.

de Vreese, C.H., Boomgaarden, H.G., and Semetko, H.A. (2008) "Hard and Soft: Public Support for Turkish Membership in the EU," *European Union Politics,* 9(4): 511–30.

Delanty, G. (2003) "The Making of Post-Western Europe: A Civilizational Analysis," *Thesis 11*, 72(8): 8–25.

Delanty, G. and Rumford, C. (2005) *Rethinking Europe. Social Theory and the Implications of Europeanization*, London: Routledge.

Delsoldato, G. (2002) Eastward Enlargement by the European Union and Transnational Parties," *International Political Science Review*, 23(3): 269–89.

Diez, T. (1999) "'Speaking 'Europe': The Politics of Integration Discourse," *Journal of European Public Policy* 6(4): 598–613.

—— (2000) "The Imposition of Governance: Transforming Foreign Policy through EU Enlargement," *Copenhagen Peace Research Institute,* Working Paper 24.

Doğan, M. (2001) *Batılılaşma İhaneti.* Istanbul: İz Yayıncılık [1975].

Doğan, Y.P. (2009a) "Amendments Do Not Cure Constitutional Problems," *Today's Zaman,* 11 May: 6.

—— (2009b) "Bağış: EU's Naysayers Will Be Mere Footnotes in History," *Today's Zaman,* 13 April: 6.

—— (2009c) "EU Expert Says Clear-Cut Accession Date Key for Turkey," *Today's Zaman,* 26 January: 6.

—— (2009d) "Lagendijk Says Some EU States Hiding Behind Cyprus," *Today's Zaman,* 20 April: 1, 6.

Donnelly, S. (2006) "Federal, Socialist and Christian Founding Myths of the European Union and Prospects for Turkish Accession," in N. Neuwahl and H. Kabaalioğlu (eds) *European Union and Turkey: Reflections on the Prospects for Membership,* Ankara: TOBB.

Drulák, P. (2001) *National and European Identities in EU-Enlargement,* Prague: Ústav mezinárodních vztahů.

Dümanli, E. (2005) "Basic Dilemma of EU Opponents," *Zaman Daily News,* 21 October. Online. Available HTTP: http://www.todayszaman.com/tz-web/yazarDetay. do?haberno=25310 (Accessed 17 July 2006).

Durakbaşa, A. (2002) *Halide Edib. Türk Modernleşmesi ve Feminizm,* Istanbul: İletişim.

Dürr, J., Marek, D. and Šaradín, P. (2004) "Europeizace české politické scény – politické strany a referendum o přistoupení k Evropské unii," *Mezinárodni vztahy,* 39(1): 27–49.

Düzel, N. (2007) "M. Kemal gelse, bu Kemalistleri sopayla kovalar," *Radikal,* 4 June.

Elgün, Ö. and Tillman, E.R. (2007) "Exposure to European Union Policies and Support for Membership in the Candidate Countries," *Political Research Quarterly,* 60(3): 391–400.

Enginün, İ. (1995) *Halide Edip Adıvar'ın Eserlerinde Doğu ve Batı Meselesi,* Istanbul: Milli Eğitim Bakanlığı.

EPACVAW (2009) "Country Focus – Turkey." Online. Available HTTP: http://www. epacvaw.org/spip.php?rubrique79 (Accessed 12 May 2009).

Epstein, R. (2007) "International Institutions and the Democratization of Central and East European Civil-Military Relations," paper submitted for the 10th biennial international EUSA conference, Montreal, May.

Eriksson, J. (1999) "Observers or Advocates? On the Political Role of Security Analysts," *Cooperation and Conflict,* 34(3): 311–33.

EurActiv (2005) "Budget 2007–13: Prospects for Deal Look Bleak." Online. Available HTTP: http://www.euractiv.com/en/future-eu/budget-2007-2013-prospects-deal-look-bleak/article-138571 (Accessed 1 May 2009).

—— (2006) "Status of Women in Turkey." Online. Available HTTP: http://www.euractiv. com/en/enlargement/status-women-turkey-black-white/article-153186 (Accessed 27 May 2009).

—— (2008) "Topolánek: vstup Turecka do EU bezvýhradně podporujeme." Online. Available HTTP: http://www.euractiv.cz/budoucnost-eu/clanek/topolanek-vstup-turecka-do-eu-bezvyhradne-podporujeme (Accessed 20 March 2009).

European Commission (1989) "Commission Opinion on Turkey's Request for Accession to the Community," SEC(89) 2290 final/2, Brussels 1989.

—— (1990) "Central and Eastern Eurobarometer." Online. Available HTTP: http://europa.
eu.int/comm/public_opinion/archives/ceeb_en.htm (Accessed 15 April 2005).

—— (1997) "European Commission Public Opinion." Online. Available HTTP: http://europa.
eu.int/comm/public_opinion/archives/ceeb/ceeb8/ceeb08.pdf (Accessed 15 April 2005).

—— (2002) "Candidate Countries Eurobarometer First Results. European Commission
Public Opinion." Online. Available HTTP: http://ec.europa.eu/public_opinion/archives/
cceb/2002/cceb_2002_highlights_en.pdf (Accessed 15 April 2005).

—— (2004a) "Commission Staff Working Document: Issues Arising from Turkey's
Membership Perspective," *COM* (2004) 656 final.

—— (2004b) "Eurobarometer 2003.5 – Identities and Values in the Acceding and Candidate
Countries." Online. Available HTTP: http://ec.europa.eu/public_opinion/archives/
cceb/2003/cceb_2003.5_identity.pdf (Accessed 13 April 2009).

—— (2004c) "Eurobarometer 62 – National Report Turkey. Executive Summary,"Online.
Available HTTP: http://ec.europa.eu/public_opinion/archives/eb/eb62/eb62_tr_exec.pdf
(Accessed 18 July 2006).

—— (2005a) "Eurobarometer 63." Online. Available HTTP: http://ec.europa.eu/public_
opinion/archives/eb/eb63/eb63_en.pdf (Accessed 18 July 2006).

—— (2005b) "Eurobarometer 64." Online. Available HTTP: http://ec.europa.eu/public_
opinion/archives/eb/eb64/eb64_first_en.pdf (Accessed 18 July 2007).

—— (2005c) "Eurobarometer 64 – Národní zpráva Česká republika." Online. Available
HTTP: http://ec.europa.eu/public_opinion/archives/eb/eb64/eb64_cs_nat.pdf (Accessed
17 May 2009).

—— (2006a) "Attitudes towards European Union Enlargement. 255. Eurobarometer."
Online. Available HTTP: http://ec.europa.eu/public_opinion/archives/ebs/ebs_255_
en.pdf (accessed 6 March 2009).

—— (2006b) "Communication from the Commission to the European Parliament and the
Council: Enlargement Strategy and Main Challenges," COM (2006) 649.

—— (2006c) "Eurobarometer 65 – National Report Turkey. Executive Summary. Online.
Available HTTP: http://ec.europa.eu/public_opinion/archives/eb/eb65/eb65_tr_exec.pdf
(Accessed 18 July 2007).

—— (2006d) "Eurobarometer 66." Online. Available http://ec.europa.eu/public_opinion/
archives/eb/eb66/eb66_en.pdf (Accessed 18 July 2007).

—— (2006e) "Eurobarometer 66 – Avrupa Birliği'nde Kamuoyu." Online. Available HTTP:
http://ec.europa.eu/public_opinion/archives/eb/eb66/eb66_tr_nat.pdf (Accessed 5 July
2007).

—— (2007a) "Eurobarometer 67 – National Report Turkey." Online. Available HTTP:
http://ec.europa.eu/public_opinion/archives/eb/eb67/eb67_tr_exec.pdf (Accessed 18
July 2007).

—— (2007b) "Eurobarometer 68 – National Report Turkey." Online. Available HTTP:
http://ec.europa.eu/public_opinion/archives/eb/eb68/eb68_tr_exec.pdf (Accessed 6 July
2008).

—— (2008a) "Eurobarometer 69." Online. Available HTTP: http://ec.europa.eu/public_
opinion/archives/eb/eb69/eb69_en.htm (Accessed 25 April 2009).

—— (2008b) "Eurobarometer 69 – National Report Turkey." Online. Available HTTP:
http://ec.europa.eu/public_opinion/archives/eb/eb69/eb69_tr_exe.pdf (Accessed 6 July
2008).

—— (2008c) "Eurobarometer 70 – National Report Turkey." Online. Available HTTP:
http://ec.europa.eu/public_opinion/archives/eb/eb70/eb70_tr_exec.pdf (Accessed 16
March 2009).

—— (2008d) "Regional Features in Turkey." Online. Available HTTP: http://ec.europa.eu/regional_policy/sources/docoffic/official/reports/pdf/p324_boxturkey_en.pdf (Accessed 9 April 2009).

—— (2008e) "Special Eurobarometer 291. The Attitudes of Europeans towards Corruption." Online. Available at HTTP: http://ec.europa.eu/public_opinion/archives/ebs/ebs_291_en.pdf (Accessed 15 March 2009).

—— (2009) "Five Years of an Enlarged EU. Economic Achievements and Challenges." Online. Available HTTP: http://ec.europa.eu/economy_finance/publications/publication14078_en.pdf (Accessed 30 March 2009).

European Parliament (1999) "Briefing No 41 Public Opinion on Enlargement in the EU Member States and Applicant Countries." Online. Available HTTP: http://www.europarl.europa.eu/enlargement/briefings/41a3_en.htm (Accessed 25 May 2005).

—— (2007) "Report on the Composition of the European Parliament (2007/2169(INI))." Online. Available HTTP: http://www.europarl.europa.eu/sides/getDoc.do?pubRef=-//EP//NONSGML+REPORT+A6-2007-0351+0+DOC+WORD+V0//EN&language=EN (Accessed 25 October 2007).

Euroskop (2009) "Schwarzenberg podpořil vstup Turecka do EU," 9 January. Online. Available HTTP: http://www.euroskop.cz/38/10198/clanek/schwarzenberg-podporil-vstup-turecka-do-eu/ (Accessed 9 March 2009).

Eurostat (2009a) "GDP per Capita in PPS." Online. Available HTTP: http://epp.eurostat.ec.europa.eu/tgm/table.do?tab=table&init=1&plugin=0&language=en&pcode=tsieb010 (Accessed 9 March 2009).

—— (2009b) "People by Age Classes; Proportion of Population Aged 0–14 Years." Online. Available HTTP: http://epp.eurostat.ec.europa.eu/tgm/table.do?tab=table&init=1&plugin=0&language=en&pcode=tps00010 (Accessed 28 February 2009).

—— (2009c) "Population change." Online. Available HTTP: http://epp.eurostat.ec.europa.eu/tgm/table.do?tab=table&init=1&plugin=0&language=en&pcode=tps00006 (Accessed 6 March 2009).

—— (2009d) "Population Projections." Online. Available HTTP: http://epp.eurostat.ec.europa.eu/tgm/table.do?tab=table&init=1&plugin=0&language=en&pcode=tps00002 (Accessed 28 February 2009).

—— (2009e) "Proportion of Population Aged 65 and over." Online. Available HTTP: http://epp.eurostat.ec.europa.eu/tgm/table.do?tab=table&init=1&plugin=0&language=en&pcode=tps00028 (Accessed 28 February 2009).

—— (2009f) "Total Population." Online. Available HTTP: http://epp.eurostat.ec.europa.eu/tgm/table.do?tab=table&init=1&plugin=0&language=en&pcode=tps00001 (Accessed 6 March 2009).

Eylem, A.E. (2007) "Mona Lisa in Veils: Cultural Identity, Politics, Religion and Feminism in Turkey," *Feminist Theology* 16(1): 11–20.

Eylemer, S. and Taş, I. (2007) "Pro-EU and Eurosceptic Circles in Turkey," *Journal of Communist Studies and Transition Politics,* 23(4): 561–77.

Falbr, R. (2004) "Turecko do Evropy nepatří," *Rovnost.* Online. Available HTTP: http://www.falbr.cz/clanky_2004_I.php (Accessed 14 October 2007).

Featherstone, K. and Kazamias, G. (2000) "Introduction: Southern Europe and the Process of 'Europeanization,'" *South European Society & Politics*, 5(2): 1–24.

—— (2001) "Introduction: Southern Europe and the Process of Europeanization," in K. Featherstone and G. Kazamias (eds) *Europeanization and the Southern Periphery,* London: Frank Cass.

Featherstone, K. and Radaelli, C.M. (2003) *The Politics of Europeanization,* Oxford: Oxford University Press.

Filip, V. (2006) "Hlavní je prý strategická poloha," *Haló noviny*, 29 December.

Findley, C.V. (2005) *The Turks in World History*, New York: Oxford University Press.

Forest, M. (2006) "Emerging Gender Interest Groups in the New Member States: The Case of the Czech Republic," *Perspectives on European Politics and Society*, 7(2): 170–84.

*Gazeta Wyborcza (*2005) "Kampania przeciwko wpuszczeniu Turcji do Unii," 17 May. Online, Available HTTP: http://serwisy.gazeta.pl/swiat/1,34174,2713680.html (Accessed 17 May 2009).

Genel, S. and Karaosmanoglu, K. (2006) "A New Islamic Individualism in Turkey: Headscarved Women in the City," *Turkish Studies* 7(3): 473–88.

Gerhards, J. (2007) *Cultural Overstretch? Differences between Old and New Member States of the EU and Turkey*, Abingdon, Oxon: Routledge.

Gillespie, P. and Laffan, B. (2006) "European Identity: Theory and Empirics," in M. Cini and A.K. Bourne (eds) *European Union Studies*, London: Palgrave Macmillan.

Girzyński, W. (2008) "Dlaczego Turcja powinna wejść do Unii Europejskiej?" *Salon24*. Online. Available HTTP: http://girzynski.salon24.pl/98746,dlaczego-turcja-powinna-wejsc-do-unii-europejskiej (Accessed 1 May 2009).

Goetz, K. (2001) "Making Sense of Post-Communist Central Administration: Modernization, Europeanization or Latinization?," *Journal of European Public Policy*, 8(6): 1032–51.

—— (2005) "The New Member States and the EU" in: S. Bulmer and C. Lequesne (eds) *Member States and the European Union*, Oxford: Oxford University Press.

Gökalp, Z. (1970) *Türkçülüğün Esasları*. Istanbul: Milli Eğitim Basımevi [1923].

Gökarıksel, B. and Mitchell, K. (2005) "Veiling, Secularism and the Neoliberal Subject: National Narratives and Supranational Desires in Turkey and France," *Global Networks,* 5(2): 147–65.

Göle, N. (1997) *The Forbidden Modern. Civilization and Veiling*. Ann Arbor: The University of Michigan Press.

—— (2000) "80 Sonrasi Politik Kültür," [Political Culture after 1980s], in E. Kalaycioglu and A.Y. Saribay (eds), *Turkiye'de Politik Degisim ve Modernlesme [Political Change and Modernization in Turkey]*, Istanbul: Alfa, 309–318.

Gordon, P. and Taspinar, O. (2006) "Turkey on the Brink," *Washington Quarterly*, 29(3): 57–70.

Grabbe, H. (2001) "How Does Europeanization Affect CEE Governance? Conditionality, Diffusion and Diversity," *Journal of European Public Policy* 8(6): 1013–31.

—— (2002) "European Union Conditionality and the Acquis Communautaire," *International Political Science Review* 23(3): 249–68.

—— (2004) "EU Expansion and Democracy," *Politics and Democracy*, Summer/Fall: 73–79.

Grapard, U. (1997) "Theoretical Issues of Gender in the Transition from Socialist Regimes," *Journal of Economic Issues*, 21(3): 665–686.

Green Cowles, M. and Risse, T. (2001) "Conclusion," in M. Green Cowles, J. Caporaso and T. Risse (eds) *Transforming Europe. Europeanization and Domestic Change,* Ithaca/ London: Cornell University Press.

Green Cowles, M., Caporaso, J., and Risse, T. (eds) (2001) *Transforming Europe. Europeanization and Domestic Change,* Ithaca/London: Cornell University Press.

Grigoriadis, I. (2008) "On the Europeanization of Minority Rights Protection: Comparing the Cases of Greece and Turkey," *Mediterranean Politics*, 13(1): 23–41.

Gros, D. (2005) "Economic Aspects of Turkey's Quest for EU Membership," *CEPS Policy*

Brief, 69. Online. Available HTTP: http://aei.pitt.edu/6611/01/1217_69.pdf (Accessed 19 March 2009).

Grote, J. (2009) "Transactionalism and Civil Society in the Czech Republic. From the Exceptionalism of Pre-Accession towards the 'Normal Politics' of Post-Accession," paper presented at Enlargement – Five Years After: The State of European Integration and New Challenges for the Discipline, Budapest, May.

Gülmez, S. (2008) "The EU Policy of the Republican People's Party: An Inquiry on the Opposition Party and Euro-Skepticism in Turkey," *Turkish Studies,* 9(3): 423–36.

Gultasli, S. (2009) "Lagendijk: Olli Rehn Supports Ergenekon Case," *Today's Zaman,* 16 May: 17.

Güntekin, R.N. (n.d.) *Yeşil Gece,* Istanbul: İnkılâp [1928].

Güsten, S. (2005) "Fears Grow that EU Membership Would Equate to a Sell-Out of National Interests," *Quantara.* Online. Available HTTP: http://www.qantara.de/webcom/show_article.php/_c-476/_nr-358/i.html?PHPSESSID=5 (Accessed 18 July 2006).

Gyárfášová, O. (2008) "Turecko a EÚ," *Zahraničná Politika,* Online. Available HTTP: http://www.zahranicnapolitika.sk/index.php?id=667&tl=13 (Accessed 27 March 2009).

Hanioğlu, Ş. (1992) "Batılılaşma," in *Türkiye Diyanet Vakfı İslâm Ansiklopedisi,* cilt 5, Istanbul: Türkiye Diyanet Vakfı, 148–152.

Hanley, S. (2002) "Party Institutionalisation and Centre-Right Euroscepticism in East Central Europe: the Case of the Civic Democratic Party in the Czech Republic," paper presented at Workshop Opposing Europe: Euroscepticism and Political Parties ECPR Joint Sessions of Workshops, Turin, March.

Harris, C.D. (1993) "New European Countries and Their Minorities," *Geographical Review,* 83(3): 301–20.

Haşim, A. (1992) *Bize Göre,* Istanbul: İnkılâp.

Hašková, H. (2003) "Czech Women´s Civic and Political Participation in the Process of the EU Enlargement," paper presented at the 5th European Feminist Research Conference, Lund University, Sweden, August.

Haughton, T. (2007) "When Does the EU Make a Difference? Conditionality and the Accession Process in Central and Eastern Europe," *Political Studies Review* 5: 233–46.

Helvacioglu, B. (1996) "Allahu Ekber We Are Turks: Yearning for a Different Homecoming at the Periphery of Europe," *Third World Quarterly,* 17(3): 326–42.

Heritier, A. (2005) "Europeanization Research East and West: A Comparative Assessment," in F. Schimmelfennig and U. Sedelmeier (eds) *The Europeanization of Central and Eastern Europe,* New York: Cornell University Press.

Hoffmann, J. (2005) "Integrating Albania: The Role of the European Union in the Democratization Process," *Albanian Journal of Politics* I(1): 55–74.

Hokovský, R. (2004) *Česko a Slovensko v diskusi o členství Turecka v Evropské unii.* Online. Available HTTP: http://www.visegradinfo.wz.cz/?q=cs/node/103 (Accessed 23 March 2009).

Hospodářské noviny (2006) "Chorvatsko do EU, Turecko ne, říkají občané," iHNed.cz. Online. Available HTTP: (Accessed 23 October 2007).

Howard, W.J. (2002) "Southern Europe, Eastern Europe, and Comparative Politics: 'Transitology' and the Need for New Theory," *East European Politics & Societies,* 15(3): 485–501.

Hrušovský, P. (2004) "Stanovisko KDH k správe EK o začatí prístupových rokovaní s Tureckom," *KDH Vyhlásenia a stanoviská.* Online. Available HTTP: http://www.kdh.sk/article.php?7 (Accessed 12 April 2009).

Hughes, J., Sasse, G., and Gordon, C. (2004) *Europeanization and Regionalization in the EU's Enlargement to Central and Eastern Europe. The Myth of Conditionality*, New York: Palgrave Macmillan.

Hughes, K. (2004) "Turkey and the European Union: Just Another Enlargement? Exploring the Implications of Turkish Accession," *A Friends of Europe Working Paper*. Online. Available HTTP: http://www.cdu.de/en/doc/Friends_of_Europe_Turkey.pdf (Accessed 14 July 2008).

Huland, A. (2001) "Western Standards for Post-Communist Women?," *Features*. Online. Available HTTP: http://www.eumap.org/journal/features/2001/dec/westernst (Accessed 12 June 2009).

Hürriyet Daily News (2009a) "Istanbul Home to the Largest Number of NGOs," 5 January. Online. Available HTTP: http://arama.hurriyet.com.tr/arsivnews.aspx?id=10697678 (Accessed 9 January 2009).

—— (2009b) "Love-Hate Relationship of Turkey with the EU," 1 June. Online. Available HTTP: http://www.hurriyet.com.tr/english/domestic/11765414.asp (Accessed 1 June 2009).

—— (2009c) "NGOs, Gov't Meet to Advance Turkey's EU Bid," 9 March. Online. Available HTTP: http://www.hurriyet.com.tr/english/domestic/11154284.asp (Accessed 9 March 2009).

Inaç, H. (2004) "Identity Problems of Turkey during the European Union Integration Process," *Journal of Economic and Social Research*, 6(2): 33–62.

Inglehart, R. (1970) "Cognitive Mobilization and European Identity," *Comparative Politics,* 3(1): 45–70.

İrem, N. (2002) "Turkish Conservative Modernism: Birth of a Nationalist Quest for Cultural Renewal," *International Journal of Middle East Studies*, 34(1): 87–112.

Işik, T. (2009) "Erdoğan: Farklı etnik kimliktekilerin kovulması faşizanlıktı," *Radikal*, May 24. Online. Available HTTP: http://www.radikal.com.tr/Radikal.aspx?aType=Rad ikalHaberDetay&ArticleID=937352&Date=24.05.2009&CategoryID=98 (Accessed 25 May 2009).

Jachtenfuchs, M. (1995) "Theoretical Perspectives on European Governance," *European Law Journal* 1(2): 115–33.

Janssen, J.I. (1991) "Postmaterialism, Cognitive Mobilization and Public Support for European Integration," *British Journal of Political Science* 21: 443–68.

Joch, R. (2005) "Radikální islamismus ohrožuje západní společnost," *CEP*. Online. Available HTTP: http://www.cepin.cz/cze/prednaska.php?ID=732&PHPSESSID=aada 7f3%C5%9999c3d79919 (Accessed 15 November 2007).

Johns, M. (2003) "'Do as I Say, Not as I Do': The European Union, Eastern Europe and Minority Rights," *East European Politics & Societies,* 17(4): 682–99.

Jones, R (2008) "An Interview with Pinar Ilkkaracan from Women for Women's Human Rights – New Ways," *Women's Human Rights in Turkey – Challenges and Prospects,* Association for Women's Rights in Development. Online. Available HTTP: http://www.awid.org/eng/Issues-and-Analysis/Library/Women-s-human-rights-in-Turkey-challenges-and-prospects (Accessed 12 May 2009).

Joseph, J.S. (2006) *Turkey and the European Union: Internal Dynamics and External Challenges*, Basingstoke and New York: Palgrave Macmillan.

Kaczynski, L. (2007a) "The Concept of Solidarity in International Relations," *President of the Republic of Poland Press Office*. Online. Available HTTP: http://www.president.pl/x.node?id=7543091 (Accessed 19 March 2009).

—— (2007b) "TRUE January 2007," *President of the Republic of Poland Press Office.* Online. Available HTTP: http://www.president.pl/x.node?id=7543036 (Accessed 19 March 2009).

Kahraman, H.B. (2002) "İçselleştirilmiş, Açık ve Gizli Oryantalizm ve Kemalizm," *Doğu Batı* 20: 153–178.

—— and Keyman, F. (1998) "Kemalizm, Oryantalizm ve Modernite," *Doğu ve Batı*, 2: 65–77.

Kaldor, M. and Vejvoda, I. (1997) "Democratization in Central and East European Countries," *International Affairs* 73(1): 59–82.

Kaliber, A. (2005) "Securing the Ground through Securitized 'Foreign' Policy: The Cyprus Case," *Security Dialogue*, 36(3): 319–37.

Kamiński, M. (2009) "Michał Kamiński: będę bronił spraw Polski i Polaków w UE," *Wirtualna Polska*. Online. Available HTTP: http://wiadomosci.wp.pl/kat,1022313,pag e,2,title,Michal-Kaminski-bede-bronil-spraw-Polski-i-Polakow-w-UE,wid,11099331,w iadomosc.html?ticaid=18354&_ticrsn=3 (Accessed 2 June 2009).

Kamp, K. (2009) "Turkey's Top NGOs," *Today's Zaman*, 18 March: 12.

Karabat, A. (2009a) "Demilitarization of Education Has Begun, but Still Has a Long Way to Go," *Today's Zaman*, 21 April.

—— (2009b) "Turkish Women's Awareness of Gender Equality Increasing," *Today's Zaman*, 4 May: 1, 17.

Karaosmanoğlu, A. (2000) "The Evolution of the National Security Culture and the Military in Turkey," *Journal of International Affairs*, 54(1): 198–216.

Karaosmanoğlu, Y.K. (2005) *Atatürk*, Istanbul: İletişim [1946].

Kárpát, D.Z. (2005) "Vétót Törökország EU-csatlakozásával szemben!," *Jobbik*. Online. Available HTTP: http://www.jobbik.hu/rovatok/kozlemeny/vetot_torokorszag_eu-csatlakozasaval_szemben (Accessed 20 June 2009).

Kasaba, R. (1997) "Kemalist Certainties and Modern Ambiguities," in S. Bozdoğan and R. Kasaba (eds) *Rethinking Modernity and National Identity in Turkey*, Seattle and London: University of Washington Press, 15–36.

Kaźmierczak, L. (2005) "Oni zaraz tu będa," *Przewodnik Katolicki*. Online. Available HTTP: http://www.przk.pl/nr/spoleczenstwo/oni_zaraz_tu_beda.html (Accessed 1 May 2009).

KDH (2006) "Stanovisko k vstupu Turecka do EÚ." Online. Available HTTP: http://www. kdh.sk/article.php?191 (Accessed 30 March 2009).

KDU-ČSL (2006) "Volební program KDU-ČSL 2006–10." Online. Available HTTP: http://www.kdu.cz/videa/Media_15075_2006_2_27_13_35_22.pdf (Accessed 30 March 2009).

Kemmerling, A. (2008) "When 'No' Means 'Yes, But': Why Some Poles Voted Against Enlargement but for EU Accession," *Rationality and Society*, 20(3): 283–309.

Kentel, F. and Poghosyan, G. (2006) *Turkish-Armenian Citizens Mutual Perception and Dialogue Project*. Istanbul: TESEV.

Ker-Lindsay, James (2007) "The Policies of Greece and Cyprus towards Turkey's EU Accession," *Turkish Studies* 8 (1): 71–83.

Keyman, F. E. and Icduygu, A. (2005) *Citizenship in a Global World: European Questions and Turkish Experiences*, Abingdon, Oxon: Routledge.

Királyi Séta (2005) "Törökország EU-csatlakozása ellen tüntettek magyar fiatalok Brüsszelben." Online. Available HTTP: http://kiralyiseta.szekesfehervar.hu/index. php?pg=news_17087 (Accessed 1 May 2009).

Klaus, V. (2004) "Turecko, Evropa a Evropská unie," *Václav Klaus články a eseje*. Online. Available HTTP: http://www.klaus.cz/klaus2/asp/clanek.asp?id=sEBCHZLTMcX3 (Accessed 25 March 2009).

—— (2005a) "Forum Istanbul: Turkey, European Union and the 'Knowledge Society,'"

Václav Klaus English Pages. Online. Available HTTP: http://www.klaus.cz/klaus2/asp/clanek.asp?id=OZuks3qgzeK2 (Accessed 25 March 2009).

—— (2005b) "Mýtus 'tureckého nebezpečí,'" *Václav Klaus články a eseje*. Online. Available HTTP: http://www.klaus.cz/klaus2/asp/clanek.asp?id=bbYGXTYqClrM (Accessed 26 March 2009).

—— (2005c) "Teze projevu Prezidenta Republiky Václava Klause 'Turecko a Evropská unie,'" *Václav Klaus projevy a vystoupení*. Online. Available HTTP: http://www.klaus.cz/clanky/1791 (Accessed 23 October 2007).

—— (2006a) "Enlargement of the EU: What to Say in Turkey?," *Václav Klaus English Pages*. Online. Available HTTP: http://www.klaus.cz/klaus2/asp/clanek.asp?id=F3msL4KmelYG (Accessed 25 March 2009).

—— (2006b) "Projev Prezidenta Republiky Václava Klause u příležitosti státní návštěvy Turecka," *Václav Klaus projevy a vystoupení*. Online. Available HTTP: http://www.klaus.cz/klaus2/asp/clanek.asp?id=EFJJVEIhVTzc (Accessed 26 March 2009).

Kočová, K. (2007) "Předseda ČSSD jednal s tureckým premiérem," Tisková zpráva ČSSD. Online. Available HTTP: www.cssd.cz/s14983/tiskove-zpravy/a15169.html (Accessed 17 November 2007).

Kohn, H. (1937) "The Europeanization of the Orient," *Political Science Quarterly*, 52(2): 259–70.

Kopeček, L. (2004) "Euroskeptici, europeanisté, euroentuziasté, eurofobové – jak s nimi pracovat?," *Politologický časopis*, 11(3): 240–62.

Kopecká, K. (2005) "Rozhovor s Janou Hybáškovou o vstupu Turecka do EU, multikulturalismu a dalších." Online. Available HTTP: http://www.eurabia.cz/ShowArticle.aspx?Artid=1028 (Accessed 14 October 2007).

Kopecky, P. and Mudde, C. (2002) "The Two Sides of Euroscepticism. Party Positions on European Integration in East Central Europe," *European Union Politics*, 3(3): 297–325.

Kossuth Radio (2008), "Szili Katalin Törökország uniós csatlakozása mellett." Online. Available HTTP: http://www.mr1kossuth.hu/index.php?option=com_content&task=view&id=15933&Itemid=95 (Accessed 1 May 2009).

Kotlandova Koenig, D. (1997) "Moderate and Sensible: Higher Education and the Czech Women's Rights Movement," *Central Europe Review* 1(14). Online. Available HTTP: http://www.ce-review.org/99/14/koenig14the.html (Accessed 23 May 2009).

Köylü, H. (2009) "Bağış: AB'de havlu atmayacağız," *Radikal*, 23 May. Online. Available HTTP: http://www.radikal.com.tr/Radikal.aspx?aType=RadikalHaberDetay&ArticleID=937253&Date=23.05.2009&CategoryID=97 (Accessed 23 May 2009).

Král, D. (2006) *Česká debata o perspektivách členství Turecka a Ukrajiny v EU*, Praha: Institut pro evropskou politiku EUROPEUM.

—— (2009) "Mýty a realita budoucího rozšíření Evropské Unie." Online. Available HTTP: http://www.euroskop.cz/45/10723/clanek/myty-a-realita-budouciho-rozsireni-evropske-unie/ (Accessed 15 March 2009).

Kubeczka, J. (2006) "Miloš Zeman radil," *Radio Praha*. Online. Available HTTP: http://www.radio.cz/cz/clanek/76118 (Accessed 12 September 2007).

Kubicek, P. (2005) "The European Union and Grassroots Democratization in Turkey," *Turkish Studies* 6(3): 361–77.

Kundera, M. (1993) *The Art of the Novel,* New York: HarperCollins.

Kurt, S. (2007) "Parties Remain Silent on Foreign Policy at Rallies," *Zaman Daily News*, 14 July: 4.

Kwak, A. and Pascall, G. (2009) "Gender Regimes in Transition: Gender Equality in

CEE Countries?," paper presented at the Enlargement – Five Years After: The State of European Integration and New Challenges for the Discipline, Budapest, May.

Kwaśniewski, A. (2005) "Wizyta oficjalna Prezydenta RP z Małżonką w Republice Cypryjskiej," *Aleksander Kwaśniewski*. Online. Available HTTP: http://www.kwasniewskialeksander.pl/int.php?mode=view&id=2175 (Accessed 17 November 2008).

Ladrech, R. (2002) "Europeanization and Political Parties: Towards a Framework for Analysis," *Party Politics*, 8(4): 389–404.

LaGro, E. (2007) "The Temporality of Enlargement: Comparing East Central Europe and Turkey," paper presented at EUSA conference, Montreal, May. Online. Available HTTP: http://www.unc.edu/euce/eusa2007/papers/lagro-e-04h.pdf (Accessed 17 November 2008).

LaGro, E. and Jørgensen. K.E. (2007) *Turkey and the European Union: Prospects for a Difficult Encounter*, Basingstoke: Palgrave Macmillan.

Lake, M. (ed.) (2005). *The EU and Turkey: A Glittering Prize or a Millstone?*, London: Federal Trust for Education & Research.

Lane, D. (2007) "Post-Communist Countries and the European Union," *Journal of Communist Studies and Transition Politics* 23(4): 461–77.

Le Goff, J. (1990) *The Medieval World,* London: Parkgate.

Lendvai, N. (2004) "The Weakest Link? EU Accession and Enlargement: Dialoguing EU and Post-Communist Social Policy," *Journal of European Social Policy* 14(3): 319–33.

Lewis, B. (1968) *The Emergence of Modern Turkey,* London: Oxford University Press.

Lewis, G. (1999) *The Turkish Language Reform. A Catastrophic Success*. New York: Oxford University Press.

Lipschutz, R. (1995) "On Security," In R. Lipschutz (ed.) *On Security*, New York: Columbia University Press.

Lundgren, Å. (2002) "The Limits of Enlargement," paper prepared for the ARENA Conference on Democracy and European Governance, Oslo, March. Online. Available HTTP:http://www.arena.uio.no/events/Conference2002/documents/Lundgren.doc (Accessed 17 May 2008).

——— (2006) "Are Some Candidates More 'European' than Others?," in H. Sjursen (ed.) *Questioning EU Enlargement. Europe in Search of Identity,* London: Routledge.

McLaren, L. (2002) "Public Support for the European Union: Cost/Benefit Analysis or Perceived Cultural Threat?" *The Journal of Politics*, 64(2): 551–66.

Magyar Koztarsasag Nagykovetsege (n.d.) "Civil társadalmi párbeszéd." Online. Available HTTP: http://www.mfa.gov.hu/kulkepviselet/TR/hu/torokeucsat/civil_tarsadalmi_parbeszed.htm (Accessed 1 May 2008).

Mahçupyan, E. (2009) "Elections, Ergenekon and the EU," *Today's Zaman*, 2 April.

Maksudyan, N. (2005) *Türklüğü Ölçmek*. Istanbul: Metis.

Manning, N. (2004) "Diversity and Change in Pre-Accession Central and Eastern Europe Since 1989," *Journal of European Social Policy,* 14(3): 211–32.

Mardin, S. (1973) "Center-Periphery Relations: A Key to Turkish Politics?," *Daedalus: Journal of the American Academy of Arts and Sciences*, 102(1): 169–91.

Márkus, G. (1998) *Party Politics, Party System and the Dynamics of Political Cleavages in Hungary,* Final Report to NATIP on the Research Project. Online. Available HTTP: http://www.nato-otan.org/acad/fellow/96–98/markus.pdf (Accessed 20 November 2008).

Marušiak, J. and Godársky, I. (2009) "13+1 odpovedí: Monika Beňová (Smer-SD)," *Volebný infoservis*. Online. Available HTTP: http://www.infovolby.sk/index.php?base=data/euro/2009/strany/rozh/smer-sd/1243969715.txt (Accessed 20 June 2008).

Matthews, O. (2002) "Europe's Orphan," *Newsweek,* 139(16): 24–27.

*MF Dnes (*2006) "Evropská civilizace není v krizi, ovšem jistá nebezpečí tu jsou," 29 April.

Miłosz, C. (1992) *Native Realm,* New York: Farrar, Straus and Giroux.

Ministerstwo Spraw Zagranicznych (2006) "W dniu 19 maja br. Minister Spraw Zagranicznych Anna Fotyga wzięła udział w konferencji 'Europe as a Global Power,' organizowanej przez Centrum Europejskie Natolin oraz Instytut nad Bezpieczeństwem UE w Paryżu." Online. Available HTTP: http://www.msz.gov.pl/W,dniu,19,maja,br.,Minister,Spraw,Za granicznych,Anna,Fotyga,wziela,udzial,w,konferencji,Europe,as,a,Global,Power,organi zowanej,przez,Centrum,Europejskie,Natolin,oraz,Instytut,nad,Bezpieczenstwem,UE,w, Paryzu.,6072.html (Accessed 1 May 2009).

Ministry of Foreign Affairs of the Republic of Hungary (2005) "EU Foreign Ministers' Decision on Croatia and Turkey." Online. Available HTTP: http://www.mfa.gov.hu/kum/ en/bal/actualities/spokesman_statements/051005_eu_croatia_turkey.htm (Accessed 20 April 2009).

Moravčík, L. (2009) "Slovensko a Turecko." E-mail (28 April 2009).

MSD (2004) "Turecko prispeje k vytváraniu multikultúrnej Európy." Online. Available HTTP: http://www.mladi.sk/clanky/219/vyhlasenia/turecko-prispeje-k-vytvaraniu-mul-tikulturnej-europy (Accessed 20 April 2009).

Mufti, M. (1998) "Daring and Caution in Turkish Foreign Policy," *The Middle East Journal,* 52(1): 32–50.

Müftüler-Bac, M. (2005) "Turkey's Political Reforms and the Impact of the European Union," *South European Society & Politics,* 10(1): 16–30.

MZV ČR (2004) "Tiskové prohlášení MZV ČR k výsledkům referend o sjednocení Kypru," Portál veřejné správy České republiky. Online. Available http://portal.gov.cz/wps/por-tal/_s.155/7226/_s.155/10202?docid=431 (Accessed 5 May 2009).

Napoli, D. (1995) "The European Union's Foreign Policy and Human Rights," in N.A. Neuwahl and A. Rosas (eds) *The European Union and Human Rights*, Hague: Martinus Nijhoff Publishers.

Nelsen, B.F., Guth J.L., and Fraser, C.R. (2001) "Does Religion Matter?: Christianity and Public Support for the European Union," *European Union Politics,* 2(2): 191–217.

Neumayer, L. (2008) "Euroscepticism as a Political Label: The Use of the European Union Issues in Political Competition in the New Member States," *European Journal of Political Research*, 47: 135–60.

Novinky (2004) "Petice sbírá podpisy proti vstupu Turecka do EU." Online. Available HTTP: http://www.novinky.cz/04/34/48.html (Accessed 12 September 2007).

Oberling, P. (1991) *Negotiating for Survival*, New Jersey: The Aldington Press.

ODS (2006) "Ke Zprávě o pokroku Turecka při přistoupení k EU." Online. Available HTTP: http://www.ods.cz/eu/zprava.php?ID=3874&page=31 (Accessed 7 November 2007).

Öğün, S.S. (1997) "Türk Muhafazakârlığının Kültür Kökleri ve Peyami Safa'nın Muhafazakâr Yanılgısı," *Toplum ve Bilim,* 74: 102–55.

Oğutçu, M. (2009) "A 'Devil's Advocate' Perspective on EU Accession (1)," *Today's Zaman,* 1 June: 14.

Okey, R. (1992) "Central Europe/Eastern Europe: Behind the Definitions," *Past & Present,* 137: 102–33.

Öniş, Z. and Grigoriadis, I. (2009) "Europe and the Impasse of Centre-Left Politics in Turkey: Lessons from Greek Experience," paper presented at Changing Party Political Constellations and Public Policy Reform in Southern Europe Workshop, March. Online. Available HTTP: http://www.eliamep.gr/wp-content/uploads/2009/04/ws09-onis-grigoriadis.pdf (Accessed 17 June 2009).

Öniş, Z. and Yılmaz, S. (2009) "Between Europeanization and Euro-Asianism: Foreign Policy Activism in Turkey during the AKP Era," *Turkish Studies,* 10(1): 7–24.

Özerkan, F. (2007) "Time to Manifest Yourself to Europe," *Turkish Daily News,* 24 July. Online. Available HTTP: http://hurarsiv.hurriyet.com.tr/goster/haber.aspx?id=-610787 (Accessed 18 June 2008).

—— (2009a) "CHP Targets Lack of Progress in EU," *Hurriyet Daily News,* 5 June. Online. Available HTTP: http://www.hurriyet.com.tr/english/domestic/11799682.asp (Accessed 5 June 2009).

—— (2009b) "Czech Gov't Crisis Hampers EU Talks," *Hürriyet Daily News,* 3 May. Online. Available HTTP http://www.hurriyet.com.tr/english/domestic/11568379.asp (Accessed 9 May 2009).

Pachta, L. (2004) "Proč musí Turecko vstoupit do EU?," *Europeum.* Online. Available HTTP: http://www.europeum.org/disp_article.php?aid=41&cid=3&nolang=0&type=0 &page=2 (Accessed 23 October 2007).

Parlatır, I. and Çetin, N. (eds) (1999) *Genç Kalemler Dergisi,* Ankara: Türk Dil Kurumu.

Parliamentary Assembly Council of Europe (2004), "Cyprus," Ordinary Session. Online. Available HTTP: http://assembly.coe.int/Main.asp?link=/Documents/Records/2004/ E/0404291500E.htm (Accessed 5 May 2009).

Paroubek, J. (2006) "Bůh do politiky nepatří," *MF DNES.* Online. Available HTTP: http:// zpravy.idnes.cz/domaci.asp?c=A060428_172902_domaci_ad (23 October 2007).

Piana, D. (2009) "The Power Knocks at the Courts' Back Door: Two Waves of Postcommunist Judicial Reforms," *Comparative Political Studies,* 42(6): 816–40.

Polat, R.K. (2009) "The 2007 Parliamentary Elections in Turkey: Between Securitization and Desecuritization," *Parliamentary Affairs,* 62(1): 129–48.

Pope, N. (2004) "Los derechos de la mujer en Turquía como indicadores de cambio social: logros y desafíos," *Revista CIDOB d'Afers Internacionals* 75: 125–33.

Přibáň, J. (2005) "Ústavní proces, svrchovanost a politická identita. Poznámky k procesu evropské integrace," in M. Hrubec (ed.) *Spravedlnost a demokracie v evropské integraci,* Praha: Filosofia.

Pridham, G. (1999) "Complying with the European Union's Democratic Conditionality: Transnational Party Linkages and Regime Change in Slovakia, 1993–98," *Europe-Asia Studies,* 51(7): 1221–44.

—— (2006) "European Union Accession Dynamics and Democratization in Central and Eastern Europe: Past and Future Perspectives," *Government and Opposition,* 41(30): 373–400.

—— (2007) "Change and Continuity in the European Union's Political Conditionality: Aims, Approach, and Priorities," *Democratization* 14(3): 446–71.

—— (2008) "Securing Fragile Democracies in the Balkans: The European Dimension," *Romanian Journal of European Affairs,* 8(2): 56–70.

ProEuropa.info (n.d.) "Wywiad Ministra SZ RP Pana Włodzimierza Cimoszewicza." Online. Available HTTP: http://www.msz.gov.pl/Wywiad,dla,ukrainskiego,portalu,inter netowego,www.ProEuropa.info,1487.html (Accessed 1 May 2009).

Putnová, A. (2005) "Women in the Labour Market – Case Study from the Czech Republic," *Regional Studies Association.* Online. Available HTTP: www.regional-studies-assoc. ac.uk/ events/presentations04/putnova.pdf (Accessed 19 April 2005).

Quadras, A.V. (2004) "EU-Turkey: A Good Match?," *Turkish Policy Quarterly* 2(4). Online. Available HTTP: http://www.turkishpolicy.com/images/stories/2003–4-EUforeignpolicy/TPQ2003–4-quadras.pdf (Accessed 21 August 2008).

Quaisser, W. and Reppegather, A. (2004) "EU-Beitrittsreife der Turkei und Konsequenzen einer EU-Mitgliedschaft," *Osteuropa-Institut Munich Working Paper,* 252. Online. Available HTTP: http://www.osteuropa-institut.de/ext_dateien/wp252k.pdf (Accessed 15 March 2009).

Radio Praha (2007) "As Erdogan Visits Prague, Czech PM Backs Turkey's Bid to Join EU." Online. Available HTTP: http://www.radio.cz/en/news/97618 (Accessed 15 March 2009).

Rangelova, R. (2003) "Gender Labour Relations and EU Enlargement," in A. Pusca (ed.) *European Union: Challenges and Promises of a New Enlargement,* New York: International Debate Education Association.

Rechel, B. (2008) "What Has Limited the EU's Impact on Minority Rights in Accession Countries?," *East European Politics and Societies,* 22(1): 171–91.

Rehn, O. (2006) "Building a New Consensus on Enlargement: How to Match the Strategic Interest and Functioning Capacity of the EU?," *Press Releases RAPID,* 19 May. Online. Available HTTP: http://europa.eu/rapid/pressReleasesAction.do?reference=SPEECH/06/316&format=HTML&aged=0&language=EN&guiLanguage=en (Accessed 16 March 2009).

Riishøj, S. (2004) "Europeanisation and Euro-scepticism. Experiences from Poland and the Czech Republic," *Central European Political Studies Review,* VI(4): 1–44.

Risse, T. and Grabowsky, J.K. (2008) "European Identity Formation in the Public Sphere and in Foreign Policy," *RECON Online Working Paper,* 04. Online. Available HTTP: http://www.reconproject.eu/main.php/RECON_wp_0804.pdf?fileitem=16662546 (Accessed 10 July 2008).

Robejšek P. (2007) "Mělo by Turecko vstoupit do Evropské unie?," *CEVROREVUE,* 6/7. Online. Available HTTP: www.cevro.cz/. . ./196541-melo-turecko-vstoupit-evropske-unie.html (Accessed 7 November 2007).

Rochtus, D. (2004) "'Turkestroika' as Precondition for Turkey's European Dream," in I. Bal (ed.) *Turkish Foreign Policy in Post Cold War Era,* Boca Raton: Brown Walker Press.

Rose, R. and Shin, D.C. (2001) "Democratization Backwards: The Problem of Third-Wave Democracies," *British Journal of Political Science* 31(2): 331–54.

Rumelili, B. (2005) "Civil Society and the Europeanization of Greek-Turkish Cooperation," *South European Society & Politics,* 10(1): 45–56.

Rumford, C. (2003) "Resisting Globalization?: Turkey-EU Relations and Human and Political Rights in the Context of Cosmopolitan Democratization," *International Sociology,* 18(2): 379–94.

Rupnik, J. (1989) *The Other Europe,* London: Weidenfeld and Nicolson.

Sadurski, W. (2002) "Charter and Enlargement," *European Law Journal* 8(3): 340–62.

—— (2004) "Accession's Democracy Dividend: The Impact of the EU Enlargement upon Democracy in the New Member States of Central and Eastern Europe," *European Law Journal* 10(4): 371–401.

Safa, P. (1938) *Büyük Avrupa Anketi,* Ankara: Kannat.

—— (1963) *Doğu-Batı Sentezi,* Istanbul: Yağmur Yayınevi.

—— (1988) *Türk İnkılabına Bakışlar,* Ankara: Atatürk Araştırma Merkezi [1938].

—— (2000) *Doğu-Batı Arasında,* Istanbul: Ufuk.

Saktanber, A. (2006) "Women and the Iconography of Fear: Islamization in Post-Islamist Turkey," *Signs: Journal of Women in Culture and Society* 32(1): 21–31.

Schimmelfennig, F. and Sedelmeier, U. (2002) "Theorising EU Enlargement: Research Focus, Hypotheses, and the State of Research," *Journal of European Public Policy,* 9 (4): 500–528.

—— (2005) "Introduction. Conceptualizing the Europeanization of Central and Eastern Europe," in F. Schimmelfennig and U. Sedelmeier (eds) *The Europeanization of Central and Eastern Europe*, New York: Cornell University Press.

Schimmelfennig, F., Engert, S., and Knobel, H. (2003) "Costs, Commitment and Compliance: The Impact of EU Democratic Conditionality on Latvia, Slovakia and Turkey," *JCMS*, 41(3): 495–518.

Schuck, A.R.T. and de Vreese, C.H. (2006) "Between Risk and Opportunity: News Framing and Its Effects on Public Support for EU Enlargement," *European Journal of Communication*, 21(1): 5–32.

Schwellnus, G. (2006) "Double Standards? Minority Protection as a Condition for Membership," in H. Sjursen (ed.) *Questioning EU Enlargement. Europe in Search of Identity,* London: Routledge.

—— (2009) "It Ain't Over When It's Over – The Adoption and Sustainability of Minority Protection Rules in New EU Member States," paper presented at the Enlargement – Five Years After: The State of European Integration and New Challenges for the Discipline, Budapest, May.

Shaw, S. and Shaw, E.K. (1985) *History of the Ottoman Empire and Modern Turkey – Vol. II,* Cambridge: Cambridge University Press.

Şenol-Cantek, F.L. (2003) *Yaban'lar ve Yerliler. Başkent Olma Sürecinde Ankara*, Istanbul: İletişim.

Şenyuva, Ö. (2006) "Turkish Public Opinion and European Union Membership: The State of Art in Public Opinion Studies in Turkey," *Perceptions*, Spring: 19–32.

Simma, B., Aschenbrenner, J.B., and Schulte, C. (1999) "Human Rights Considerations in the Development Cooperation Activities of the EC," in P. Alston (ed.) *EU and Human Rights,* Oxford. Oxford University Press.

Sjursen, H. (2006) "Introduction. Enlargement and the Nature of the EU Polity," in H. Sjursen (ed.) *Questioning EU Enlargement. Europe in Search of Identity,* London: Routledge.

Slomczynski, K. and Shabad, G. (2003) "Dynamics of Support for European Integration in Post-Communist Poland," *European Journal of Political Research*, 42: 503–39.

SNS (2004) "SLOTA: Európa pre Europanov." Online. Available HTTP: www.sns.sk/clanky/slota-europa-pre-europanov-216.htm l (Accessed 1 May 2009).

—— (2006) "Slota: SNS je proti vstupu Turecka do EÚ." Online. Available HTTP: http://www.sns.sk/clanky/slota-sns-je-proti-vstupu-turecka-do-eu-671.html (Accessed 12 April 2009).

Sofos, S.A. (2001) "Reluctant Europeans? European Integration and the Transformation of Turkish Politics," in K. Featherstone and G. Kazamias (eds) *Europeanization and the Southern Periphery*, London: Frank Cass.

Sözen, A. (1998) *The Cyprus Conflict and the Negotiations: A Political and International Law Perspective,* Turkey: Can Reklam, Ankara.

—— (1999) *Cyprus Conflict: Continuing Challenge and Prospects for Resolution in the Post-Cold War Era*, Missouri, USA: University of Missouri.

—— (2005a) "Turkish Cypriot Early General Elections of February 2005: The Rise of CTP/BG," *South European Society & Politics*, 10(3): 465–75.

—— (2005b) "Turkish Democratization in Light of its EU Candidate Status," in K. Inglis and A. Ott (eds) *The Constitution for Europe and an Enlarging Union: Union in Diversity?*, Amsterdam: Europa Law Publishing.

Stearns, M. (1992) *Entangled Allies: U.S. Policy Towards Greece, Turkey, and Cyprus*, New York: Council on Foreign Relations Press.

Steiner, G. (2005) *The Idea of Europe*, Tilburg: Nexus Institute.

Strazay, T. (2003) "The Incongruent Culture? Nationalist-Populism and Democratization of Post-Communist Central Europe," *TCDS*. Online. Available HTTP: http://www. newschool.edu/tcds/Tomas%20Strazay.pdf (Accessed 27 January 2009).

Süssheim, K. (1938) "Abd Allah Djewdet," *Encyklopaedie des Islam*, Ergänzungsband, Leiden: E.J. Brill, 55–60.

Sychra, Z. (2006) "Perspektivy dalšího rozšiřování EU z hlediska zájmů ČR: dopady extenze počtu členů EU na pozici ČR v EU," in V. Dočkal, P. Fiala, P. Kaniok, and M. Pitrová (eds) *Česká Republika v Evropské Unii. Evropský integrační proces a zájmy České Republiky*, Brno: International Institute of Political Science of Masaryk University.

Szczerbiak, A. (2001) "Polish Public Opinion: Explaining Declining Support for EU Membership," *Journal of Common Market Studies*, 39(1): 105–22.

Szczerbiak, A. and Taggart, P. (2004) "Contemporary Euroscepticism in the Party Systems of the European Union Candidate States of Central and Eastern Europe," *European Journal of Political Research*, 43(1): 1–27.

—— (2007) "Theorising Party-Based Euroscepticism: Problems of Definition, Measurement and Causality," *European Parties Elections and Referendums Network*, Working Paper 12; *SEI*, Working Paper 69. Online. Available http: http://www.sussex.ac.uk/sei/documents/wp69.pdf (Accessed 14 October 2007).

Szigetvári, T. (n.d.) *Törökország Trianonja és az örmény népirtás*. Online. Available HTTP: http://www.kre.hu/kremlinologia/Torokorszag_Trianonja_es_az_ormeny_nepirtas.pdf (Accessed 1 June 2009).

—— (2006) "Törökország az Európai Uniós csatlakozási tárgyalások kezdetén," *Világgazdasági Kutatóintézet*, Budapest: MTA. Online. Available HTTP: http://www.vki. hu/mt/mh-72.pdf (Accessed 1 June 2009).

Szymański, A. (2006a) "Turkey and Poland – Two Different Countries in the Process of European Integration?" in N. Neuwahl and H. Kabaalioğlu (eds) *European Union and Turkey: Reflections on the Prospects for Membership*, Ankara: TOBB.

—— (2006b) "Turkey's Future Membership of the European Union and its Consequences for Poland," *The Polish Quarterly of International Affairs*, 4: 64–82.

—— (2007a) "Alternatives to EU Membership. The Case of Turkey," *The Polish Quarterly of International Affairs*, 4: 55–72.

—— (2007b) "The Position of Polish Political Elites on Future of EU Enlargement," *Journal of Communist Studies and Transition Politics*, 23(4): 548–60.

—— (2008) "Szymański: oczekujemy od Turcji odpowiedzialności za ludobójstwo Ormian," *PiS*. Online. Available HTTP: http://www.pis.org.pl/article.php?id=12563 (Accessed 1 May 2009). Also available HTTP: http://archiwum.europa21.pl/Article12162.html (Accessed 3 January 2010).

Taggart, P. (1998) "Touchstone of Dissent. Euroscepticism in Contemporary Western European Party Systems," *European Journal of Political Research*, 33(3): 363–88.

Taggart, P. and Szczerbiak, A. (2002) "The Party Politics of Euroscepticism in EU Member and Candidate States," paper presented at Workshop Opposing Europe: Euroscepticism and Political Parties ECPR Joint Sessions of Workshops, Turin, March.

Tamkoç, M. (1988). *The Turkish Cypriot State: The Embodiment of the Right of Self Determination*. London: K. Rüstem & Brother.

Tanasoiu, C. and Colonescu, C. (2008) "Determinants of Support for European Integration: The Case of Bulgaria," *European Union Politics*, 9(3): 363–77.

Tanyici, S. (2003) "Transformation of Political Islam in Turkey: Islamist Welfare Party's Pro-EU Turn," *Party Politics*, 9(4): 463–83.

Taşpinar, O. (2007) "Kuzey Irak ile diyalog şart," *Radikal*, 4 June.

Tekin Alp, M. (1937) *Le Kemalisme*, Paris: Alcan.

TEPAV (2009) *Toplumun Kamu Yönetimine ve Kamu Hizmetlerine Bakışı (Public Attitudes towards Public Management and Public Service)*, Ankara: TEPAV.

Tocci, N. (2003) "Turkey's Strategic Future. Anchoring Turkey to Europe: The Foreign Policy Challenges ahead," *Turkey's Strategic Future*, ESF Working Paper, 13. Online. Available HTTP: http://shop.ceps.eu/BookDetail.php?item_id=1056 (Accessed 15 July 2007).

—— (2007) "Report. Unpacking European Discourses: Conditionality, Impact and Prejudice in EU-Turkey Relations," in N. Tocci (ed.) *Conditionality, Impact and Prejudice in EU-Turkey Relations,* Roma: Quaderni IAI.

—— (2008) "The European Union as a Normative Foreign Policy Actor," *CEPS Working Document 281.* Online. Available HTTP: http://aei.pitt.edu/7582/01/Wd281.pdf (Accessed 21 January 2009).

Today's Zaman (2009a) "Ankara Takes another Slow Step in EU Accession Talks," 1 July: 4.

—— (2009b) "Poll Shows Support for EU on the Rise," 30 March: 4.

—— (2009c) "Turkey's EU Process 'One-Way Road,' Declares Davutoğlu," 21 May: 4.

—— (2009d) "Verheugen Criticizes EU's Turkey Stance," 3 March: 4.

Tomský (2007) "Turecko do Evropy nepatří," *euRabia.* Online. Available HTTP:http://www.eurabia.cz/Articles/1340-turecko-do-evropy-nepatri.aspx (Accessed 1 November 2007).

Topidi, K. (2009) "Exporting Tolerance from the EU: Turkey's Europeanization as a Test Case," paper presented at the Enlargement – Five Years After: The State of European Integration and New Challenges for the Discipline, Budapest, May.

Topolánek, M. (2005) "Rezoluce k návštěvě předsedy ODS Mirka Topolánka v Chorvatsku," Prohlášení klubu ODS. Online. Available HTTP: http://www.ods.cz/eu/zprava.php?ID=2050&page=32 (Accessed 7 November 2007).

—— (2009) *"Five Years of Success,"* *EU2009.CZ.* Online. Available HTTP: http://www.eu2009.cz/en/news-and-documents/speeches-interviews/speech-by-the-prime-minister-of-the-czech-republic-mirek-topolanek-five-years-of-success-11262/ (Accessed 10 April 2009).

Transparency International (2008) "Persistently High Corruption in Low-Income Countries Amounts to an 'Ongoing Humanitarian Disaster.'" Online. Available HTTP: http://www.transparency.org.ro/politici_si_studii/indici/ipc/2008/Press%20release%20Transparency%20International.pdf (Accessed 17 April 2009).

TRT (2009) "Gül Pays a Visit to Czech Republic." Online. Available HTTP: http://www.trtenglish.com/international/newsDetail.aspx?HaberKodu=b3d6a6b9–25cf-4ef9-b270–773781e98657 (Accessed 12 May 2009).

TRT-World (2009) "The Role of Civil Society in Turkey-EU Relations," 11 March. Online. Available HTTP: http://www.trtspanish.com/International/newsDetail.aspx?HaberKodu=4a93c470-6596-451e-b715-e757a1d7831d (Accessed 12 March 2009).

Tüccarzâde, İ.H. (1997) *Avrupalılaşmak. Felâketlerimizin Esbâbı*, Istanbul: Gündoğan.

Tunaya, T.Z. (2002) "Türkiye Cumhuriyeti Rejiminde Batılılaşma Olayları ve Fikirleri," *Türkler*, cilt 17, Ankara: Yeni Türk Yayinlari, 798–809.

Tuncer, H. (2007) *History Education and the "Other" in History*, Istanbul: Yurt Yayinlari.

Tunkrová, Lucie (2006) "Soft Eurosceptic Parties in the East Central Europe," *Acta Politologica* 5: 219–36.

—— (2008) "Imagining Europe: European Identity and Turkish Accession Process," *The International Journal of the Humanities*, 6: 1–8.

Turkish Daily News (2007a) "CHP Announces its Election Manifesto," June 21.

—— (2007b) "Who to Vote for and Why?," 14 July. Online. Available HTTP: http://www.turkishdailynews.com.tr/vote2007/article.php?enewsid=22 (Accessed 14 July 2009).

TÜSIAD (2007) "*Türk Demokrasisi'nde 130 Yıl (1876–2006): Prof. Dr. Bulent Tanor'un Anisina Turkiye'de Demokratiklesme Perspektifleri 10. Yil Guncellemesi,*" Istanbul.

Uğur, M. (2001) "Europeanization and Convergence via Incomplete Contracts? The Case of Turkey," in K. Featherstone and G. Kazamias (eds) *Europeanization and the Southern Periphery,* London: Frank Cass.

Uğur, M. and Yankaya, D. (2008) "Policy Entrepreneurship, Policy Opportunism, and EU Conditionality: The AKP and TUSIAD Experience in Turkey," *Governance: An International Journal on Policy, Administration and Institutions*, 21(4): 581–601.

Ülken, H.Z. (2001) *Türkiye'de Çağdaş Düşünce Tarihi,* Istanbul: Ülken Yayınları [1966].

United Nations Population Division (2009) "World Population Prospects. The 2008 Revision Population Database." Online. Available HTTP: http://esa.un.org/unpp/ (Accessed 30 March 2009).

Uslu, E. (2008) "The Kurdistan Workers' Party Turns against the European Union," *Mediterranean Quarterly,* 19(2): 99–121.

—— (2009) "Turkey and Armenia Move Closer to a Deal on Formal Diplomatic Relations," *Eurasia Daily Monitor*, 10 February. Online. Available HTTP: http://www.jamestown.org/programs/edm/single/?tx_ttnews[tt_news]=34487&tx_ttnews[backPid]=27&cHash=4e78beadc6 (Accessed 10 February 2009).

Uslu, N., Toprak, M., Dalmis, I., and Aydin, E. (2005) "Turkish Public Opinion toward the United States in the Context of the Iraq Question," *MERIA*, 9(3). Online. Available HTTP: http://meria.idc.ac.il/journal/2005/issue3/jv9no3a5.html (Accessed 7 July 2006).

Vaknin, S. (2002) "Women in Transition in Eastern and Central Europe," *World in Conflict and Economies in Transition.* Online. Available HTTP: http://samvak.tripod.com/brief-women01.html (Accessed 21 May 2009).

Vaněk, P. (2005) "Pochybná lekce z demokracie," *Literární Noviny.* Online. Available HTTP: http://www.literarky.cz/index_o.php?p=clanek&id=337 (Accessed 23 October 2007).

Verez, J.-C. (ed.) (2005) *D'un élargissement à l'autre: la Turquie et les autres candidats*, Paris and Istanbul: L'Harmattan, Université de Galatasaray.

Verney, S. (2006) "Justifying the Second Enlargement: Promoting Interests, Consolidating Democracy or Returning to the Roots?," in H. Sjursen (ed) *Questioning EU Enlargement. Europe in Search of Identity,* London: Routledge.

Víšková, J. (2006) "Ministr Gandalovič jednal s tureckým vyjednavačem Babacanem," *Ministerstvo pro místní rozvoj.* Online. Available HTTP: http://www.mmr.cz/Pro-media/Tiskove-zpravy/2006/Ministr-Gandalovic-jednal-s-tureckym-vyjednavacem- (Accessed 20 April 2009).

Vlachová, K. and Řeháková, B. (2009) "Identity of Non-Self-Evident Nation: Czech National Identity after the Break-Up of Czechoslovakia and before Accession to the European Union," *Nations and Nationalism*, 15(2): 254–79.

Vláda České republiky (2008) "Premiér M. Topolánek v turecké Ankaře podpořil vstup Turecka do Evropské Unie," 8 October. Online. Available HTTP: http://www.vlada.cz/scripts/detail.php?id=43090 (Accessed 20 March 2009).

Vláda Slovenskej republiky (2004) "Návrh stanoviska Slovenskej Republiky k začatiu prístupových rokovaní Európskej Únie s Tureckou republikou." Online. Available HTTP: http://www.rokovania.sk/appl/material.nsf/0/2AA5AAB0D8FAA985C1256F550042DDB7/$FILE/Zdroj.html (Accessed 27 March 2009).

Wæver, O. (1995) "Securitization and Desecuritization," in R. Lipschutz (ed.) *On Security,* New York: Columbia University Press.

—— (2000) "The EU as a Security Actor: Reflections from a Pessimistic Constructivist on Post-sovereign Security Orders," in M. Kelstrup and M. Williams (eds), *International Relations Theory and European Integration: Power, Security and Community*, London: Routledge.

Warning, M. (2006) "Neighborhood and Enlargement Policy: Comparing the Democratization Impact of the European Union in Morocco and Turkey," WP 4, *CIRES.* Online. Available HTTP: http://www.cires-ricerca.it/upload/sub/PUBBLICAZIONI/WP/Warning_4_06.pdf (Accessed 17 June 2009).

Wiener, A. (2006) "The Constitution of Europe: Assessing European Constitutionalism in the Light of Turkish Accession," in N. Neuwahl and H. Kabaalioglu (eds) *European Union and Turkey: Reflections on the Prospects for Membership*, Ankara: TOBB.

Williams, M. C. (2003) "Words, Images, Enemies: Securitization and International Politics," *International Studies Quarterly,* 47(4): 511–31.

"Women in Transition," (1999) *The Monee Project Regional Monitoring Report* 6. Online. Available HTTP: www.unicef-icdc.org/publications/pdf/monee6sume.pdf (Accessed 11 May 2005).

World Bulletin (2009) "Czech Delegation Visits Turkey over EU Talks." Online. Available HTTP: http://www.worldbulletin.net/news_detail.php?id=40411 (Accessed 12 May 2009).

World Public Opinion (2008) "International Poll Finds Large Majorities in All Countries Favor Equal Rights for Women." Online. Available HTTP: http://www.worldpublicopinion.org/pipa/articles/btjusticehuman_rightsra/453.php (Accessed 8 March 2008).

Yanatma, S. (2009) "European Union Says It's on Same Page with Turkey on Foreign Policy," *Today's Zaman*, 9 May: 1.

Yapp, M.E. (1992) "Europe in the Turkish Mirror," *Past & Present*, 137: 134–55.

Yavuz, E. (2008) "Turkey Struggles to Fight Corruption," *Today's Zaman*, 31 August. Online. Available HTTP: http://www.todayszaman.com/tz-web/detaylar.do?load=detay&link=1 51717 (Accessed 7 July 2009).

Yeni Şafak (2009) "Türkiye karşıtlığı AB güvenliğine zarar verir," 24 May. Online. Available HTTP: http://yenisafak.com.tr/Dunya/?t=25.05.2009&c=4&i=188178 (Accessed 25 May 2009).

Yeşilada, B. and Sözen, A. (2002) "Negotiating a Resolution to the Cyprus Problem: Is Potential EU Membership a Blessing or a Curse?" *Journal of International Negotiation*, 7(2): 261–85.

Yılmaz, H. (2004) "Turkey: Within or Outside Europe: An Historical Perspective," paper presented at the conference Betwixt and Between: Europe and the Mediterranean: New Stakes and New Challenges, Durham, July.

—— (2006) "Two Pillars of Nationalist Euroskepticism in Turkey: The Tanzimat and Sevres Syndromes," in I. Karlsson and A.S. Melin (eds) *Turkey, Sweden and the European Union: Experiences and Expectations*, Stockholm: SIEPS.

Zaborowski, M. (2006) "More than Simply Expanding Markets: Germany and EU Enlargement," in H. Sjursen (ed.) *Questioning EU Enlargement. Europe in Search of Identity,* London: Routledge.

Zahradil, J. (2006) "Jan Zahradil: Tempo reforem má být zvoleno Ankarou," Prohlášení klubu ODS. Online. Available HTTP: http://www.ods.cz/eu/prispevek.php?ID=3244&page=34 (Accessed 7 November 2007).

Zaman (2009) "Kanunlar özgürlükçü yorumlanmadığı için AİHM'ye şikayet azalmıyor," 2 April.

Zieleniec, J. (2005) "Petice proti vstupu Turecka do Evropské unie," *Josef Zieleniec.* Online. Available HTTP: http://www.zieleniec.eu/index.php?dok=00830000000271,det (Accessed 7 November 2007).

—— (2007) "Projev Josefa Zieleniece ke vztahům EU – Turecko," *Josef Zieleniec.* Online. Available HTTP: http://www.zieleniec.eu/index.php?dok=00820000000744,det (Accessed 7 November 2007).

Index